1987

Poets, Poems, Movements

Studies in Modern Literature, No. 64

A. Walton Litz, General Series Editor

Professor of English
Princeton University

Other Titles in This Series

Poets, Poems, Movements

by
Thomas Parkinson

UMI Research
Press

Ann Arbor, Michigan

Produced and distributed by
UMI Research Press
an imprint of
University Microfilms, Inc.
Ann Arbor, Michigan 48106

Library of Congress Cataloging in Publication Data
Parkinson, Thomas Francis, 1920-
Poets, poems, movements.

(Studies in modern literature ; no. 64)
Includes bibliographical references and index.
1. American poetry—20th century—History and criticism. 2. English poetry—20th century—History and criticism. I. Title. II. Series.
PS323.5.P28 1987   821'.91'09   86-30910
ISBN 0-8357-1783-6 (alk. paper)

Contents

Literary Movements

Some American Poets

Preface

The essays in this book are selected from the work of over forty years, with the addition of two new essays (one on Lowell and one on Everson). They have been brought together not only to make them more accessible and to provide an overview of my critical work, but also to give a more complete view of the poets and the movements I have studied. The earliest essay is on Yeats and Pound, and one of the most recent, on Yeats and the limits of modernity, can be construed as bringing up to date the material in the earlier work. Yeats looms large in the book because I have been studying his poetry since childhood and have written two books on him. Nothing in this book is from those studies, and I have deliberately excluded other essays on Yeats that would not be pertinent to the structure of the present work.

This book begins with an essay that examines the nature and burden of the poet, moving from loneliness to community through the medium and magic of poetic art, and in the process destroying the loneliness of the reader, bringing him into a more full and rewarding knowledge of being. The essay attempts to define my sense of the nature of the human lot, especially in this century but as it has been endured at all times, and my sense of the reward and glory of the poetic enterprise.

The second section treats the relations between poets, as audiences for each other and as creative artists. The aim of this group of essays is to explore the artistic and human relations between poets and the artistic and social consequences. These essays rely on the extant correspondence between the poets and on the poetic texts that they wrote at the time of that correspondence. In such a context, poets are compelled to see their work more fully and intimately as another poet acts as audience. Hence this section treats the close relations between important poets and their individual poetic motives in order to clarify the motivation and intent that reside in poems of genuine weight and quality. In those essays my aim was to understand each poet, his poetry, and through his relation with the other poet, the consequences of his work. It was a genuine pleasure to experience, through texts that had not at the time been published, some of which (Crane's letters to Winters) were assumed to have been destroyed, so close a relation to the creative process.

The third section takes three grand poems and examines in detail their structure, texture, tone, and quality. They are poems of some length and different from each other in quality and impact, Whitman's rhapsodic tone contrasted with Yeats's prophetic motives, and with Stevens's meditative and philosophical and often playful methods. For me, they are norms of excellence as poems and as serious human articulations of basic human problems.

The fourth section moves to the treatment of the work and career of a great poet followed by examination of younger Irish poets whose work is emerging rather than fully accomplished and ended by death. This section on Yeats and contemporary Irish poetry follows a treatment of Yeats's career and accomplishment with discussion of the three current Irish poets who seem to me to have shaped genuinely large accomplishments, Heaney, Kinsella, and Montague. My clear impression is that current Irish poetry has greater richness and density than the general run of poetry from England and the United States because it is facing more directly and with greater objectivity many of the major problems of personal and cultural identity.

The fifth section then considers some poetic movements in order to place poetry in a wider social and artistic context. Poetry begins and ends in a person, and the person necessarily shapes his being within a web of social and economic and political realities. The attempt in this section is to explore ways in which poetry and society interact, an interest that motivates most of my work. The point where the soul meets history is the point where the grandest poetry emerges.

The final section examines the work and in some instances the personal life of some contemporary poets. These essays are plainly more subjective than the bulk of the preceding matter. Commentary on contemporary poetry is by its nature personal and immediate in its response to the work presented to or chosen by the critic. The two essays on Robert Lowell grow from my long concern with and interest in his work, as do the essays on Rexroth, Duncan, Snyder, Ginsberg, and Everson. The essay on Burroughs is included partly because it fits with the essay on the beat writers in section four and partly because of the extended portrait of Allen Ginsberg with which it opens.

Writing on contemporary work should attempt to distinguish the qualities of the work involved. Judgment is secondary and grows from the qualitative description, so that the critical function is to explore. It seems evident that poetry with the scope of Lowell's or Duncan's or Snyder's or Rexroth's embodies social and moral judgments that shape an imagined world. That world in turn comments on the social and moral realities that underlie our current lives. The critic is thereby compelled toward reactions that are personal because he in turn is involved inextricably with the world that all men and women now endure. At that point, the scholar, critic, and person become one.

If I were to acknowledge debts to those persons who have been important to my work, I should be committed to an unwieldy autobiography. What has emerged from my writing is a deep respect for the community of the world of letters, notably my debt to such helpful and intelligent women as the late Georgia Yeats, who gave me access to so much material and helped in ways that gave me the deepest sense of what generosity really means, and Janet Lewis Winters, who spent long hours in interviews with me on details and designs of her husband's life that should otherwise have been inaccessible. But beyond those great personal aids, I think of the entire community of people ranging from librarians and research assistants to scholars and critics and poets who have given so much of themselves to the art and understanding of poetry. Criticism and scholarship are impossible without the cooperation of a large body of people, many of whom labor in obscurity.

Poetry and the Art of Loneliness

1

Poetry and the Art of Loneliness

Loneliness begins with the recognition of one's singularity—the fact that a deep communication of one's self and recognition by others of its legitimacy is not fully possible. Individualization is painful, and individuality is therefore a mixed boon. The sense of being a voice in a void—speaking in a vacuum—is unsettling and disturbing. With this sense comes the desire for comrades, of homesickness for one's own kind. This desire for companions grows from a sense of exile, of being part of the social world that does not resonate in harmony with the buried genuine self that we take to be our most certain reality. Realizing our separateness, we are moved toward understanding—a noncensorious passion, a fellow feeling that asserts that the world really is a community of spirits who all know one another. Mature men and women of sensitivity are often delighted on meeting another who is inhabiting the same world and can thus mitigate the sense of being banned from one's proper milieu. The imagination, the capacity for seeing others as other and yet as part of our being, and ourselves as part of theirs, leads to work, study, and affections that extend, subtilize, and confirm the initial sense of separateness.

The classics of modern literature by Joyce, Pound, Proust, and Eliot are largely populated by characters who live in isolation. They are encapsulated and walled in so that meaningful relations are canceled for them. They do not find the comradeship that relieves the burden of individuality. They have no place. Their condition is further aggravated by the sense of helplessness that has permeated literature and life in the last half of the twentieth century. W. H. Auden could speak of the 1940s as the Age of Anxiety. Perhaps we are in the Age of Panic in which the human condition in the world is without the supports of the firm, unchangeable natural order, without a set of ordered rituals and sacraments. For as the general human ability to control the environment increases, the specific individual capacity to control the forces of the world diminishes to the vanishing point. The individual vanishes into a condition of laconic impotence.

The poet suffers less from this condition than most men. This may be one of the major reasons for the sudden growth of interest not only in reading poetry or attending poetry readings, but in the actual writing of poetry. Twenty years ago the student who wanted to write had idle dreams of becoming another Ernest Hemingway, living a romantic life, and drinking gin with the international set on the Riviera. Now the more attractive model is the more private figure of the poet working modestly without publicity and social status. The freedom for contemplation and exploration is more attractive to such students than the glare of public attention. Nor is this privacy viewed as mere self-indulgent solitude; it is rather a mode of entry into the basic human condition.

The subject of much poetry is loneliness. The writing of poetry is a solitary operation. But that very loneliness is among the primary rewards of the poet. Writing to a young poet who complained of his loneliness, Rilke said:

> What is needed is just this. Loneliness, vast inner loneliness. To walk in one's self and to meet no one for hours on end. That is what one must be able to attain. To be lonely the way one was lonely as a child, when the grown-ups moved about, involved in things that appeared important and big because the big ones looked so busy and because one understood nothing of what they were doing. If one day one comes to perceive that their occupations are miserable, their professions moribund and no longer related to life, why not go on regarding them like a child as something alien, looking out from the depths of one's own world from the expanse of one's own loneliness which is itself work and rank and profession. Why want to exchange a child's wise understanding for defensiveness and contempt when not understanding means being alone, while defensiveness and contempt mean participating in that from which one is trying by their means to separate one's self.

Rilke asks the young poet to return to the freedom of the child so that he might accept the conditions of life without defensiveness and contempt. The capacity for perceiving and accepting those conditions depends on the ability to recognize the basic reality of human loneliness.

In spite of the carrying power of tradition that allows any serious poet to live in a community that extends back to the earliest of human experience, the poet in action lives in essential loneliness. He shares this domain with all other discovering workers, whether artists or scientists. In work, in knowledge, even in love, we approach the loneliness of death in which the world ceases to function in any hitherto meaningful fashion. The world's modes and forms lose their inner authority, their power to support. The work of vision and knowledge destroys even those ties and affections that have made the work possible. Those powers are strangely depersonalized so the testimony to the force of revelation is possible only in the articulated, revealed artifacts. Looking back on the process of creation, the poet himself or his critic may perceive the weight of traditional lore, the habits of prosody that are the poet's personal style. But in honesty one has to admit that there is a leap, a point of breaking, where tradition and personality equally cease to have determining power. The loneliness of the poet and the loneliness of any discoverer is a form of death, both for the tradition of learning and the world it refers to, and for the personality itself.

What renders the poet's work specialized is the social character of language. Critics talk about the vocabulary of forms used by painters or architects or musicians, but poetry really has a vocabulary—a word hoard that all men can more or less employ for purposes of communication. The poet may aim beyond communication to communion. He may try to create linguistic silence, but he still does so with familiar materials. This reliance on a vocabulary of words cuts across the grain of normal human expectation to a greater extent than the vocabulary of forms developed by painters.

When language undergoes distortion, such as even the most conventional poetry must effect, men react to it very deeply or at least passionately. Nothing is more admired or resented than poetry. Like music, it is an incisive art that makes intimate impact. Poetry imposes a rhythm that entails the opening of new nervous channels. The range of human possibility is limited by kinesthetic habit, and part of the resistance to poetry comes from a deep and justified conviction that it will make an exorbitant claim, ask that we change our lives, or with overwhelmingly dangerous intimacy force us to move in designs that we had never previously imagined or entertained. The poet's lonely discovery menaces the social reliance on defensiveness and contempt because it is rendered in designs of language that have a design on the audience. The ideas are only as profound as their impact. Men are threatened only by incisive arts.

The loneliness described by Rilke as the poet's destiny and reward has its articulation in poetic forms that destroy solitude. The same loneliness was described by Yeats in many different essays as a descent into the true self that was deeper than anarchic individualism or social character. Yeats saw that deeper self as personal and typical, and as an embodiment of a universal role or function more meaningful than the social life. In his phrasing, "The rhetorician would deceive his neighbors, / The sentimentalist himself; while art / Is but a vision of reality." Or in another passage derived from John Stuart Mill, "Rhetoric is heard, poetry overheard." T. S. Eliot, in distinguishing the voices of poetry, described first the poet speaking to himself. In Yeats' sense that activity would constitute poetry. Rilke, Yeats, and Eliot all insist on the solitude of the poet's activity, its asocial character, and Yeats exquisitely emphasizes the visionary nature of poetic art. Poets often stress that their art requires that one share the vision, undergo the experience of poetry. They are, in Susan Sontag's phrase, "against interpretation." They are convinced that the poem means exactly what it says. They share the kind of frustration that the scientist undergoes when he sees his work confused with technology and engineering, rather than related to the contemplative action of artist and saint. Anyone who has undergone the experience of science or of religion in a genuine manner understands immediately the irritation of a poet when asked to explain what he is communicating.

When we turn from the essential loneliness of the contemplative life in which the poet participates, we encounter another isolating factor—the relation of the poet to a paramount, transcendent structure, a vision of reality that at once underlies and is expressed or articulated in his artifacts. Embodying this vision in language is the aim of the prophetic poet. Many of the great poets, especially those since the eighteenth century, have been occupied in constructing a vision of the world that will have elegance, harmony, cogency, and inclusiveness. Living as we all do in a world where the standard options have become unacceptable to thinking people, each man has to construct a satisfactory accounting for phenomena. If that man has representative quality and great gifts of articulation, then he is paid attention. In the modern world, men live in multiple spheres to such an extent that each is a universe unto himself. This may be our greatest burden. The poet's singular vision serves to bring us an extension and subtilizing of our own limited and partial view, and once again the vision is communicated with unequaled incisiveness.

Modern men are bound by a special kind of loneliness that is related to the multiplicity of philosophical and religious options available to them. I have already mentioned the Age of Panic and the sense of isolated helplessness that is so prevalent as to be typical. Poets do have a socially representative role that to them is ancillary, but to readers often primary. The kind of loneliness that one finds in Robert Lowell's recent lyrics falls in the category that he calls "the existential dark night." And in the early poetry of Ginsberg, particularly in such well-known poems as "Howl," there is a sense of moral and social outrage at his own solitude and the solitude of others he has known. He tries to utilize his sense of separation to identify himself with the insulted and injured of the world. Thus the refrain of "Howl" in the Rockland section is, "Carl Solomon, I am with you in Rockland," an insane asylum in New York. Ginsberg is saying that he identifies with the suffering, the mutilated, and the damaged. He projects his sense of outrage into a general social view.

Ginsberg's work is very complicated and there are other kinds of solitude and loneliness expressed in it. Some of it is the loneliness of the visionary and the loneliness of the man who is emotionally stifled and emotionally unsatisfied, both by the experience of his body and by the society in which he lives. You see that most clearly in his poem to the terribly sad loneliness of his mother, the Kaddish poem in which he describes a funeral service, her life and death. Then there is the kind of loneliness that comes from a vision that he cannot communicate. There is the loneliness that comes from the lack of love he feels in himself and in those with whom he associates. There is also a heroic loneliness of the sort that Walt Whitman exalted. In his extension of Whitman's vision, Ginsberg looks out a Pullman window and declares, "America, I will haunt you with my beard," a characteristic piece of wry wit. What he is really haunting America with is his eccentricity, his idiosyncracies, his isolating qualities that underline the national isolation and make possible the peculiarly American poem.

So far I have stressed the poet's attitude toward loneliness as a necessary condition of his work, as an arena for struggle where he can find his demons or angels, as the isolation of discovery, as a result of his effort to find and construct a controlling vision of experience, and as an inevitable consequence of his fierce perception of the immediate.

But loneliness is also a primary subject of poetry because it is a major human problem. Most human beings do not share the poet's protection against, or reward for, his loneliness. The poet, moreover, as man rather than artist, suffers as all men do from loss, from the failure of communication, and from the sense of being locked within himself. The poet, too, is one of those that Matthew Arnold spoke of when he wrote, "We mortal millions live alone." Indeed many of Matthew Arnold's best poems have as their substance the fact of unrewarding solitude, the sense of strangeness in a strange land, or the conviction that his buried life may never emerge into a fruitful relation with his daily conscious self. In his poetry, nature becomes a backdrop for the tears of the solitary man. Love normally fails and leaves the individual isolated in the sea of life. Love merely embodies the construction of a sad duo, and the love of this duo is no more than an assertion against the violent dark world where ignorant armies clash by night. Arnold looks with envy on the community of silence of the Carthusian monks and sees it in contrast to the noisy, divided world of his own being as illustrated in a phrase often quoted from the "Stanzas from the Grand Chartreuse": "Wandering between two worlds, one dead, / The other powerless to be born." Or Arnold takes the solitary gypsy scholar as a norm of happy loneliness that his lack of faith will now allow him to attain. He mourns the death of his friend, Arthur Hugh Clough, who did not bring to fullness his entire promise. Solitude is the normal human condition for Arnold. It fills him with misery and, alas, a certain amount of self-pity. This last, the tendency toward self-pity, was so disturbing to Arnold that he deleted one of his finest and most extensive poems, "Empedocles on Etna," from his first large collection, explaining the deletion in his preface on the following grounds:

> What are the situations, from the representations of which, though accurate, no poetical enjoyment can be derived? They are those in which the suffering finds no vent in action; in which a continuous state of mental distress is prolonged, unrelieved by incident, hope, or resistance; in which there is everything to be endured, nothing to be done. In such situations there is inevitably something morbid, in the description of them something monotonous. When they occur in actual life, they are painful, not tragic; the representation of them in poetry is painful also.

Most contemporaries might dismiss this as a priggish Victorian shying away from the difficulties of life. But William Butler Yeats justified excluding Wilfred Owen from *The Oxford Book of Modern Verse* on the grounds that passive suffering is not a proper subject for poetry. Something more than prudery lies behind Arnold's attitude; it was probably that very attitude that led Arnold to give up writing poetry entirely. From our point of view what is even more alarming is that the situation outlined in that selection from his 1853 preface is not very remote from the existential dark night that Robert Lowell described as underlying one of his most representative later poems. I have characterized Arnold's view at length because I should like to inspect the question of whether loneliness is not in fact a kind of passive suffering that poets as great as Arnold or Yeats found a subject so improper for poetry that when it became a dominant obsession of poetry, a man of such intellectual integrity as Arnold stopped writing poetry entirely and became an inspector of schools and a literary critic.

I shall now examine two extreme poetic perceptions of loneliness, Percy Shelley's "Stanzas Written in Dejection near Naples," and William Carlos Williams' "Danse Russe." Shelley's poem used to be part of every survey course in English literature, but fashion has now decreed that it should be forgotten. The poem begins with the description of an exhilarating day, perfect in its Italian fullness of life, and then focuses on the poet, "I sit upon the sands alone." He reflects on the beauty of the scene and then he says with some ambiguity, "How sweet! did any heart now share in my emotion," which I take to mean that his loneliness makes it impossible for him really to experience the fullness of beauty. His loneliness casts a pall over the scene. He describes his inner condition, and when one tries to think about what the worst inner condition might be, one imagines it as a state without peace or calm, contentment, or inner glory, and certainly one lacking fame, power, love, or leisure. Other men may take pleasure in life, but as Shelley says, "To me that cup has been dealt in another measure." There follows the key stanza that has been widely discussed in literary criticism generally and by Shelleyans in particular. I shall reproduce the whole poem because I like it. I first read it when I was about sixteen and have come back to it over and over again. It is beautifully wrought and though not in the current style, still very lovely:

> The sun is warm, the sky is clear,
> The waves are dancing fast and bright,
> Blue isles and snowy mountains wear
> The purple noon's transparent might,
> The breath of the moist earth is light,
> Around its unexpanded buds;
> Like many a voice of one delight,
> The winds, the birds, the ocean floods,
> The City's voice itself, is soft like Solitude's.

> I see the Deep's untrampled floor
> With green and purple seaweeds strown;
> I see the waves upon the shore,
> Like light dissolved in star-showers, thrown:
> I sit upon the sands alone—
> The lightning of the noontide ocean
> Is flashing round me, and a tone
> Arises from its measured motion,
> How sweet! did any heart now share in my emotion.

> Alas! I have nor hope nor health,
> Nor peace within nor calm around,
> Nor that content surpassing wealth
> The sage in meditation found,
> And walked with inward glory crowned—
> Nor fame, nor power, nor love, nor leisure.
> Others I see whom these surround—
> Smiling they live, and call life pleasure;
> To me that cup has been dealt in another measure.

> Yet now despair itself is mild,
> Even as the winds and waters are;
> I could lie down like a tired child,
> And weep away the life of care
> Which I have borne and yet must bear,
> Till death like sleep might steal on me,
> And I might feel in the warm air
> My cheek grow cold, and hear the sea
> Breathe o'er my dying brain its last monotony.

> Some might lament that I were cold,
> As I, when this sweet day is gone,
> Which my lost heart, too soon grown old,

> Insults with this untimely moan;
> They might lament—for I am one
> Whom men love not—and yet regret,
> Unlike this day, which, when the sun
> Shall on its stainless glory set,
> Will linger, though enjoyed, like joy in memory yet.

The lovelessness of Shelley does bring him at that point to genuine self-pity, and his suffering is passive.

Now let us alter our humor entirely and turn from this poem to a celebration of loneliness written a century later by the jovial doctor of Rutherford, New Jersey, William Carlos Williams. The shift, let me warn you, is abrupt:

> If I when my wife is sleeping
> and the baby and Kathleen
> are sleeping
> and the sun is a flame-white disc
> in silken mists
> above shining trees,—
> if I in my north room
> dance naked, grotesquely
> before my mirror
> waving my shirt round my head
> and singing softly to myself:
> "I am lonely, lonely.
> I was born to be lonely,
> I am best so!"
> If I admire my arms, my face
> my shoulders, flanks, buttocks
> against the yellow drawn shades,—
>
> Who shall say I am not
> the happy genius of my household?

Williams' poem transcends its own subject by a happy denial of the very sufferings in the Shelley poem. It is amusing. It is fun and it has a cheerful objectivity about it that is charming. Yet I suspect that it is as objectionable to some as the Shelley poem is to others. At least I hope it is. It is autoerotic to the point of onanism. It is vulgar and smug and posturing as much as the Shelley lines are sentimental and self-pitying and posturing. Can we say, though, that these lines or the Shelley lines are excessive to their subjects? If we object to either poem, we might say that it is tasteless. We are reduced to making this matter a question of taste and judgment. It does not do much good to argue that the Shelley lines are immature. So are the Williams lines. Perhaps the concept of social maturity is simply not applicable to the poetic process.

Very few poems approach the question of loneliness as directly as these do. Often what we take to be loneliness resulting from the loss of love or the loss of an admired leader or friend becomes in the poet's hands something quite different. Catullus really is more concerned with his own passion and the character of Lesbia than with his loneliness. In his elegy for Lincoln, "When Lilacs Last in the Door-Yard Bloom'd," Whitman is more concerned with the intimate panorama of the American nation unified in suffering than with the loss of Lincoln. There is only the most general reference to the character of Lincoln, while the sanctified earth of the nation and the nature of death itself are the real subjects of the poem. Loneliness, then, is the arena where the poet in his inner wandering finds his subject, where his angels and demons rise up for the creative clash that brings him to full awareness. Loss is antecedent to discovery. It is only the alienated who seek and create community either politically or imaginatively. Poems are based on the invisible, barely audible community of the great, lonely figures of tradition. When loneliness becomes the subject of poetry as it is in the works by Shelley and Williams, it does not embody the attitude of the poet or the controlling form of his poetic production. In these cases, the passive suffering of loneliness is thus not the poem, but what the poem treats or starts from. The Shelley poem, therefore, is not really about loneliness but about despair, which is a much more important human condition. The Williams poem, conversely, is about joy.

What then do poets have to say about loneliness? Everything, I would say. For, once the poet has gone through the purifying process of his discipline, of which loneliness is no small part, he speaks to and for others. Man's fate is controlled and limited not only by the strictures of the social order or milieu, but by his nature—his limited capacity for knowing himself and the limited nature of his language.

I should like to consider in more detail two of the great poems of the twentieth century, Rilke's *Duino Elegies*, and D. H. Lawrence's "The Ship of Death." Thanks to the brilliant translation of Leishman and Spender, the *Duino Elegies* have become part of the English-speaking tradition. In the elegies, loneliness is a major subject which is now more and now less explicit, but always a resonant tone. One metaphor the elegies use (much as D. H. Lawrence uses death in "The Ship of Death") is love: the frustration of love and the reward that results from such frustration. For Rilke, requited love is insufficient. He reminds us that the human capacity for the unsatisfied may be our saving grace. It makes our loneliness meaningful. What is more important, "human beings do not love singly nor in pairs, / Their love wells up from immemorable instances." It is invaded by memories they as men cannot evoke normally. In love, human beings look beyond the lover to a reality that the lover only suggests. For human beings, as Rilke sees it, love is a total action, a kind of thorough responsibility for the universe they inhabit. In love, the beloved is left behind. Rilke speaks of what lovers could see if only the other were not there always spoiling the view.

> Look, we don't love like flowers, with only a single
> season behind us; immemorial sap
> mounts in our arms when we love. Oh, maid,
> *this:* that we've loved, *within* us, not one, still to come, but all
> the innumerable fermentation; not just a single child,
> but the fathers, resting like mountain-ruins
> within our depths;—but the dry river-bed
> of former mothers;—yes, and the whole of that
> soundless landscape under its cloudy or
> cloudless destiny:—*this* got the start of you, maid.

> And you yourself, how can you tell,—you have conjured up
> prehistoric time in your lover. What feelings
> whelmed up from beings gone by! What women
> hated you in him! What sinister men
> you roused in his youthful veins! Dead children
> were trying to reach you . . . Oh gently, gently
> show him daily a loving, confident task done,—guide him
> close to the garden, give him those counter-
> balancing nights. . . .
> Withhold him . . .

Love is therefore at its best when unsatisfied; it is most selfless and noble when, like the arrow, it outlives the bowstring. It is described here as total human action involving a temporal continuum that extends back to the very origin of human beings.

Now this is a model of the way in which poetry effectively destroys the loneliness of its reader. Poetry, like all literature, has the therapeutic function of making the human condition more bearable, even a source of fun and joy because it presents the full, incisive indication of human speech acting in the world. Poetry, and indeed all literature, destroys our solitude by placing it intimately in contact with another solitude. It embodies a spatial and temporal continuity. All men may live in loneliness, but no one who can read need be alone. A once useful word has unfortunately become a shibboleth recently: the misuse of language has tainted a perfectly good word like "community." Yet the only way to describe what the *Duino Elegies* do is to say that they provide an entry into a larger and more worthy community of spirit.

The finished poem takes on a social function that contrasts with the loneliness that fuels the poetic process. In talking about poetry on different occasions, I often find myself shifting back and forth from explaining poetry as the work of a poet involved in psychological and technological processes highly specialized and individualized, to explaining poetry as a social event. Poetry is a form of social action even when the poet writes only to be overheard. It may be, as Auden observed, that poetry makes nothing happen but it does make poetry happen. What happens in poetry concerns the courageous and joyful actions with which man faces the mystery of human destiny, of love or death, of external nature, of the otherness of things and beings. He may face his own death as Yeats does in the last stanza of one of his last poems:

> When a man grows old his joy
> Grows more deep day after day,
> His empty heart is full at length,
> But he has need of all that strength
> Because of the increasing Night
> That opens her mystery and fright.

Or the poet may face his own death with a quiet, insistent tone that makes it represent all deaths.

A paradigm of such poetry is Lawrence's "The Ship of Death." D. H. Lawrence is not adequately known as a poet, but some of his best energies went into the poetic enterprise. His stories and novels take much of their vigor from his deep, continuous immersion in the poetic process. Certainly Lawrence's greatest poems are media for seeing and apprehending the human condition and grant us entry to a more generous and delicate life than we could have imagined without them. The poems of death are poems in which the calmness of suffering and the acceptance of fate appear most tenderly. One of them is fairly short, "Bavarian Gentians." He wrote it during the last weeks of his life when he knew he was dying.

> Not every man has gentians in his house
> In soft September, at slow, sad Michaelmas.
>
> Bavarian gentians, tall and dark, but dark
> Darkening the day-time torch-like with the smoking blueness of
>   Pluto's gloom,
> Ribbed hellish flowers erect, with their blaze of darkness
>   spread blue,
> Blown flat into points by the heavy white draught of the day.
>
> Torch-flowers of the blue-smoking darkness, Pluto's dark-
>   blue blaze
> Black lamps from the halls of Dis, smoking dark blue

Giving off darkness, blue darkness, upon Demeter's yellow-
pale day
Whom have you come for, here in the white-cast day?

Reach me a gentian, give me a torch!
Let me guide myself with the blue, forked torch of a flower
Down the darker and darker stairs, where blue is darkened on
blueness
Down the way Persephone goes, just now, in first-frosted
September
To the sightless realm where darkness is married to dark
And Persephone herself is but a voice, as a bride
A gloom invisible enfolded in the deeper dark
Of the arms of Pluto as he ravishes her once again
And pierces her once more with his passion of the utter dark.
Among the splendor of black-blue torches, shedding fathomless
darkness on the nuptuals.

Give me a flower on a tall stem, and three dark flames,
For I will go to the wedding, and be wedding guest
At the marriage of the living dark.

There is a curious pride in his uniqueness that is qualified and placed
in a wider perspective. His death becomes identified with the death of
the year and the reception into darkness that is inevitable and, as he
shows it, worthy of celebration. There is neither self-pity nor bravado
in treating a situation that tempts to both. The relation between man,
brief beautiful flower, and death becomes a sacramental rite.

"The Ship of Death" takes its origin in Etruscan burial practices,
but the association of the longest voyage and the voyage into death
is widely diffused throughout the various cultures of the world.
Lawrence places himself in the framework of these wide human associations, and sees his individual death in the perspective of all preceding
voyagers. His use of the metaphor of the seasons makes for the identification of life and death; he sees the entire world in those terms.
When we approach and face death we are reminded of our ultimate
vulnerability and divested of armor. Death is the final democracy. The
ship of the poem is the vehicle of the journey that is life, that is death,
and that brings us to the verge of human possibility. What matters
most in the poem is the expression of a love of life that makes death
itself an object of love. There is a splendid mild resignation, an abdi-
cation of any property rights to experience. In such a poem, the poet
consoles, reveals, and makes the exigencies of life endurable. He destroys our solitude.

I

Now it is autumn and the falling fruit
and the long journey towards oblivion.

The apples falling like great drops of dew
to bruise themselves an exit from themselves.

And it is time to go, to bid farewell
to one's own self, and find an exit
from the fallen self.

II

Have you built your ship of death, O have you?
O build your ship of death, for you will need it.

The grim frost is at hand, when the apples will fall
thick, almost thundrous, on the hardened earth.

And death is on the air like a smell of ashes!
Ah! can't you smell it?
And in the bruised body, the frightened soul
finds itself shrinking, wincing from the cold
that blows upon it through the orifices.

III

And can a man his own quietus, make
with a bare bodkin?

With daggers, bodkins, bullets, man can make
a bruise or break of exit for his life;
but is that a quietus, O tell me, is it quietus?

Surely not so! for how could murder, even self-murder
ever a quietus make?

IV

O let us talk of quiet that we know,
that we can know, the deep and lovely quiet
of a strong heart at peace!

How can we this, our own quietus make?

V

Build then the ship of death, for you must take
the longest journey, to oblivion.

And die the death, the long and painful death
that lies between the old self and the new.

Already our bodies are fallen, bruised, badly bruised,
already our souls are oozing through the exit
of the cruel bruise.

Already the dark and endless ocean of the end
is washing in through the breaches of our wounds,
already the flood is upon us.

Oh build your ship of death, your little ark
and furnish it with food, with little cakes, and wine
for the dark flight down oblivion.

VI

Piecemeal the body dies, and the timid soul
has her footing washed away, as the dark flood rises.

We are dying, we are dying, we are all of us dying
and nothing will stay the death-flood rising within us
and soon it will rise on the world, on the outside world.

We are dying, we are dying, piecemeal our bodies are dying
and our strength leaves us,
and our soul cowers naked in the dark rain over the flood,
cowering in the last branches of the tree of our life.

VII

We are dying, we are dying, so all we can do
is now to be willing to die, and to build the ship
of death to carry the soul on the longest journey.

A little ship, with oars and food
and little dishes, and all accoutrements
fitting and ready for the departing soul.

Now launch the small ship, now as the body dies
and life departs, launch out, the fragile soul
in the fragile ship of courage, the ark of faith
with its store of food and little cooking pans
and change of clothes,
upon the flood's black waste
upon the waters of the end
upon the sea of death, where still we sail
darkly, for we cannot steer, and have no port.

There is no port, there is nowhere to go
only the deepening blackness darkening still
blacker upon the soundless, ungurgling flood
darkness at one with darkness, up and down
and sideways utterly dark, so there is no direction any more
and the little ship is there; yet she is gone.

She is not seen, for there is nothing to see her by.
She is gone! gone! and yet
somewhere she is there.
Nowhere!

VIII

And everything is gone, the body is gone
completely under, gone, entirely gone.
The upper darkness is heavy as the lower,
between them the little ship
is gone.

She is gone.

It is the end, it is oblivion.

IX

And yet out of eternity a thread
separates itself on the blackness,
a horizontal thread
that fumes a little with pallor upon the dark.

Is it illusion? or does the pallor fume
A little higher?
Ah wait, wait, for there's the dawn,
the cruel dawn of coming back to life
out of oblivion.

Wait, wait, the little ship
drifting, beneath the deathly ashy grey
of a flood-dawn.

Wait, wait! even so, a flush of yellow
and strangely, O chilled wan soul, a flush of rose.

A flush of rose, and the whole thing starts again.

X

The flood subsides, and the body, like a worn sea-shell
emerges strange and lovely.
And the little ship wings home, faltering and lapsing
on the pink flood,
and the frail soul steps out, into the house again
filling the heart with peace.

Swings the heart renewed with peace
even of oblivion.

Oh build your ship of death. Oh build it!
for you will need it.
For the voyage of oblivion awaits you.

One of the difficulties and challenges of writing about the poet's loneliness has been to make a narrow, arbitrary channel through the immense diversity of poetic literature. In a sense the only subject of poetry is human loneliness, seen under the aspect of an inclusive vision and rendered in language that incises its vision deeply and completely in the receptive mind. If we should like to be among those on whom nothing is lost, poetry can show us what we might be missing. Out of this enlightenment issues beauty and the only kind of power that matters, the power over ourselves that transforms mere external fate to inner destiny and gives us that sense of sudden growth, of love, and of courage that only the dignity of full human knowledge can grant. If after that moment of sharing in the sense of glory we find ourselves alone and perhaps lost and wondering, the example remains. The ability to know and appreciate and lovingly accept our loneliness may be the ability of the wisest and best men. At their best poets are precisely such men.

Reprinted from *The Anatomy of Loneliness*, eds. Hartog, Audy, and Cohen (New York: International Universities Press, 1980), by permission of the publisher. An earlier version appeared in *Ohio Review*, Spring/Summer 1977.

"Danse Russe" reprinted from William Carlos Williams, *Collected Earlier Poems* (New York: New Directions, 1938), by permission of the publisher. "The Ship of Death" reprinted from D. H. Lawrence, *The Complete Poetical Works* (New York: Viking Penguin, 1964), by permission of the publisher.

Poets as Poets and Audiences

2

Yeats and Pound: The Illusion of Influence

"How the hell many points of agreement," Ezra Pound asks a correspondent, "do you suppose there were between Joyce, W. Lewis, Eliot
and yrs. truly in 1917; or between Gaudier and Lewis in 1913; or between me and Yeats, etc.?"[1] The question was rhetorical and it is
perhaps impolite to answer it; but it has been answered with apparent
conviction by several critics recently, and answered too simply, especially with respect to Pound and Yeats. Thus John Berryman says of
the change in Yeats' style that he has "always supposed Pound the
motor";[2] and though Hugh Kenner and F. R. Leavis are more restrained in their conclusions, Leavis finds that Pound "influ-
enced . . . . Yeats beneficently at a crucial moment . . ."[3] and Kenner
that Pound "effected some transfusion of ironic discipline into
Yeats. . . ."[4] A. N. Jeffares and Vivienne Koch also argue that Pound's
influence on Yeats was profound, and it is fast becoming a platitude
that Pound was one major—if not *the* major—force in creating Yeats'
later style. Like all such platitudes it will not bear close inspection, but
on critical examination alters to a hypothesis that bears little re-
semblance to the original flat statement. There is little evidence pointing to Pound's influence on Yeats; there is not much more indicating
that Yeats was very important to Pound; and there is a great deal to
support the view that the two men present the unusual instance of
master and disciple outgrowing one another in areas eccentric to the
original points of agreement. Yet they remained bound to one another
by affection and the tension of fruitful disagreement.

The tension is exhibited in a letter from Pound to Sarah Perkins
Cope (1934) in which he betrays his uneasiness in dealing with Yeats'
later poetry: "Are you still young enough to read Ole Uncl. William
Yeats? Or at least to tell me how it strikes the young and tender of your
generation?"[5] Pound, with his admirable and almost compulsive desire
to keep up with and remain capable of instructing "les jeunes," is here
betraying a certain uneasiness before a poetry that, while not to his

taste, had an apparent and puzzling vital attainment to recommend it. Nor is it any mere habit of thinking antithetically that compelled Yeats to write, in *A Packet for Ezra Pound*, that Pound was a man "whose art is the opposite of mine, whose criticism commends what I most condemn, a man with whom I should quarrel more than with anyone else if we were not united by affection. . . ."[6] When Pound was at work on the *Cantos* and Yeats at work on *A Vision* and his later poems, the two men regarded one another with respect tinged by suspicion.

This ultimate disagreement indicates that perhaps the relations between the pair in the period 1908–17 were not so simple and unilateral as Kenner and others now assume. For if Pound taught Yeats how to write major poetry there is something a little unsettling in his judgment of Yeats—after the publication of *The Wild Swans at Coole*. With this first of Yeats' later books available to him, Pound wrote to William Carlos Williams that Yeats had "faded." Apparently he was a little annoyed with his pupil, as he was in the 1930s when he returned to Yeats the lyrics from *The King of the Great Clock Tower* with the single comment "putrid." His lack of sympathy for Yeats' later poems and Yeats' dubious appreciation of the *Cantos* tend to undermine the view that Pound could radically alter the poetry of a man some twenty years older than himself, a man distinguished, Irish, and stubborn.

Yeats and Pound first met in 1909, but until 1911 the two men were not close friends, perhaps because, as Pound said, "Only after five years of acquaintance does he [Yeats] learn to distinguish one member of the race from another member."[7] The period of their intimate relation began in May of 1911 when they met in Paris while Yeats was free of the pressures that beset him in the British Isles:

> Yeats I like very much. I've seen him a good deal, about daily, and he has just gone back to London. As he was here for quiet, one got a good deal more from him than when, as before, he has been occupied with other affairs. He is as I have said once before, a very great man, and he improves on acquaintance.[8]

Before this chance meeting their relations had been distant and formal. Arriving in London at the age of twenty-three, Pound was awed by Yeats' achievement and reputation; to him Yeats was the greatest living poet, and in his letters he mentions him with a curious mixture of reverence and pride. When Pound gave his series of courses at the Polytechnic in 1909, Yeats was the only contemporary that he found significant enough for inclusion. When rumor had it that Yeats intended to say something "nice" about Pound in a public lecture, Pound was elated.[9] With some possible exceptions on the continent, Pound then thought, Yeats was "the only living man whose work has more than a most temporary interest."[10]

This judgment was based on *The Wind Among the Reeds* and a few short lyrics in some of the other collections.[11] These poems proved to him that Yeats was one of the few nineteenth-century English poets who could teach him anything about the technique of verse. He learned from Yeats, taking up similar subjects, even his metrical tricks. Yet he used archaic diction and inverted syntax almost at will in his early poems, devices that Yeats had scrupulously shunned after 1890. Thus Pound:

> Nathless I have been a tree amid the wood
> And many a new thing understood . . .

The inversion in the second line exists purely in order to purchase a rhyme for *wood*, and the archaic *nathless* and *amid* show that the early Pound was farther from modernity than was his master. Moreover, the dominant milieu of Yeats' verse—the Irish and the cabalistic—differs markedly from that of Pound's—Provence and the Middles Ages generally. What they share is the very special attitude of weariness and distrust of experience, of nostalgia for a happier and more interesting time, of isolation in the service of art, that distinguished English poetry of the 1890s. Since Pound neither imitated Yeats' diction or syntax nor followed him into the *anima mundi* with its Symbolist implications, it seems likely that he admired Yeats' poetry because it combined craftsmanlike excellence with a congenial tone.

By 1911, when the two men became intimate friends, both had outgrown Yeats' early style. If we are to understand properly the relation between the two in the years 1911–17, we must realize first that Yeats had become, by 1899, a master of the poetic mode of the 1890s; second that, between 1899 and 1910, he had served an apprenticeship in the theater, attaining dramatic mastery in the process; and, third, that a complex of factors—his personal life, his theater experience, his constitutional will toward self-regeneration—all had conspired to direct a concerted criticism of himself, his thought, and the methods of his early verse. Pound did in time outgrow the early Yeats; but it is also true that Yeats himself—before meeting Pound—had outgrown the early Yeats.

In 1911, when Pound first came to be on intimate terms with Yeats, he had become, under the stimulus of T. E. Hulme and Ford Madox Hueffer (Ford), interested in the type of poetry that we know under the label "Imagism." Yeats' refusal to have any truck with Imagism grew from his preoccupation with the symbolic, and in Pound's mind he became the prototype of the Symbolist; as he wrote in 1937 to William Carlos Williams: "Yeats for symbolism Hueffer for clarity."[12]

But Hueffer stood for more than clarity; as he wrote in 1911, his ideal poet would "voice the life of dust, toil, discouragement, excitement, and enervation that I and many millions lead today";[13] he would "reflect his own day."[14] Hueffer did not apply this criterion foolishly; he stipulated the legitimacy of Hardy and of the early Yeats. But Yeats' indifference to Hueffer and his *English Review* was, to Pound's mind, one of his blind spots.[15] For Yeats was interested in his own day. He did write occasional satirical poems on Abbey Theatre controversies or on the Hugh Lane fight; but Ireland was his chief social reality and the occult, spiritualism, and alchemy the chief spiritual reality. Moreover, Imagism, with its stress on the intellectual-emotional complex caught in a moment of time, was at odds with his stress on the enriching conflict between temporal and eternal reality. Yeats wrote that he wished "to live a passionate life, and to express the emotions that find one thus in simple rhythmical language,"[16] and he said also that "The words should be the swift natural words that suggest the circumstances out of which they rose."[17] This is not Imagism, but an expression of Yeats' interest in the dramatic nature of lyric poetry, an interest that had become an increasingly major motivation in his verse from 1899 onward. His verse from 1912 to 1917 develops, refines, elaborates the techniques of the dramatic lyric that he had already firmly established in main outline with the publication of the *Green Helmet* in 1911 and carried further in *Responsibilities* (1914).

One basis for the belief that Pound had a profound influence on Yeats rises from the fact that for three winters—1913–14, 1914–15, 1915–16—Pound acted as Yeats' secretary at Stone Cottage in Sussex. That Yeats thought Pound was helping him is suggested by his statement to Lady Gregory that working on a poem with Pound was like working on a sentence in Irish dialect with her; and, despite the lack of any real evidence, it is probably true that their intimate association had an impact on Yeats' poetics. But when Pound offered to read contemporary literature to Yeats, he preferred to hear Browning and Morris. And though Pound, at Yeats' suggestion, did go through the early poems and point out the "abstractions" (unneeded epithets), Yeats did not revise those poems until about 1923. When he did revise them, the resultant poetry was very similar in texture and design to the poetry of his 1911 and 1914 volumes, poetry for the most part written before the winters in Sussex. The lyrics written by Yeats from 1913 to 1916 are mainly occult or Irish in subject, in techniques similar to those of his lyrics written between 1903 and 1912. If Pound had any effect on Yeats' lyrics during the Sussex winters, it is not visible.

Pound did not find Yeats an eager disciple. Reviewing *Responsibilities* for *Poetry*,[18] Pound shows a certain reluctance to praise, growing out of his rapidly developing sense that Yeats (being a Symbolist) was, for all his personal friendship, in the other camp. He points out that there is no reason to expect a man to be a leader in two distinct literary movements. His main point, however, is dual: Yeats made important contributions to English poetry in his early work; he may not be in the "movement" at present, but his recent poetry has a new hardness. After praising Yeats for having "driven out the inversion," he describes a "new note" and "change of manner," a certain freedom from neo-Celtic "glamour" and a new "quality of hard light," all of which he approves. He stresses the fact that Yeats is a Symbolist, *not* an Imagist, though he points out that he has written "*des Images* as have many good poets before him." Pound seems, for him, very tentative in his judgment, certainly reluctant to blame but at the same time hesitant to praise. He is sympathetic, he is even hopeful, he is certainly respectful, but he is not—as he clearly was in an article on Hueffer written at the same time—celebrative and warm.

As becomes plain from Pound's published and unpublished correspondence, his early awed reverence for Yeats was gradually changing, under the pressure of intimacy, to admiration tempered by impatience. To Pound's mind, Yeats was more than a great and useful friend—though he was that, he was also a source of encouragement and support—he encouraged Pound's intransigence and supported his impulse to tell people to go to Hell.[19] At the same time Pound found Yeats something of a bore with his incessant talk about spiritualism and his refusal to look with much interest on poetry after Morris. He could not stomach Yeats' occult experiments or accept his interest in the rhetorical and abstractly didactic modes of poetic discourse, his need for stanzaic formality, his use of the widely suggestive symbol, the cogent general statement.

From 1913 through 1915, while Yeats doggedly continued working on Irish and occult material in the manner of the dramatic lyric, Pound was busy on a series of works that typically sprawl over six or seven literary modes: continuation of the Provence poems, some new yawps and blasts in the Whitman manner, experiments in the Imagist mode, imitations of the classic Latin epigram, the *Cathay* translations from the Fenollosa manuscripts, and, from the same source, the translations of the Japanese Noh drama. Of these various works Pound was least satisfied with the Noh translations ("it's all too damn soft")[20] but Yeats was, perversely, most smitten by them. They answered his constitutional need for a theater but did not require that he stand for the insults and injuries attendant on a popular stage. Of his adaptations of the Noh form Yeats could say with characteristic aloofness, "I have invented a form of drama, distinguished, indirect, and symbolic, and having no need of mob or press to pay its way—an aristocratic form. . . ."[21] Pound deals with the matter more practically:

> He [Yeats] has done a play of his own on the Noh model, and is preparing a new dramatic movement, plays which won't need a stage, and which won't need a thousand people for 150 nights to pay the expenses of production. Yeats seems to expect the new drama to do something, at least there will be no compromise, actors will wear masks, scenery will be mostly imagined, at most a cloth or a screen. . . .[22]

Yeats had already been using minimal scenery—the 1911 version of *The Countless Cathleen* used a painted cloth as background—and he had long been meditating on the occult significance of the mask and considering also the stage possibilities of masks. The Noh drama made extensive use of supernatural figures, gods and spirits; and to Yeats, with his abiding preoccupation with the relation between the temporal and the eternal, it was very exciting to hear that the crises in the plays often came with the revelation that one of the characters was in fact a god or spirit. The translations from the Noh drama fell into ready hands.

Yet it was not mere arrogance that prompted Yeats to assert that "I have invented a form of drama." The basic structure of the Noh drama had already been present in his *Plays for an Irish Theatre* (1911), though not so formally, so ritualistically, fixed. In *Deirdre* (1907), for instance, the scene opens with songs by two musicians; a subsidiary character then enters and talks, chiefly to himself with occasional asides to and from the musicians. He then meets the two main characters, who engage in a dialogue; the supernatural then intervenes, the play reaches its climax, the singers conclude with a choral comment. The general pattern of the action is similar to that of many Noh plays, and it was a pattern toward which Yeats was by temperament inclined, allowing for a brief intense action dramatized mainly in dialogue, accompanied by song. *At the Hawk's Well* and *The Dreaming of the Bones*, both written after Pound's translation of the Noh drama, merely carry this pattern to a more rarefied level of abstraction while retaining the basic verse textures of Yeats' Abbey plays. The Noh drama provided a form allowing for the natural development of certain tendencies in Yeats' early plays; it encouraged and strengthened, it did not shape and change.

After 1917 and Yeats' marriage—at which Ezra Pound served as best man—the literary winters in Sussex came to a halt, and the poets drifted apart. Pound had already started the *Cantos* and Yeats with the aid of his wife began the series of psychical experiments and historical and philosophical studies that would culminate in *A Vision*. Both men were committed to differing modes of writing, and what strength they had gained from intimate association was to result in major but basically differing poetries. Yeats would seek a symbolic system that would let him dramatize both the circularity of history and the occasional intrusion of immortal upon mortal. Pound would create ideograms that would let him criticize by juxtaposed images the straight line of decay of usury-ridden monotheistic civilizations. Yeats would cultivate the inner vision of the magician, attempting by incantation to evoke heroic images from the *anima mundi* as models of emulation for the Irish. Pound would, by compelling his readers to *see* economic fact, purify the language and intellect of Western Europe. Perhaps the difference between the two poets is best evinced by their interest in Oriental thought, Pound praising the political perspicacity of Confucius and the clear sense of fact underlying it, Yeats praising the logical and boundless forms of Hindu thought and the symbolic sense of eternal reality that it vindicates.

Between Yeats the advocate of the symbol and Pound the champion of the ideogram lies an unbridgeable gap. Once Pound found what he wanted to become, and that it was *not* a Symbolist, that it was something new and other, something clear, definite, hard, limited, he could not accept the bias of a Yeats. For Yeats fundamentally disliked certainty and definiteness, liked the suggestive force of the unconsciously directed symbol. Pound thought metaphysics and theology were bosh, and yielded to no Marxist in his persuasion that reality was essentially political and economic. Yeats, on the other hand, could—as Rilke urged—"assume the metaphysical," though he was careful not to confine himself to one or two metaphysics, fluctuating between vitalism, pure idealism, and dualism with a splendid disregard for system.

The two men grew apart, their basic differences in temperament and poetic intention gradually forcing a basic divergence of judgment. From this initial awed reverence, through respect tinged by impatience, Pound came eventually to the conclusion that Yeats was, aesthetically though not personally, an enemy. In 1946 he wrote to E. E. Cummings that he remembered very little that Yeats said in print after 1908; from 1920 on his estimate of Yeats' later poetry sank lower and lower, though he never denied the importance of his early poetry. In 1935 he referred to Yeats as a "historic munnymint,"[23] and in 1936 wrote to Basil Bunting that Yeats is "dead," that his "stuff [is] slop," and that he is merely "clinging to [the] habit of being a writer."[24] His chief complaint was against Yeats' "fade out and increasing difficulty of reading the buzzard."[25]

Yeats during this same period remained interested in, and puzzled by, Pound's poetry. He liked *Mauberley*,[26] and once told Pound that he could have outdone Eliot in writing an introduction to Pound's *Selected Poems*.[27] But Yeats' two major public statements on the *Cantos* were not favorable. His celebrated paragraph on the *Cantos* in *A Packet for Ezra Pound* elicited some Poundean invective: "Yeats' bloody paragraph. Done more to prevent people reading Cantos for what is *on the page* than any other one smoke screen."[28] His reaction to Yeats' introduction to the *Oxford Book of Modern Verse* is not recorded, but it was probably vigorous, for in that essay Yeats comes to certain unflattering conclusions about Pound's verse. Pound's work as a whole suffers because it has "more style than form; at moments more style, more deliberate nobility and the means to convey it than in any contemporary poet known to me, but it is constantly interrupted, broken, twisted into nothing by its direct opposite, nervous obsession, nightmare, stammering confusion."[29] Considering the *Cantos*, Yeats confesses: "Like other readers I discover at present merely exquisite or grotesque fragments."[30] And he asks the basic aesthetic question that must give pause to any reader of the poem: "Can impressions that are in part visual, in part metrical, be related like the notes of a symphony: has the author been carried beyond reason by a theoretical conception?"[31] Though he suspends judgment for the moment, it is clear that Yeats distrusts the *Cantos*, distrusts indeed the whole body of Pound's poetry. He finds in Pound the chief source of "that lack of form and consequent obscurity which is the main defect of Auden, Day Lewis, and their school. . . ."[32]

This final disagreement was unavoidable. With it and the other evidence presented in this chapter in mind, it should be plain that, if Pound exerted an "influence" on Yeats, it was minor and adventitious. A summary of their relation would read as follows: For a period the two men were capable—in a very limited sense—of learning from one another; and, though a sharp, fundamental opposition of temperament and interests doomed them to ultimate disagreement, they did strengthen one another. Yeats strengthened Pound by his technical accomplishments, by his selfless dedication to the life of poetry, and by his personal affection. Pound encouraged in Yeats certain tendencies that were already strong in Yeats' poetry and gave him his generous loyalty and admiration as well as his criticism and disagreement. The relation is complicated by the fact that Pound took the early Yeats for his master at a time when Yeats, tired of his own early accomplishments, wished to grow into a fresh set of possibilities. Both poets from 1908 to 1917 were starting from Yeats' early poetry, but they moved from this starting point to ends that were in fact mutually incompatible. They met, profited, grew apart aesthetically, but remained tenuously joined by personal affection. It is a literary relation that is, so far as I know, unique. But Yeats—*not* Pound—made Yeats a major poet.

Reprinted from *Comparative Literature*, Summer 1953.

Notes

1. *The Letters of Ezra Pound, 1907–1941*, ed. D. D. Paige (New York, 1950), p. xxii.

2. John Berryman, "The Poetry of Ezra Pound," *Partisan Review* (April 1949), p. 379.

3. F. R. Leavis, "Ezra Pound: The Promise and the Disaster," *Partisan Review* (Nov.– Dec. 1951), p. 730.

4. Hugh Kenner, "Remember That I Have Remembered," *Hudson Review*, III (1951), 603.

5. *Letters*, p. 730.

6. W. B. Yeats, *A Vision* (New York, 1938), p. 3.

7. *Letters*, p. 96.

8. Unpublished letter in the American Literature Collection of the Yale University Library. The present chapter is based largely on materials in this collection, to which I have had access through the courtesy of the Yale University Library. The letter is dated May 1911 and addressed to Pound's father, Homer L. Pound.

9. Yale Collection, Mar. 2, 1910, to Pound's mother, Isabel W. Pound.

10. Ibid., Jan. 1, 1910, to Isabel W. Pound.

11. Ibid., around Sept. 1909, to Homer L. Pound.

12. Ibid., some time in 1937, to William Carlos Williams.

13. Ford Madox Hueffer, *Collected Poems* (London, 1913), p. 342.

14. Ibid., p. 340.

15. Yale Collection, Oct. 18, 1936, to H. Swabey.

16. Richard Ellman, *W. B. Yeats, The Man and the Masks* (New York, 1948), p. 210.

17. Ibid., pp. 210–11.

18. *Poetry: A Magazine of Verse* (May 1914), pp. 64–69.

19. *Letters*, p. 178.

20. Ibid., p. 137.

21. *Certain Noble Plays of Japan*, translated by Ezra Pound and with an introduction by W. B. Yeats (Dundrum, 1916), p. ii.

22. Yale Collection, Feb. 1916, to Homer L. Pound.

23. Ibid., Mar. 1935, to M. D. Zabel.

24. Ibid., Mar. 1936, to Basil Bunting.

25. Ibid., May 1936, to Basil Bunting.

26. Ibid., Sept. 1, 1920, to Homer L. Pound.

27. Ibid., Nov. 27, 1928, to Olga Rudge.

28. *Letters*, p. 321.

29. *The Oxford Book of Modern Verse*, ed. W. B. Yeats (Oxford, 1936), p. xxv.

30. Ibid., p. xxiv.

31. Ibid.

32. Ibid., p. xxiv.

3

Pound and Williams

Relations between poets are never simple, but the relations between Pound and Williams have a rich complexity that gives them symbolic importance in the history of American poetry. They were friends from their university days until the death of Williams. In the world of contemporary poetry they remain among the greatest resources available to the young writer; what they have given to the American tradition has not been exhausted and probably never will be. They were among our great liberators, and they are among the great contrasts in the American legacy, equivalent to Whitman and James in their achievements and in the charge that their testaments leave to their godchildren. Pound once wrote to Williams that it was "possibly lamentable that the two halves of what might have made a fairly decent poet should be sequestered and divided by the—buttocks of the arse-wide Atlantic Ocean."[1] Pound is responding to the appearance of *Kora in Hell* in 1920 and to Williams' using their relationship in his "Prologue" as symbolic of problems in poetics for American writers. That is a good starting point for considering the special nexus of poetic agreement and tension that distinguishes the art and affection of Dear Bill, Deer Bull, My dear William, My Dear Old Sawbukk von Grump and Dear Ezra, Dear Ez, Liebes Ezrachen, Dear Esq, Dear Editor, You poor dumb cluck, No Ezekiel, Dea Rez—those are some of the salutations used in their correspondence.

The salutations are playful, and even when the correspondence treats questions of treason and imprisonment, the tone is that of two young men, in one of the above instances ("You poor dumb cluck") young men in their sixties. They were always amazingly youthful, and in reading their special conspiratorial works, I sometimes feel that they were in a deep sense emotionally arrested at the age of twenty, which in part accounts for the attraction they exert even after their deaths for the young, and for their willingness to pay so much time and attention to those young who came knocking at their doors.

Eventually, however, this impression dwindles and the abiding seriousness of their positions becomes clear. Their youthfulness is one of their limitations, but it is not crippling. The bouncy tone of puppy conduct and language dwindles when they approach the center of their agreements and dissensions, that is, the life of the imagination.

In spite of the steady creative tension that bound them together, their professional relations were happy and productive. Pound dedicated *Ripostes* (1912) "To William Carlos Williams" and a year later arranged with Elkin Mathews the publication of Williams' first mature book *The Tempers* and reviewed it with praise and prophecies of future distinguished work. When Pound conceived of the *Bel Esprit* project in 1921 to relieve Eliot of economic troubles, he thought of Williams as another poet to be liberated from irrelevant labors. Williams' *A Voyage to Pagany* (1928) was prefaced by the dedication "To the first of us all / my old friend / EZRA POUND / this book is affectionately dedicated." In spite of some breaks, an especially long one after the outbreak of World War II in 1939 until 1946, they were cheerful conspirators, acting as each other's agents, reviewing each other's work, praising one another's work to editors, critics, and other poets, and jointly promoting Major Douglas' theories of Social Credit.

They shared common ground, memories of youth, disenchantment with the dominant economic system of capitalism, the urge to invent and the sense of ordering art and of a continuous tradition that transcended mere convention because it was the fundamental life of the imagination. They were remarkably free with each other, engaging in the frankness of equals. There were occasional outbursts, especially when Williams wearied of Pound's more dogmatic instigations and replied brusquely and truculently. Their affectionate long association inevitably won out over such moments. For long periods of Williams' life, Pound was a lifeline, and it was more than professional respect that led him to call Pound "the first of us all": Ezrachen was "my old friend," and whatever stresses that friendship underwent, it remained unbreakable. Pound was emotionally tied to Williams, but for both of them their affections were qualified and enriched by their symbolic relationship as "two halves of what might have been a fairly decent poet." Pound cast Williams, very properly, in the role of the American friend who, unlike Eliot and H. D., remained tied to the American continent, thus evoking for Pound a sense of doubt and a figure complemental to himself. And Williams accepted the role.

In fact he leaped to it. When *Al Que Quiere* was published in 1917, he turned his attention toward the improvisations that would ultimately form *Kora in Hell* (1920). Those poems were the occasion for bringing his entire relation to poetry into focus, and the ultimate prologue defined a distinctive poetics. In the prologue he uses Pound as the center for distinguishing his work from that of the expatriates Pound and Eliot. Williams provoked Pound into writing him a letter that he quotes selectively, a very funny intimate letter that Williams edits so that Pound seems like a bumptious elitist. But Williams' main fire is reserved for Edgar Jepson, a tool of Pound's in his cheerful vendetta against Harriet Monroe. Williams simply borrowed a page from Pound's book on how to run literary conspiracies.

In fact, Williams added a paragraph to the effect that if one cannot find a fellow conspirator, it is proper to use an intimate personal letter by an adversary, written in the innocent belief that personal letters are not public material. In the correspondence that followed the publication of *Kora in Hell*, after citing the judgment of *Hugh Selwyn Mauberley* by an ungrateful protegé, Pound wrote, "I must cross the proper names out of this, as you're such a devil for printin' one's private affairs."[2] Obviously Pound thought Williams an admirable rogue, but he did take seriously the argument posed by *Kora in Hell* and its ancillary material.

The prologue to *Kora in Hell* is a complex document, but one important point is that it is the first public statement by Williams critical of Eliot and, by implication, of certain facets of Pound. Basically, the differences are established in Williams' anecdote of a typical argument in their early days: "I contended for bread, he for caviar. I became hot. He, with fine discretion, exclaimed: 'Let us drop it. We will never agree, or come to an agreement.' He spoke then like a Frenchman, which is one who discerns."[3] This was the base for their continued mutual aid; the differences that appear when Williams treats Jepson's admiration for Eliot's "La Figlia che Piange" are differences of principle. When Pound uses Jepson as his "bolus" to purge Harriet Monroe, then Williams can say of him "E. P. is the best enemy United States verse has. He is interested, passionately interested—even if he doesn't know what he is talking about. But of course he does know what he is talking about. He does not, however, know everything, not by more than half."[4] The issue can be summarized very clearly and on one point: that of residence, which in turn means cultural identity:

> I praise those who have the wit and courage, and the conventionality, to go direct toward their vision of perfection in an objective world where the signposts are clearly marked, viz., to London. But confine them in hell for their paretic assumption that there is no alternative but their own groove.[5]

Kora in Hell was a programmatic work that asserted the supremacy of the innovative imagination over received associations, but the primary target was the conventional view of poetry in English, with its local habitation in London and its embodiment in the poetry of Eliot and the attitudes of H. D. and Pound. Williams was not one bit troubled by the fact that the improvisations of *Kora* had an earlier parallel in the *Illuminations* of Rimbaud and Baudelaire's *Le Spleen de Paris*; Williams accepted his affiliations with French culture, both its experimental literature and its inventive painting. What he could not endure was the conventionality and the remove from experience that he saw in Edgar Jepson's admiration for Eliot's "La Figlia che Piange," surely an odd choice for a poem to vindicate a specifically American poetic achievement.

The programmatic aspect of *Kora in Hell* was important but at the same time intentionally humorous. Williams made use of Pound wittily and amicably, and Pound reacted accordingly. When *Kora in Hell* was published in full in 1920, Pound wrote three friendly analytical letters to Williams. He knew that there was, as they say in the Mafia, nothing personal involved, just business. What annoyed him most, oddly, was Williams' sly statement that he was "the best enemy of American verse." His defense in his letter to Williams of September 11, 1920, shows the rightness of Williams' argument, affirming his enmity to the faults of American verse and confessing the inadequacy of Jepson's mind: "there was no one else whose time wasn't too valuable to waste on trying to penetrate Harriet Monroe's crust. That silly old she-ass with her paeans for bilge."[6] Pound's irritation with her was endless and far too often justified, but more important than such political literary judgment was Pound's definition of his relation to America.

Pound's reactions to American poetry were not merely aesthetic but in the fullest sense cultural, and his reaction to Williams as a person differentiates him from Williams in a strange and troubling manner. It probably troubles people of this epoch more than it would the contemporaries of Pound and Williams, who were more naturally concerned with immigration and the question of national connection. Pound's argument seems to be that the longer one's family inhabits the American continent, the worse the virus that infests the blood. Hence, Williams, coming from stock only recently introduced to the continent, has a greater richness because a greater freedom from the plague that is Americanism.

> There is a blood poison in America: you can idealize the place (easier now that Europe is so damd shaky) all you like, but you haven't a drop of the cursed blood in you, and you don't need to fight the disease day and night; you never had to. Eliot has it perhaps worse than I have—poor devil!
>
> You have the advantage of arriving in the milieu with a fresh flood of Europe in your veins, Spanish, French, English, Danish. You had not the thin milk of New

York and New England from the pap; and you can therefore keep the environment outside you, and decently objective.

With your slower mental processes, your later development, you are very likely, really of a younger generation; at least of a later couche.

Different from my thin logical faculty.[7]

The metaphor shifts from blood poison to blood thinning—perhaps a king of cultural leukemia?—that comes with several generations of residence in America. Williams as the son of immigrants had an ambiguous advantage. He was an American, newly arrived, mixed in blood. Pound manages to express an emotion new to me, that is, snobbish self-derision. He really does admire Williams, and he really believes that Williams' position is more advantageous than his own or Eliot's—his own mind moved too quickly, had no checks that impelled it toward hesitations, doubts, natural density that derives from lingering over the strangeness of experience. Williams had opaqueness, the density that comes from original perception, while Pound's mind moved unchecked from abstraction to abstraction, logic aborting perception. Common wisdom reminds us that we tend to accuse others of the sins we find potential in ourselves and the cause of gravest guilt, and here in a rare self-critical moment, Pound reveals one reason for his hatred and distrust of abstraction: it was a tempting and inevitable personal vice.

Pound's responses to *Kora in Hell* and its prologue came at a time when he was in serious doubt. The magnificent collaboration of the arts that he had looked forward to in 1913, that miraculous year when all seemed possible, had been destroyed by the war, so that London did not seem habitable. Yeats admired *Mauberley*, but Pound was no longer satisfied with the praise of the greatest living poet; he wanted understanding responses from a respected contemporary, and he asked Williams for just that. Williams was a testing point, both in his work and as representative of the American culture that at once intrigued and appalled Pound. He thought vaguely of returning to the United States but ultimately chose Paris, where his presence would evoke more trouble in Williams' truculent urgencies. Williams became a focal point where Pound's interests and doubts could coalesce.

By 1921 Pound was in the process of abandoning London for Paris, and Williams, tired to death by his work as physician and as midwife to *Contact* and mortician for *Others*, yearned for some escape. His judgments and feelings focussed on Pound. He urged him to come to America and lecture to the populace, and Pound, with eminent practicality, asked what the economic benefits would be and evidently found them not attractive. Williams wrote to Pound in an attempt, as he said, "to normalize myself by addressing you":

It is growing bitter to think of you there far off where I cannot see you or talk to
you. It would be as if—It would be the sun coming up to see you again. . . . I wish
I were in Paris with you tonight. I am a damned fool who sees only the light
through a knothole. I resist, it's about the most I can say for myself. Yet I remember
moments of intense happiness—no it wasn't happiness.[8]

Williams' position seems a variation of Descartes: I resist, therefore I
am. His depression with the state of America grew deeper. Pound was
committed to Europe. McAlmon emigrated into his dreadful marriage,
and the practice of medicine became more demanding and irritating
and preoccupied attention and energy that might better have gone into
his quest for an indigenous American culture. Hence his ambivalence
toward his life increased, and when Pound spoke of Europe the invitation became ever more seductive. His personal status coincided with
the quality of life in America and the attractive exchange rate.

Williams was not alone with his troubles.

Pound could resolve his doubts and escape his disappointment
with the artistic life of England by yet another emigration. T. S. Eliot
had no such escape, and the strains of his life led to a serious breakdown, which Pound diagnosed as the result of overwork. Pound responded by organizing support for artists, especially poets, with Eliot
being the first beneficiary of that *Bel Esprit*. Williams was to act not
only as a donor and possible organizer of an American system of donor-
ship but as a potential candidate for at least enough support to grant
him a summer of leisure in Paris. Pound had in mind a long range conspiracy: "the struggle is to get the first man released."[9]

Williams was not impressed and responded with amiable irrever-
ence: "Oh why don't you go get yourself crucified on the Montmartre
and will the proceeds to art? I'll come to Paris and pass the hat among
the crowd. What the hell do I care about Eliot?"[10] In the body of his responding letter, Williams carries on his battle with Pound and asks
whether he should trade his illusions for Pound's. Pound had taunted
Williams with the offer of freedom as successor to Eliot:

I wd. back you for the second, if you wished. But I don't really believe you want
to leave the U.S. permanently. I think you are suffering from nerve; that you are
really afraid to leave Rutherford. I think you ought to have a year off or a six
months' vacation in Europe. I think you are afraid to take it, for fear of destroying
some illusions which you think necessary to your illusions. I don't think you ought
to leave permanently, your job gives you too real a contact, too valuable to give up.
But you ought to see a human being now and then.[11]

This passage shows Pound's relationship with Williams in much of its
complexity, for Pound is genuinely fond of Williams and at the same
time enjoys pushing him toward a violent reaction. He can show an

understanding of what Williams' medical practice meant to him, something more than a source of income, while renewing the conflict between them that Williams had already made public in the prologue to *Kora in Hell*. This paragraph affected Williams deeply, and after his initial annoyance, he wrote a postscript that committed him to a European venture, that although it would not occur until over two years later, may never have occurred without this challenge. He responded, ultimately, with a sense of liberation to Pound's letter with its statement that the aim of *Bel Esprit* was the "release of energy for invention and design." Pound's generous offer of housing for a summer was itself a release of energy.

The first extended postscript of five hundred words (the original letter was about half that length) was followed by yet another equally long: Pound's description of *Bel Esprit* evoked thought after thought. Williams was deeply grateful to Pound for recognizing that his medical practice had value for him. Pound had had the beneficent effect of leading him to a definition of his life and his future.

> My pace is a slow one but as I am gifted by nature with an inflexible stubbornness and an excessively adherent youthfulness I have not worried about that. If I am to succeed in any kind of valuable work I shall succeed in spite of advancing years.
>
> If I am defeated by sickness or accident I shall always know that I have kept company with my imagination through thick and thin.[12]

He could, now and thanks to Pound's suggestion, realize that he must, even so, go abroad, and soon.

> Now the time has come when I want to go abroad; I do not say that I feel starved for a trip or cramped in any way. I simply feel a strong desire to move in among a few others more or less like myself. I suppose it is really ridiculous to imagine they are any more in the sun than I am. They cannot be so, not today. But they are more used to it. I like good manners and good company. In fact—if life had been more amenable to reason and more luxurient [sic] where I have happened to be in the world reality might have found me—I would have enjoyed the happiest existence conceivable . . .[13]

Williams included with this letter twenty-five dollars as his first semi-annual contribution to *Bel Esprit*. The contribution comes with a special irony, for Eliot, with help from Pound, had just completed *The Waste Land*, which Williams much later would describe as "the greatest catastrophe to our letters." Pound's project continued until early 1923 when Eliot declined to participate and took over the editorship of the *Criterion*. Williams, whether through self-interest or not, maintained his support of the project even after the publication of *The Waste Land*.

In December of 1922, Williams wrote a spirited defense of Pound after the *New York Tribune* published a particularly nasty editorial attacking Pound's project. Williams' answer was not published and it is just as well, for it was ill-tempered and impatient and not very effective. The real impact of the project did not come in any direct impact on Eliot or Williams but because it awakened both a sense of community and affection among writers and, for Williams, acted as an opening to an expanded set of possibilities, beyond Rutherford. Pound was the seminal force, not so much causing as revealing Williams' true feeling and motives. Williams, in time, would go to France, but it seems reasonably certain that without the instigations of Pound and without his affectionate generosity, that time might never have come. In July of 1922 Williams had to give up the idea of a summer in Paris: "It's no use. Can't be done. One hundred and seven dollars to Paris. THIRD class plus the same for return trip. At least fifty dollars in the city—AT LEAST. And I'd only be there ten days."[14] He promised Pound that he would be there in 1923, but in July of 1923 he wrote from Rutherford that he would positively see Pound in Paris or Italy in the spring. And so, during his sabbatical year of release from the practice of medicine, he would. Williams found himself in the awkward position of being published, largely through the agency of his expatriate friends McAlmon and Pound, in France, and France became increasingly his second homeland, much more than it ever was for Pound.

The Great American Novel and *Spring and All* preceded Williams' stay in France, the first published under Pound's editorship and part of a series printed in Paris by William Bird, the second edited and published by Robert McAlmon and printed in Dijon. Two products came from the stay in France, showing the two sides of Williams, the first being the completion of his American recording *In the American Grain* and the second his first novel, *Voyage to Pagany*, very rightly dedicated to Ezra Pound when it appeared in 1928. I say rightly dedicated because without the urging of Pound and without the questioning stirred in Williams by that urging, he might never have made the move to Europe that provided the material and impetus for the book.

It is paradoxical, however, that Pound's instigations of Williams to travel to Europe gave them very little time together. Pound could not see Williams at Rapallo and arrived in Paris a bare ten days before Williams' departure. Although Williams spent six months on the Continent, they saw little of each other, and on Williams' final day of June 12, 1924, he could call on Pound only in the very early morning; Pound was sleeping, and it would be fifteen years before the two would meet again. Pound would shortly establish himself in Rapallo with his complicated domestic life and his dedication to the *Cantos*. Williams after his sabbatical year had a fresh body of experience to bring home with him, but home was Rutherford.[15]

Williams and Pound were then fixed in their geographically defined cultural positions. They continued their transatlantic collaboration, Williams writing laudatory reviews of the *Cantos* in 1931 and 1935.
Pound edited twenty-one poems and eighteen prose pieces by Williams under the title "The Descent of Winter" to form the bulk of the
Autumn 1928 issue of *Exile*, thus complementing Williams' dedication
to Pound of *A Voyage to Pagany*. In the same year Pound wrote an appreciation of Williams for *The Dial*. In 1933 Pound included a generous
selection from Williams' poetry in his *Active Anthology*.

Through the 1920s and well into the 1930s Pound and Williams
were allies, but as Pound became more rigidly fascist in his attitudes,
especially during the Spanish Civil War, Williams drew back from him,
so that in 1939 when Pound came to the United States to avert any possible conflict between his native country and Italy, they had very little
to say to one another. Their friendship would eventually survive their
differences, but from 1939 to 1946 Williams lost patience with Pound.

The relations between Williams and Pound were tripartite: first,
they were friends, loyal to their past associations; second, they were
culturally divided and represented for each other opposing sets of possibility, and finally, they were politically united in their espousal of social credit and its attendant simplified labor theory of value and politically divided by Pound's admiration for Mussolini and Williams'
hatred of authoritarian brutality. Even after the bombing of Guernica
(and Williams, because of his family connections, identified his well-
being with that of Republican Spain), he defended Pound but his patience was running very thin, and he became more assertive about the
rightness of his cultural commitment. In March of 1938 he affirmed the
superiority of his life, as a full unit, to that of the merely literary:

> What the hell have you done that I haven't done? I've stayed here, haven't I, and
> I've continued to exist. I haven't died and I haven't been licked. In spite of a tough
> schedule I've gone on keeping my mind on the job of doing the work there is to
> do without a day of missing my turn. Maybe I haven't piled up a bin of superior
> work but I've hit right into the center of the target first and last, piling up some
> work and keeping it right under their noses. I've interpreted what I could find out
> of the best about me, I've talked and hammered at individuals, I've read their stuff
> and passed judgment on it. I've met a hell of a lot more of all kinds of people than
> you'll even get your eyes on and I've known them inside and outside in ways you'll
> never know. I've fought it out on an obscure front but I haven't wasted any time.[16]

Such a letter practically sets aside friendship for a superior cultural reality, as if Williams' larger identity superceded the personal life. Increasingly Williams came to speak and think as a distinct being who
represented a complex of realities antipathetic to those that Pound represented. He found it increasingly difficult to separate Pound the fas-

cist from Pound the generous and inventive contributor to the modern arts. The disconnection between Pound's art and his politics sickened Williams, so that with the collapse of Republican Spain in 1939 Williams had effectively broken off his connections with Pound.

When Pound did come to the United States in 1939, he and Williams spent very little time together, though Williams at first greeted him with a hearty hug after their fifteen years of separation. But he saw Pound only once again before his return to Italy. At that time he saw in Pound the lunatic of a set of fixed ideas, moving toward a kind of logical and abstract insanity, or so he wrote to James Laughlin:

> The logicality of fascist rationalization is soon going to kill him. You can't argue away wanton slaughter of innocent women and children by the neoscholasticism of a controlled economy program. To hell with Hitler who lauds the work of his airmen in Spain and so to hell with Pound if he can't stand up and face his questioners on this point.[17]

The questioner, about Guernica, was Williams himself. A final wedge was being driven between Williams and the two always forgivable aspects of Pound, the old friend and the poet:

> He's an old friend and an able poet, perhaps the best of us all, but his youthful faults are creeping up on him fast and—you can't avoid issues forever by ignoring them or attempting to change the topic of conversation. Even the lion finally gets a horn through the guts.[18]

The wedge was politics, expressed in the greatest war of human history. It would be, except for a few brief exchanges, the cause of their separation from 1939 until Pound's incarceration at St. Elizabeth's. Williams had no sympathy for Pound, old friendship and poetic achievement becoming irrelevant.

When the United States entered the war after the bombing of Pearl Harbor, Williams was to see his two sons inducted into the Navy and undergo the anxiety of their absence in the Pacific. He had his medical practice and he worked on his long poem. The relations between Pound and Williams took on symbolic weight, so that *Paterson* became an effective act of war. Taking the larger works by Pound, Williams, and Eliot written during and immediately after the war, *Four Quartets* taken as a whole, and especially the last three quartets, affirm Eliot's ultimate identification with the culture of England. The *Pisan Cantos* define Pound as the last remnant of the broken ant-hill of Europe. *Paterson* embodies Williams' commitment to the culture of the American Locale:

"Paterson," I know, is crying to be written; the time demands it; it has to do just with all the peace movements, the plans for international infiltration into the dry mass of those principles of knowledge and culture which the universities and their cripples have cloistered and made a cult. It is the debasing, the keg-cracking assault upon the cults and the kind of thought that destroyed Pound and made what it has made of Eliot. To let it into "the city," culture, the benefits of culture, into the mass as an "act," as a thing. "Paterson" is coming along—this book is a personal finger-practicing to assist me in that: but that isn't all it is.[19]

The book in question was ultimately published not by Laughlin but by Cummington Press as *The Wedge*.

Williams saw two wars before him, the terrible political war and, obliquely related to it, the second and long-term cultural war that came between him and Pound, the war between received convention and innovative tradition, between the socially acceptable and the imagination. Even personal affection dwindled in importance, not because of the social embarrassment caused Williams by Pound's broadcasts from Rome and the subsequent visits from the F.B.I. questioning Williams about his political views and his relation to the Second World War after Pound mentioned Williams by name during one broadcast—the annoyance was real, and three visits from the F.B.I. would unsettle even a patriotic doctor with two sons in the service. But when Pound was returned to the United States for trial and incarcerated at St. Elizabeth's, Williams had simply let friendship go, and the cultural war continued, trailing with it elements from the political war. His indifference to Pound is clear in the letter he wrote on February 1 of 1946 to Dorothy Pound:

Dear Dorothy:
    Your letter of December 10th received, there is nothing I can do for Ezra who, as you may know, is now confined at St. Elizabeth's Hospital, Washington, D.C. as insane. Laughlin, who spent a day with him there recently seems to feel that this represents the true situation.
    I have no desire to write to Ezra. I don't think he'd want to hear from me in the first place and in the second I don't think anything I could say would do him any good. Laughlin is trying to get some money together, I understand, for medical care to be administered to Ezra in the hospital. That's all I know.
    If Ezra wants me to do anything for him as an old friend and you communicate his wishes to me yourself, I'll write and even go to Washington to see the man, not until then.

Sincerely
Bill[20]

The coolness of the letter becomes even more evident when one realizes that Pound had been in St. Elizabeth's for over a month, that

Laughlin had been kept in touch with events through the lawyer that he had procured for Pound, and that in spite of his knowledge of Pound's situation, Williams had remained silent. When the correspondence resumed, the tone and subject matter briefly returned to the old question of their separation, Williams wishing that Pound could have been with him in the United States while recognizing the necessity, however tragic the outcome, of Pound's following another course. At first it seemed that they would work back toward their old relationship, but some new stubborn independence in Williams, some truculence, made him unwilling to gloss over their troubles. Even the recognition of Pound's terrible problems at St. Elizabeth's and the mollifying influence of his wife Flossie did not keep him from brusqueness and self-assertion. Rather than seeing Pound as a comrade he saw him as an opponent. What seemed to irritate him most was Pound's constant curiosity about what he was reading. This reaction came not from any sense that he was simply not reading enough but that much more important was the quality of perception. On July 8 of 1946 he wrote Pound two letters, the first vetoed by his wife and genuinely rude, moving toward the break that would eventually occur in the correspondence later that year. He included that letter along with one written the same day and more carefully phrased: "Flossie vetoed the enclosed letter—but I send it anyway but in a different mood from that in which it was written—for your amusement."[21] Pound could hardly have been amused that his oldest friend should tell him that he really was "cracked," that he was sick of him, that he could not learn anything or even ask an intelligent question, that he was a bully who constantly imposed his ideas on others without any concern for their needs or interests. Flossie's veto forced Williams to phrase his concerns more gently and more positively. When he did so, he was still defining the difference between the cultures that he and Pound embodied. Before satisfying Pound's curiosity about his reading, he cited a sentence from John Dewey's "Democracy and America": "Vital and thorough attachments are bred only in an intimacy of intercourse which is of necessity restricted in range."[22] The sentence meant a great deal to Williams, and my construction of it is that he took it to mean that the fullest direct perceptions and hence meanings came from the immediate and local, not the abstract. It was not reading that mattered to Williams, though he dutifully went on to indicate his reading at the time. He read and translated Eluard, kept up with the surrealists who edited *View* and read the avant-garde works of Anais Nin and Henry Miller and Parker Tyler, and occasionally he read one of the plays of Shakespeare.

So, naturally, you conclude "Poor Bill he ain't interested in ideas." 'S all right with me. But it does seem a waste of time to argue with you bastards. Yet, I must be patient—and work. Work! produce. Better stuff. If only I could do it faster. Too many things block me—you are one of them. If only your intelligence was what it was when you were younger! You were, at heart, more generous then. More alert to others.[23]

To those of us who know what Pound's general condition was at the time, this passage may seem heartless, and in extenuation it must be said that Williams had not been in Pound's presence, and, contrary to his own principles, was acting on merely verbal knowledge. He simply could not get out of the habit of treating Pound as a healthy equal.

And if I grow angry with you it is just that I do not have your help in my work, you a man with what used to be extraordinary perceptions. Now all you do is ask me, "What are you reading?" What kind of an intellect does that present to me? But, as I say, I must be patient.[24]

His patience was tried even more in succeeding months by Pound's insistence that Williams, indeed his entire culture, was living in a twenty-five year time lag. For Williams, Pound simply demanded too much from friendship: "I am half ashamed when I abuse you, knowing your unquestioned abilities, your genius even. But you assume too much. How will you ever be enlightened unless you give the other fellow at least the chance to prove that he is a man also?"[25] Finally, on November 17, Williams simply closed the correspondence, and they did not communicate for about six months.

After that point, they kept their friendship alive in the face of heart attacks, operations, madness, and public neglect and abuse. Williams resigned himself to Pound's reading lists, following out some of his suggestions, and even incorporated a section of a letter from Pound in Book Three of *Paterson* denying that he had told Williams to read Artaud and urging that he read the Loeb versions of the Greek tragedies as well as Frobenius, Gesell, Brooks Adams and the Golding Ovid: "& nif you want a readin' / list ask papa." Williams was very busy with the completion of *Paterson* and the increasing demands on his time from universities and writers' conferences, and he was working against time to bring his work to a satisfying form. But to bring his life into focus meant placing in perspective his relations with Pound. *The Autobiography* and the *Selected Essays* gave a perspective on the past, but for the remainder of this essay I will consider what Williams saw in the *Cantos* in the crucial period from 1947 to 1950. The following essay was written for Dallam Simpson's *Four Pages*, though never published in that very little magazine from Galveston, Texas.

E. P.'s Cantos:

One thing you must say of E. P., he convinces us of the presence of history. Or convinces us, at once and over all as we read him, uniquely—as no one else writing today, prose or verse, has done—that we are in the presence of history. That we stand continually in the presence of history.

His verses are expert, made up of devices of many sorts to convince us of the simultaneity of the historical present. That 6 billion or 60 billion men and women of all qualities, colors and attainments have preceded us but that through all there struck the same light—or darkness. Many were simple, elemental if you like, but exquisitely accurate and just in their perceptions and performances. But some befouled their senses, the common liars—then as today: liars, as carrion is a lie to flesh, smelling of rot. No one willingly smells rot but the just man—and is moved thereby to action by it, toward the living. E. P. insists that we whiff of it—to find many "great."

He discloses history by its odor, by the feel of it—in the words; fuses it with the words, present and past in whatever "language" (all one) to MAKE his Cantos. *Make* them. Why shall we insist that he be "right"? He is not right, he *is*. First of all he is; second, he is eyes, nose, mouth, touch and a perfume—of history: smitten by a stench of liars.

E. P. at his best seems to realize whole areas of the art which no one else more than touches. He has come to represent for me a preeminence of the work of art itself, over against [a] philosophy book or a steel mill or a political pie, which has not been conceived of in the world for many centuries. His grasp (weak as he may be) is for the world, a world of thought and feeling—and action. There is a magnificent unity or attempt at unity, a seeking to pull the world together into something distinguished and true in his great poem. Something just and worth having.

The breadth of Pound's grasp is not sufficiently realized by those who would evaluate him—how he makes you feel the details as part of a whole. The details as he uses them all contribute toward a whole—even prosaic or fragmentary catalogues, just men's names perhaps but heavily weighted with feeling, seem to gather the strength together to *make* the poem. Somehow there is a magic in them. They do NOT fall into grit and rubble but seem to hang together to make a world, an actual world—not "of the imagination" but a world imagined, which is another thing.

It is sad to think of a man so gifted falling into such bad ways. But whatever his condition may be he is yet something for us to treasure in our day as among our greatest possessions.[26]

This essay represents a simple clear act of generosity and affection by Williams, but it is plainly deeply considered. The key point of praise is that the *Cantos* hang together "to make a world, an actual world—not 'of the imagination' but a world imagined, which is another thing." Praise of that sort at that time meant the world to Pound, and Williams sent him a copy of it. Pound also saw and appreciated "The Fistula of the Law," Williams' review of *The Pisan Cantos*, written at the request of Thomas Coles for his little magazine *Imagi*.

This review is not completely enthusiastic in its praise and seems more ambiguous, but there is no question about its commitment to

Pound's work. What he stresses is "a sense of reality in the words." There is "trash" in *The Pisan Cantos*, but that trash is not in the ideas but in "incommunicable personal recollections—names, words without color." The failure is technical but is more than compensated for by "A new hygiene of the words, cleanliness." In the review Williams affirms his affiliation with Pound on the question of Usury. When one tries to condense the common set of ideas that unite, for all their differences, Pound and Williams, it might be simplest and clearest to say, "Art is the basis of reality, not the expression of it," and "In the exact dance of language that is true poetry, the basis of truth is most authentically sounded." Or, in the words of Williams' review, *The Pisan Cantos* derive their truth from being written in "the most authentically sounding language . . . of our present day speech."[27]

Williams would make one more attempt to come to terms with *The Pisan Cantos*, in January of 1950. These notes were intended for his own use, and they were not published until ten years after his death. Essentially, they affirm the integrity of the language of the *Cantos* that renders clear the greatness of Pound:

> The greatness of Ezra Pound lies not, as he grows older, in his esteemed "romantic passages," but in the common text of his *Cantos*—the excellence of the fabric, the language of woof and warp, all through. It is the fineness, the subtlety, the warmth and strength of the *material* that gives the distinction. . . .
> It is the time, the way the words are joined in the common line, common in the sense that the tissues of music are joined or, as one might speak of the book of common prayer, the general text.[28]

There was no separation between the line, the idea, and the man. The language that Pound developed could change the world, but the world would not accept the language for fear of the change:

> Pound was born with a superb ear. He also had a brain. It is the conjunction of these two which is important. In youth the art dominated, as he has grown older the intelligence (no matter how faultily coordinated) is primary. He has struck not at the branch but at the root. It is the structure, the time structure, of the poem that has been his major field. In the *Pisan Cantos* this time structure is the basic importance.[29]

Williams concedes, as he must with his impatience with anti-Semitism and fascism, the faulty coordination of the ideas in Pound, but he remains the literary comrade and personal friend. In basic ways he could conjoin his sense of the dance of language with Pound's, and though they remained always, as Pound early described them, incomplete in opposed ways, Williams could never deny Pound. He could not forgive what Pound had done but he forgave what Pound was.

Williams beyond this point made no further effort to come to terms with Pound, for in the most important sense, that of basic affection, the terms were fixed. They leave us, their godchildren, the special double legacy of the local American and the cosmopolitan American, a reminder of the great hope that we may yet some day in this troubled country develop a culture that is at once local in its origins and international in its resonance and validity. Pound and Williams shared a belief in the power of the poem that Williams in his last extended meditation on Pound's work expressed: "The poem should be read. It isn't even necessary to understand every nuance; no one can do that. Read! Read the best and the thing will come out in a cleaner, more timely, more economically adjusted business world and in better statesmen."[30] In that faith, Williams and Pound lived and died. We have their works, and we have their quarrels and their affections. They have enriched the national life.

Reprinted from *Pound among the Poets,* ed. George Bornstein (Chicago: University of Chicago Press, 1985).

Notes

1. *The Letters of Ezra Pound, 1907–41.* Edited by D. D. Paige (Harcourt, Brace and Company: New York, 1950), 160. Hereafter referred to as *L.* Letter of September 11, 1920.

2. Ibid.

3. William Carlos Williams, *Imaginations.* Edited with an introduction and notes by Webster Schott (New Directions: New York, 1970), 26.

4. Ibid., 26–27.

5. Ibid., 27.

6. *L,* 157, September 11, 1920.

7. *L,* 158, September 11, 1920.

8. Manuscripts Department, Lilly Library, Indiana University, Bloomington, Indiana. Quoted with permission of that library and of the estate of William Eric Williams and Paul Williams. Hereafter referred to as Lilly. Letter of January 4, 1921.

9. *L,* 173. Letter of March 18, 1922.

10. Lilly, letter of March 29, 1922.

11. *L,* ibid.

12. Lilly, letter of March 29, 1922.

13. Ibid.

14. Lilly, letter of July 13, 1922.

15. Lilly, letter of March 29, 1922.

16. Paul Mariani, *William Carlos Williams, A New World Naked* (New York: McGraw-Hill, 1982), 413–14.

17. Ibid., 428.

18. Ibid.

19. *The Selected Letters of William Carlos Williams.* Edited with an introduction by John C. Thirlwall (New York: McDowell, Obolensky, 1951), 214.

20. Lilly.

21. Lilly, letter of July 8, 1946.

22. Ibid.

23. Ibid.

24. Ibid.

25. Ibid.

26. Lilly, appended to letter to Pound of February 21, 1949.

27. William Carlos Williams, "The Fistula of the Law." *Imagi*, IV: 4 (Spring 1949), 10–11.

28. William Carlos Williams, "The Later Pound," edited by Paul Mariani, *The Massachusetts Review*, XIV:1 (Winter 1973), 124.

29. Ibid., 128–29.

30. Ibid., 129.

4

Hart Crane and Yvor Winters

Their Only Meeting

As Malcolm Cowley observed, the completion of "The River" marked the end of Hart Crane's development as a poet;[1] and by summer of 1927, Winters had reached the end of his first period as an experimental writer. His entry that fall into the Stanford graduate school introduced him for the first time to systematic study of the history of English literature, and though Winters is justified in saying that Stanford did not cause the development toward his later style, that it grew from his personal sense of the inadequacy of his free verse experiments to the kind of poetry he genuinely admired, that of Baudelaire, Valéry, "and Hardy, Bridges, and Stevens in a few poems each"[2] the impact of William Dinsmore Briggs and of the canon of poetry in English were, in effect, Stanford.

Early in summer Winters rejoined Janet Lewis Winters in Santa Fe, and they then went on to Palo Alto where they settled in a rustic atmosphere, with Winters' dogs, soon to be augmented by goats, and a sizable vegetable garden. Crane went through a series of abortive plans, hoping again to establish the conditions that led to the creative period on the Isle of Pines. At times he wanted to return to the island, but there was no real house to live in since the hurricane; he was impelled toward Martinique, then Mallorca, then Europe in general, or he would seek employment in New York. His father continued sending him fifty dollars a month, and in September he received a further subsidy of three hundred dollars from Otto Kahn.[3] Martinique seemed possible, but in mid-October his mother moved to Hollywood with his ailing grandmother, and she objected to his being so remote from her. He found an unsatisfying job in a bookstore in New York, and then in early November he was invited to act as secretary and companion to Herbert A. Wise, a wealthy man recovering from a nervous breakdown. Crane looked on the arrangement as the greatest possible luck.

Wise was going to Altadena, California, so that Crane could see his mother frequently without bearing the full burden of her constant presence. Winters was within reach by a twelve-hour train ride, and he was one of the first people that Crane wrote to, only two days after his arrival. At Winters' request he had visited Elizabeth Madox Roberts, whom Winters had known since his year at the University of Chicago in 1917–18. Winters had in fact contributed to her support while he was studying at Boulder and she was suffering from illness. The book that Crane had just finished reading was *My Heart and My Flesh*. The letter is dated November 23, 1927 from Mr. Wise's rented mansion at 2160 Mar Vista Ave. in Altadena.

> *2160 Mar Vista Ave.*
> *Altadena, Cal.*
> *November 23rd, 1927*

Dear Winters:

Ye Gods! what a pink vacuum this place around here is! I just arrived day before yesterday, and already I'm beginning to wish I had jumped off the train around Albuquerque. I sort of sensed it at the time—and almost did. The hybrid circumstances of my immediate environment make it all the worse: a millionaire neurotic (nice as he is) with valet, chauffeur, gardener, and all the rest. This house seems to be all bathrooms and bad furniture, about which my boss suffers about as much as I do, but apparently the president of the American Express, who rented it to him, isn't afflicted by anything. I have already limousined around enough to wince at the "sculptural" advertising which you mentioned. If the bull that advertises some eating place were only a bit more gilded, not to say gelded, I'd approve of that one piece, however, as a symbol at least, of the whole shebang. Did some one say Spanish architecture?!!!!

I won't promise not to blow off more steam before seeing you—when you'll get aplenty—but this will do for now. I'll try to keep the home fires burning somewhere within me without exploding and thereby losing my job. They say that work is hard to find in California. . . .

Yes, I went to see Elizabeth Madox Roberts. It was certainly worthwhile, and she was most cordial, though I never felt that society could torture any human being so much before, without intending to. I thought of a sibyl writhing on a tripod. No one, with any amount of deliberation, could have so taken the part. But I doubt if I should have remained any longer than I did, regardless of a previous engagement that took me away within a half hour. We talked about you, California, her book. This latter I had hurriedly read a day or so before meeting her. There is no doubt about its permanence as a major accomplishment. And one feels the sense of form, a relentless pattern, from the 20th page or so right on to the terrific torture of the climax—and then the beautiful "dying fall," the unforgettable pathos of the obscene inscriptions in the w.c. It's a marvelous book. But I don't think it necessarily diminishes the stature of *Ulysses*. Its range is more limited, and its intentions are different. Formally, yes, of course—it is more solid. Such debates are useless, however, with our present lack of any absolute critical logos.

I'm a bit muddled, and may remain so for awhile, especially as my situation demands a good deal of egg-stepping here. But I'll do my best to avoid boring you, and with the avid hope that you will support me to some extent by whatever rages, deliberations, constations, etc. may seem worthwhile putting on paper for the nonce or otherwise. I ordered your book from Four Seas months ago; has it come out yet?

Faithfully,
Hart Crane

Winters responded by suggesting that they meet at Christmas while he and Janet Lewis were visiting Winters' parents near Pasadena and close to Altadena. Crane welcomed the opportunity to meet one of his most devoted admirers, and he looked forward to some literary conversation. The review of *White Buildings* by Marichalar had appeared in the February 1927 edition of *Revista de Occidente* (Madrid). As Crane wrote to Slater Brown, he anticipated the arrival of Janet and Yvor Winters as a real event. The formality of Mr. Wise's household had a dulling effect on him. Crane wrote gratefully and with hearty anticipation to Winters on December 8:

2160 Mar Vista Ave.
Altadena
Dec. 8th

Dear Winters:

I am anticipating your Christmas visit a great deal. Please do get in touch with me right away on your arrival: phone *Niagara 2684*. I have just located a court near here, where, if I am a great deal improved in my technique by that time, we may possibly have a game or so. Right now I'm lamentable.

This locale is certainly growing on me. No, I'm not turning up my nose. For one thing I've been too much out of breath! Movie studios have so far occupied a good deal of the time, mainly owing to my boss's curiosity in that direction. And I've looked up a couple of minor constellations (Alice Calhoun and Robert Graves) whom I used to know in school in Cleveland. Your kind introductions have been unemployed so far—simply owing to the rush. The world is small. . . . Ran into a very pleasant fellow who used to know Tate at Vanderbilt, etc. Meanwhile I'm becoming gradually accustomed to the formalities of a broker's household. AND begin to worry a little about having too good a time—that is for the approbation of the muses.

But I have at least read his copies of Richards' *Principles*—and Weston's *Ritual to Romance*. The former is damned good. I look forward to a detailed talk with you about it. The latter is especially interesting as revealing to me my unconscious use in *The Bridge* of a number of time-honored symbols. Wise (my boss) has a substantial enough stack of good things to read to keep me busy for some time.

I'm enclosing a review of "W.B." which was a good while getting to me, but which opened a slight correspondence between author and critic, which, if I ever go to Spain for a visit, may be profitable. Marichalar writes the Madrid letter for the *Criterion*. Perhaps you're already familiar with his work, prolog to the trans. of Joyce's *Portrait*—, etc. I had Macauley send him a copy of the *Am. Caravan*, which, he says, interests him very much. I hope later to see what he writes about it in the *Revista de Occidente*. Please don't lose this clipping. I had to correct him about the Statue of Liberty. That was a gift from the great *République Française*, you know!

All best to you—
Crane

The meeting between Crane and Winters has excited some lurid imaginings, but it was in fact gentle and decorous. Later, Winters was to observe that Crane's appearance was not healthy when they met:

> I saw Crane during the Christmas week of 1927, when he was approximately 29 years old; his hair was graying, his skin had the dull red color with reticulated grayish traceries which so often goes with advanced alcoholism, and his ears and knuckles were beginning to look a little like those of a pugilist.[4]

What evidence Winters had of Crane's "somewhat violent emotional constitution" came largely from hearsay. During their only meeting, Crane behaved amicably and politely. There was no drinking; there were no unseemly incidents.

This information comes from Janet Lewis Winters. She and her husband traveled by train from Palo Alto to Los Angeles, and as she said recently, "That was a long trip in those days." They stayed at the home of Winters' parents in Flintridge, overlooking Pasadena, the setting of Winters' childhood:

> From the high terrace porch I watch the dawn.
> No light appears, though dark has mostly gone,
> Sunk from the cold and monstrous stone. The hills
> Lie naked but not light . . .
>
> This is my father's house, no homestead here
> That I shall live in, but a shining sphere
> Of glass and glassy moments, frail surprise,
> My father's phantasy of Paradise . . .[5]

Crane came to visit them in the afternoon. Janet Lewis was still convalescing from tuberculosis and was confined to bed each day until four o'clock. They had tea together in her room, and they talked, about California, about poetry. Crane stayed for dinner, and after dinner Winters' father took them for a drive down the famous Christmas Tree street in Pasadena, lined with deodars and decorated and lighted brilliantly for the season. Crane and Winters shared the back seat, and Crane gave a wildly vivid recitation of the new version of "The Hurricane," which Winters had seen in an earlier form. They met four times for extended periods during that Christmas week.

They talked poetry, and as Janet Lewis says, Crane was charming, as he often could be. The conversations were evidently like the letters, affectionate and respectful and amusing, but always turning toward the common ground of poetry. They argued about Blake, with Winters pointing out that Blake's "The Tyger" was composed of perceptions throughout. Winters also showed and read aloud to Crane from the Bridges edition of Hopkins, to Crane's delight.

Winters was a natural pedagogue and Crane a grateful audience and interlocutor. Winters went through a considerable body of French poetry with Crane, especially Baudelaire, Rimbaud, and Valéry, though as Janet Lewis recalls, he did not read *Ebauche d'un Serpent*. Crane had very little French, so that Winters translated passages. Janet Lewis' clear impression is that Crane would have had difficulty struggling through a poetic passage with a dictionary and that he must have got all his French through translations. With Winters' magnificent sense of the poetic line and his thorough control of the language—and his pedagogic patience—it was a revelation to Crane.

To Winters, the occasion was one of the abiding joys of his life. In his essay on "The Significance of *The Bridge* by Hart Crane or What Are

We to Think of Professor X" written some twenty years after the Christmas meeting of 1927, Winters says:

> Professor X says, or since he is a gentleman and a scholar, he implies, that Crane was merely a fool, that he ought to have known better. But the fact of the matter is, that Crane was not a fool. I knew Crane, as I know Professor X, and I am reasonably certain that Crane was incomparably the more intelligent man. As to Crane's ideas, they were merely those of Professor X, neither better nor worse; and for the rest, he was able to write great poetry. In spite of popular and even academic prejudices to the contrary, it takes a very highly developed intelligence to write great poetry, even a little of it. So far as I am concerned, I would gladly emulate Odysseus, if I could, and go down to the shadows for another hour's conversation with Crane on the subject of poetry.[6]

So deeply did Winters remember those meetings in Flintridge and Altadena, and perhaps those meetings came to his mind when he picked up the letters from Crane and contemplated their destruction. And he may well have remembered those golden days of the late twenties when he could earnestly write to Crane that they were living in a great literary period. Whatever his final judgments of Crane, from his first reading of "For the Marriage of Faustus and Helen" he saw genius in him and felt his death as a tragic waste and loss.

During the reminder of the stay their talks continued in an atmosphere of mutual respect and trust. Winters left behind several of his own poems. Crane was overwhelmed by Hopkins and asked Samuel Loveman to find him a copy, even if it cost ten dollars—a large sum at that time for anyone in Crane's financial circumstances. And, as he often did, he commented on Winters' poems. The poems should have suggested to him that some basic changes were occurring in Winters' poetics. For one thing, they were sonnets, and during their correspondence to that time, Winters had been writing in free verse. After Winters left, Crane puzzled over the sonnets and made characteristic comments. His criticism of one sonnet might have been instrumental in changes that Winters made.[7] Winters was to say that he wrote the sonnets to annoy Crane, but he took them with some seriousness.

Winters sent a copy of Hopkins to Crane and continued sending Crane poems for comment, and he also wrote a letter defending Crane from an attack by Kay Boyle in *transition* for January 1928. The attack by Boyle was balanced by a fuzzy review of *White Buildings* by Laura Riding. Apparently Winters' visit invigorated Crane's interest in poetry: he was reading Phelps Putnam's *Trinc* and MacLeish's *Streets in the Moon*, and he was weaving a tortuous passage through Ramon Fernandez's *Messages*, with little reward. The following two letters discuss the problems raised by his reading and by the January issue of *transition*.

Jan. 10 1928
Altadena

Dear Winters:

I've had a devil of a time making up my mind about the four sonnets! They are certainly not without value, possibly great value for all I can say—for I have the suspicion that some of the more obdurate lines contain concepts well beyond my scope of detection. My only complaint is that in general they strike me as but partially achieved "as harmoniously functioning units." . . . Why not work on them for a while longer, or lay them aside only, and take them up again! They have a fine, hard ring. Metrically good. But too skeletal—i.e. like a chemical formula rather than its concrete demonstration, which is an equivalent for what a poem ought to be in terms of metaphor. I have the idea that my "Atlantis" is lacking in the same sense.

"The winter stars flash into ermine dusk"—this sonnet strikes me as the best of them all, excepting perhaps "God in his loneliness—." There are as brilliant lines in others, but not as consistent a synthesis. For instance: "Screaming eternity of infinite logic is grinding down receding cold" . . . This blurs somehow. But there is perhaps no finer moment in any of them than

> Pinnacled, solitary, I can find
> your face, but not your eon: could you burn
> across my calendar that none has read,
>   etc.

I hope you got the copy of *The Bare Hills* I forwarded to you from the publisher. I'll expect the books you mentioned today or tomorrow. I'm keen about reading Hopkins so do, please, send him. And your thought about sending other books from the library is kindness itself. I may ask you for something or other soon. This is very hastily written, I hope you will forgive; for we are off for a day at Santa Monica in a few minutes. Please give my sincere regards to Janet Lewis—and try to hope for better from me when I get my head out of the configurations of the *Prophetic Books!*

Hart Crane

2160 Mar Vista
Jan. 20th '28

Dear Winters:

I can't help rejoicing that someone has come to the rescue of my Grandmother, for above and beyond the bellowing and wallowing, there was the odiously patronizing reference to one of my relatives, which I may yet feel justified in answering, albeit it can only provoke mirth, no matter what *I* may say. The admirable *temper* of your letter, however, should prompt me to leave well enough alone. After all, anyone who reads "My Grandmother's Love Letters" will notice that Kay Boyle hasn't. . . . But it's really the spectacle of anyone getting away with such snottiness that gets my goat. She apparently has no sense of pride or professional integrity.

I'm glad that Laura likes me and my work, but I hope she never gets herself (and incidentally me) so wound up in a ball of yarn. Is she trying to evolve a critical style from Gertrude Stein? My God, what prose! Honestly, if I am forced to read much more of that sort of thing I'll go back and join hands with Morley and Canby. I've got as far as *Trinc* already. Damned if I don't like that "Ballad of a Strange Thing" more and more. It has an integrity of rhythm which isn't obvious at first. And I like a number of other things in the book without, however, thoroughly approving them. Putnam really has just as much to say as MacLeish, perhaps more, but isn't quite so devious in saying it. My favorites turn out to be just those of everybody else: Memorial Rain, Selene Afterwards, Nocturne, Signature for Tempo (1), and Immortal Helix. That Fragment in *The Caravan* was the best yet. Certainly MacLeish arouses one's speculations as much as anyone these days.

The epistemology of the Fernandez book is difficult for me to grasp. I started the initial chapter several days ago and soon found myself horribly muddled. I have an idea that he is awfully long winded and somewhat pretentious—but that is no better than a prejudice, so far. Meanwhile I shall lay the blame on myself and pray for the advent of a gleam of revelation when I pick up the book again, which will be soon. Did I shock you once while you were here by the admission that I had never read *Wuthering Heights?* Well, I have made up for lost time. Captain Ahab now has a partner in my gallery of demon-heroes, for I'll not soon forget Heathcliff! You probably read Proust "in the native," but if you should care to read the translation of *Sodom & Gomorrah* which is just out let me know and I'll send you my copy. The Stanford Library will *not* have that, I feel sure, and as the edition is limited to subscribers you may not find it accessible. I've just about finished it.

I'm sorry I haven't been able to do more justice to the admirable lyrics that you have sent me lately. But as I have more than hinted by numerous actual demonstrations of critical ineptitude lately—I find myself less and less sure of a number of previous persuasions. Finding myself completely disoriented I can hardly pretend to the capacities of a firm judgment on anything but more technical details. And even these are involved in—and justified or disqualified by—the intention or direction of the work as a whole. All this may well be less evolution than involution. But until I get back on the tracks again my word isn't worth much.

Getting back to *transition*—it was a pleasure to see the two Tonita Penas, and "The Fixer" (Hemingway) story was good burlesque. His *Men Without Women* is a book you ought to read. The short story called "The Killers" makes one doff one's hat.

Please remember me to Janet Lewis—and I can't help thanking you for the letter to *transition!*

Crane

The receipt of Hopkins' poems was important to Crane, and he reacted gratefully. At the same time, his meeting with Winters and the reminder of Winters' continuous productivity urged him toward his own work. Nothing had been accomplished in California except some extended reading that was only incidentally pertinent to his interrupted work on *The Bridge*. "Cape Hatteras," which Winters was to dislike in its finished form, remained a set of incomplete notes. His troubles with his mother were coming to a head, and he was already thinking of leaving Wise. His letters to Winters were cheerful on the surface, and in this correspondence he was notably reticent about the details of his personal and family life, but this letter exhibits a basic uneasiness:

Altadena—
Jan. 27 . 28

Dear Winters:

I hope you are in no great rush for the return of that Hopkins book. It is a revelation to me—of unrealized possibilities. I did not know that words could come so near a transfiguration into pure musical notation—at the same [time] retaining every minute literal signification! What a man—and what daring! It will be long before I shall be quiet about him. I shall make copies of some of the poems, since you say the book is out of print. As yet I haven't come to the theoretical preface— nor Bridges' notes—excepting a superficial glance. Actually—I can't wean my eyes from one poem to go on to the next—hardly—I'm so hypnotized . . .

Having jumped from Proust into *this*—haven't yet got to the Fernandez vol. Nor have I had time to do justice to Janet Lewis' poems—for which, please tell her, I am most thankful—and also for the line drawing—which looks a great deal like you.

I happen to have felt a good deal in one of those parturition times lately—with the clamant [?] hope that I was about to yield "Cape Hatteras" or something equally ambitious at almost any moment . . . but have been so subject to interruptions that I guess the fit has passed off . . . leaving only an irritating collection of notes and phrases defying any semblance of synthesis. I'm going to stop all reading soon in a more-or-less desperate effort to digest and assemble what I've been consuming—or maybe to put it even out of mind. I'd like to get a little work done soon—or else take up copywriting, plastering or plumbing again. . . .

To go back beyond your last—to the mention of Tom Nashe—you named one of my greatest Elizabethan enthusiasms—though all I know of him is his *Unfortunate Traveller*.

Well thanks again to you and Janet Lewis—

Hart Crane

Almost a month intervened before the next letter, so that it opens with apologies. Crane was becoming increasingly bored with his life as companion to Wise and worried over the condition of his family. He was a little spiffed when he started the letter, and he was irritated with Fernandez's *Messages*, for which no sensible person could blame him— it is one dull book. He shared Winters' annoyance with William Carlos Williams, who singled out "See Los Angeles First" from the new poems by Winters, largely, one suspects, because it was close to what Williams himself was working on at the time. And Crane, in his turn, emphasizes "The Vigil," probably because it was close to the depressed and frustrated condition of his own mind.

2160 Mar Vista Ave
Feb 23 '28

Dear Winters:

Since I am becoming chronically remiss in responding to all the epistolary courtesies of my friends for so long a time past as to be (or to have been) long since disparaged—I make no more excuses in detail, beyond the passing recognition of that imperfection, its millionth confirmation, as it were, with the added addled protest that I am still, as always, your friend, and that silence is not more mysterious, in this instance, than (at least) cordial. Further, I have at present a little Spanish port in my noddle. And who knows (quien sabe), perhaps the wine is to blame for conceit of writing you. But enough of bows and furbelows!

Your friend Fernandez—his epistemology and indirections are on the verge of forcing me to hurl his pretentious tome into the fire— which is what Wise tells me he did long since, before enduring half so much of his insufferable prose as I have already! I have to take long vacations and dissipations between glimpses of those great messages of his, so it is taking me a long time to come to any decision about him. Meanwhile I'm susceptible to a thousand and one temptations as momentary reliefs. I am especially consoled by Wyndham Lewis's latest, *Time and Western Man*, which at least has a vigorous style, whether or not you agree with all he says: a bull-headed man, astonishingly sensitive in many ways—who is a lot better than the usual Doug Fairbanks of controversies. I advise you to read the book, even though it costs—Well, let me know, and I'll send it to you. . . .

Yes, Williams would naturally prefer such a secondary item as "See L. A. First" to your better things. I've always had my finger on that soft spot in his—no, not brain—but character! He's almost as bad as some of the "revolutionary simpletons" that Lewis lays out, excepting that I'll always concede him a first-rate talent for language. If he'd only let himself alone! He's so afraid he'll find the Zeitgeist at his heels— not realizing that by means of that very attitude it's been *riding* him for some time since.

In "The Vigil" you are at your best, in action, but at something less than that in "registration" . . . I can't help telling you that in such a poem you do not carry me beyond the level of my own station in the laboratory of a like quandary. There is a certain lack of synthesis. I'm in the same fix in regard to my "Cape Hatteras"—a bundle of smoldering notes, no more. I don't know when the proper moment may arrive to grasp them and make them a whole. . . . It's a damned hard time we live in. And I think you stand a much better chance of biding your time beyond it than I do—for a number of reasons.

Glad you liked the Blake. It really IS worth having. I am still discovering new marvels in Hopkins. Do, please, forgive me for withholding these books so long. I'll return them soon. My heartiest greetings to Janet Lewis. . . .

as ever,

Crane

The note of March 7 is little more than a note, and it does not mention any cause for Crane's state of mind. But he had made his decision

to quit Altadena, and returning books to Winters was part of the process of clearing out:

> *2160 Mar Vista Avenue*
> *Altadena, California*
> *March 7th*

Dear Winters:
   I hope you got the books all right—if not please let me know at
once, as I sent them about ten days ago. My letter probably peeved
you—in which case I'm sorry. I won't plead excuses however—
beyond the fact that I am in a rather unpleasant state of mind all round
these days—and am therefore poor company.
   I hope that all is well with you. And let me repeat my thanks for
your many courtesies.

> *Yrs.*
> *Crane*

   Crane moved in with his family, and Winters, on hearing of the ill
health and other difficulties of Kay Boyle, decided not to send his letter
of protest to *transition*. Winters' *The Bare Hills* had finally appeared
from the Four Seas Company, and it had been reviewed by Agnes Lee
Freer in *Poetry* and by Allen Tate in *The New Republic*. Agnes Freer took
the book with deep seriousness:

> Strong winds blow through *The Bare Hills*, a book inspiring in its absolute original-
> ity. To some readers, it will signify mere austerity. Others will find tenderness, as
> they find in it the gigantic conflict of the first movement of Beethoven's *Ninth Sym-
> phony*, or in the fateful tones of Brahms' *Tragic Overture*. Important and remarkable,
> it may be better understood in France than in America, for Frenchmen are not
> afraid of the dark. Yvor Winters cannot complain if, after some of the sophisticated
> cadences of today have died out, Time, the flow of which is almost a physical sen-
> sation of pain to him, but Time in the only conception the average person has of
> it, brings these sculptured poems to a place in what men call the future.[8]

   And Allen Tate, describing how the book goes "Beyond Imagism,"
found in it "a classical precision of statement, a kind of naked elegance,
which no other contemporary poet commands."[9]
   The reference to Benét has to do with one of William Rose Benét's
unfortunate attempts at humor, a review of *White Buildings* that degen-
erates into a set of impertinent parodies.[10]

1803 N. Highland
Hollywood, Calif.
March 29th '28

Dear Winters:

I'm glad you withdrew the protest in *transition* for I don't believe in booting anyone when he's disabled or "down." "Hell of a world" is right! I feel like an episode from Cervantes since going to Pedro last Sat. night to meet a friend of mine from the east who worked his way clear out to see me—as a waiter on a steamer. Five thugs waylaid us, beat us nearly insensible and robbed us of everything. I finally got him back to his bunk—but am still worried sick about his condition. The ship left next morning without my being able to get aboard to see him.

I haven't yet seen the *Poetry* review, but whatever objections I might have felt are already obviated. The Benet jibe has also escaped me— unless it is the mention of "The Tunnel," which dates back to January or earlier. I'm piqued by curiosity. Could you lend me the clipping, if you still have it? You are the best cudgel wielder I know, and I'd hate to miss the swing of your blow.

Your second-last letter would have been answered before this if my affairs had been more settled. I left Mr. Wise's mansion about a week ago. It was a very distracting place and I regardless, had come to the unshakable conviction that I was needed elsewhere. So I am remaining on here—in order to do what I can to alleviate the predicament of my mother, who is confined every moment by her attendance on my grandmother. The two are quite alone out here, and I couldn't go back east with enough mental ease to make it in any way profitable.

This decision has thrown me into the familiar scrimmage for employment. I'll secure something in the way of mechanical writing—advertising or scenario—with one of the movie companies if possible. Not that I prefer it to some other jobs, but I must secure the maximum cash to in any way fulfil my purpose in staying. My own projects in any case, will have to go hang, at least for awhile. But I hope I shall have sparks left over to redeem the waste of time that bread and butter claims.

Tate's review was well written, and to me seemed very laudatory. I know it to have been completely sincere. In a way it was more "fortunate" than his preface to my work.

I'm rushing off to an interview—so my mind is too preoccupied to do anything justice at the moment. But I owe you better, and shall try to *do* better in the next few days. Meanwhile, as always, I'm grateful for your patience!

Hastily,
Crane

Winters' review of *Fugitives: An Anthology of Verse*, appeared in *Poetry* in May 1928 and marked a departure for Winters: it was the first time that he reviewed a book of which he did not approve. His sole positive purpose was to talk with general approval of the poems of Allen Tate, and his main negative impulse was to decry the impact of T. S. Eliot on poetic style. The review occasioned a bitter response from John Crowe Ransom and a complaint from Tate. Crane liked it, not only because it attacked Eliot, whose *The Waste Land* he was attempting to counteract in *The Bridge*, but also because Winters recommended Crane—alone with Baudelaire, Corbière, Hardy, Dickinson, and Hopkins—as a proper guide for young Americans who wished to achieve anything poetically. They should look to "the spiritual *and* formal values of two poets—Hart Crane, and especially that of the most magnificent master of English and of human emotions since Thomas Hardy, William Carlos Williams."[11]

May 7th '28

Dear Winters:

Your review of *The Fugitives* is full of nails well hit and powerfully driven. And you manage to cover an amazing amount of ground! You can't imagine how much such writing means to me these days of fad and insipid compromises. It is evident that you are not reserving your onslaught against Eliot for your book of criticism announced for next year! And you are dead right in attacking Eliot's followers in manner and attitude. When you come to a man like MacLeish, though, I think you may find him harder to dispose of creatively than Eliot himself. He is really illusive—perhaps not genuinely anything—as he has displayed himself in several successive postures. . . . Anyway, I like your good solid opinions. It takes a stoic to have them nowadays.

The Benet jibes were all too obvious to do much more than point back to the idiotic mind that dared boast of such stubborn density. The Canby Crap Can is always full of such complacencies. I'd rather prompt their ridicule than their praise.

Isidor Schneider recently sent me his new poems—and wondered if you'd like a copy. I said yes. *Anthony* has vigor and confusion and a lot of other features—nearly everything but major form. But I like a few of the shorter poems—*Sunday Morning, Funeral, Whatever you seek*, etc. None of them flash or sing however as even the second-best of Williams—but Schneider's drollery is good even if heavy,—in places.

I see you have read *Wuthering Hts.* But the one apparent vagary in your review seems to me your mention of that book in connection with

Racine. It ought either to have been amplified or omitted. At least I can't relate it in any definite way to the "inadequacy of former spankings." I haven't read much by Herbert—just neglect, not lack of interest. Marvell is another that I didn't encounter until lately. Do you know the wonderful lines (57–66) in his *The First Anniversary*—where the building of Thebes is described? They have that perfection of solidity and inward movement so hard to equal in any modern forms.

Any chance of our meeting here this summer?

Yrs.

Hart Crane

There was no chance of their meeting again that summer, or ever again. On June 27, Crane would write to Winters from Patterson in a happy vein and with only a brief explanation of his precipitous departure from Hollywood.

The Last Phase

After Crane left California, the correspondence with Winters did not deteriorate—it simply dwindled away. Crane was preoccupied with his family and economic problems, which were inseparable. Leaving his mother and grandmother in Hollywood was an act of flight that he sustained for the rest of his life. He was never to see his mother again, and his grandmother died in September. From his arrival in Patterson until his departure for Europe in December, there was very little calm in his life. Now that he was famous and his work sought after by magazines, he had nothing to send; no progress was made on *The Bridge*, and after some spectacular misconduct, even Mrs. Turner could not put up with him any longer. He was cast adrift and wandered from friend to friend, getting temporary jobs in an advertising company and in a bookstore. His friends were loyal, but his depression was generally constant. Writing to Winters would remind him of his wasted poetic vocation, and that was too painful to contemplate.

His letter written shortly after arriving in Patterson is jovial enough, partly because of sustaining memories of the Mississippi and New Orleans, and more surely because of his sense of release from the clutching troubles of his mother. Winters was deep in the study of Renaissance poetry and offered his reading list and if necessary copies of texts. Crane's response was friendly but not encouraging.

Patterson, New York
June 27th, 1928

Dear Winters:

I left the Coast on the 15th of last month. I had thought that I had given the hasty signal of at least a postcard dropped off the station platform at Houston or San Antonio, but evidently not, judging by your good letter received this morning via Hollywood. I left in a hurry, but not without due deliberation. You already know my grudges against the L.A. population, but perhaps you don't know my full distaste for family turmoils. At any rate . . . here I am again in the old house with the old woman and her cats, and sneezing as strenuously as ever at the date of roses . . . and damned good and glad to rejoin a few human associates who live around here and to smell a little horse manure again.

The boat ride down the Mississippi to the Gulf was, of course, something of a heart-throb to me. One day only is enough to make one sentimental about New Orleans. I never before felt so in the presence of the "old" America—not badly "confronted" with it, as at places like Salem, Mass.—but surrounded and rather permeated by it. But I suppose pewter is the more representative, and the old tarnished gold of Orleans belongs rather to the traditions of Martinique than to the spirit of the Minute Men. I'd like to spend a winter there sometime, anyway. And the Mississippi delta is all that I ever dreamed it to be. Then I had four more days on the water before a sight of land. It's just as cheap as the northern routes, and to me a lot less tiresome, though longer.

Nathan Asch and his wife as well as the Cowleys and Josephsons are close neighbors of mine this summer. There is also a cashiered army officer turned bootlegger over on Birch Hill, who makes very good applejack. But in spite of all this whirl, not to mention the usual croquet tournaments up at Slater Brown's place, I intend to get something done before going into N.Y. later for a job. I've met Williams before, but I'm hoping to know him better when he comes out here soon as a guest of the Asches. They are also hoping to get Morley Callaghan down from Canada for a brief spell . . . but I'm beginning to sound like a maitre d'hotel.

To get back in the files a little—I am glad that my dear old Kit still gives you so much kick. I am always amazed at the glorious cornucopia that Tamburlaine shakes page after page. I enjoy the antiquated spelling even in this case, of the Oxford edition, wherein the buskins of Hero are described as a "*woo*nder to behold." Truly, the very prologue to Tamburlaine and the very first words set the key for the diviniest human feasting:

From iygging vaines of riming mother wits,
And such conceits as clownage keeps in pay . . .

What a "flourish without" to signal the whole Age of Elizabeth! and a promise that was truly kept! I have been haunted by those two lines so many times, and always wonder in what consists their strange combination of tangibility and illusions. You get it also in Keats' "Eve of St. Agnes," but not in quite so joyous, so robust a form. The very kindly jaggedness of the Marlowe lines endears them more, at least at times, than the suave perfections that somehow reached a little over the line, into death, with Keats.

The tremendous lines from Blake that you wanted are on page 763. They always strike me as about the most final lines ever written. At your mention of Traherne I have been looking over some specimens in an anthology I have and can't imagine why once, years ago, I failed to appreciate his astonishing validity. Vaughan, whom he certainly bears a likeness to, really does bore me excepting a handful of complete poems and scattered lines in others. It lies rather with a kind of Presbyterianism that infects Vaughan, I surmise; whereas Traherne's piety is more universalized, more positive. You even begin to suspect him of apocalyptic casuistry here and there, so crystalline and capable is his bended head, when lo! by adding even more wit to the occasion he convinces you of his complete absence of vanity. Almost a Brahmin in some ways.

I'll follow your advice and read more of Herbert. Cowley has a copy down the road. But please don't bother about the proferred copy of Traherne—not that I wouldn't love to have it, but I'm so near N.Y. now, that such books are once more accessible. You may be interested in watching for some forthcoming articles in the *Outlook:* Cowley on Poe; Tate on Emily; Burke on Emerson (I think), etc. I haven't been able to get advance carbons from any of them, but these three generally have something worthy of interest. Cowley has a rather slow, laborious mind that simply cannot turn out a shoddy sentence. I would rather talk to him about the sheer mechanics of poetry than anyone I know—that is since Tate has become too pontifical for any discusions whatever. Which reminds me of the protests you mention receiving for your Fugitive review. I suspect you irritated a great deal by spelling his first name Allan instead of Allen. He raised such a row with Liveright about that misdemeanor on the title page of *White Bldgs.* that the whole edition was torn up, new title pages inserted and rebound. As to the locutions of Marianne—she seems to have had at least a good time with her briefer on your book. I shall never be able to make out the meaning of "apperceptions . . . whose cumulative eloquence recedes in geometrical inverse ratio to imperativeness." For God's sake, somebody play the "Kitten on the Keys," PLEASE! All this exudes a "flabby algebraic odor"—which in one of Cummings' poems is descriptive of a good-sized c—t.

I didn't mean to end matters so oderiferously; I'm sure I can congratulate you on your pups, anyway, if not on your Turgid Mention.

All best,
            Crane

On July 31, Winters wrote to Harriet Monroe about her reaction to Crane's "Moment Fugue," after Crane had sent him her note on the poem. Winters probably destroyed Monroe's note, as he destroyed practically all his correspondence, but his letter to her is preserved in the Poetry Magazine Papers at the University of Chicago Library. It is not quite so amusing as Crane and his friends found it. Winters made a reasonable paraphrase of the poem and managed to offend the staff of *Poetry* in the process. His letter elicited an acerbic note from Jessica North, who had been responsible for the initial note to Crane. And Winters wrote a scathing reply. *Poetry* did not publish the poem.

            New York City
            Aug. 17th, 1928

Dear Winters:

Aunt Harriet deserved the justling. Cowley and some others have had a good time reading the carbon you sent, which you don't mind my having shown, I hope. . . .

I'm in the big, simmering gluepot Metropolis hunting work. Not much to say in any direction and slightly dizzy.

So you'll forgive my brevity, I hope. I'd give you my present address, but it's so uncertain for any length of time that you'd better keep me at Patterson, whence forwarding is more certain.

As ever,
            Hart Crane

Three weeks later Crane had found a job and a remedy for hay fever, but he could not forget the effrontery of Jessica North's joking (as she saw it) attempts to diagram the sentences of "Moment Fugue" and failing. Crane was too troubled to write a proper letter. His grandmother had died on September 6, bringing sorrow and new troubles.

77 *Willow St*
Brooklyn, N.Y.
Sept. 9th '28

Dear Winters:
I'm back again where I can see the harbor from my window, and Brooklyn Bridge. Also I've found a job (copywriting) as well as a remedy for hay fever that really seems to work. In regard to the last, if you have any other sneezing critters among your friends who need relief remember to tell them of the following two remedies which team beautifully—Rinex (internally) and *Estivin* (for eyes). More violent cases should apply to Miss Jessicum North, Mother Superior of Thunder Mug University, Illinois, for summary advice and parsing treatment. . . .
Have been reading Laura Riding's "Contemporaries and Snobs" (Jonathan Cape) and recommend parts of the first 100 pages as some really remarkable analysis, fumblingly expressed, but damned suggestive. *And* have you heard Bach's *Toccata & Fugue in D Minor* on the Orthophonic yet? The Philadelphia Symphony gives it wonderful volume. The pattern and purity of it are beyond praise. The sublimest rhetoric I have ever heard!
My mind is mostly a flat blank these days, that is—what is left of it after it has been crammed and unloaded several times every day, the material being CALOROIL HEATERS, FOS-FOR-US MINERAL MIXTURE (for hogs, cattle, poultry) and FLOWER OF LOVE WEDDING RINGS, etc. etc. The high tension rush of an agency office is only to be compared with a newspaper office. Inserts, folders, circulars, posters, full pages and half pages, a two-column twenty-liner here, there this there that! But I'm sorry to be working and, in fact, was damned lucky to get anything as good right now.
When I get a little back on my feet financially I'll feel a little more like a man. Meanwhile you seem to have the gracious facility of making me believe that I am possibly at least a poet.

All best, hastily,
Hart Crane

Winters was troubled by the letter and the previous silence. He was at the time busy contemplating Allen Tate's *Mr. Pope and Other Poems* and preparing a review for the *New Republic*. He wrote extensively to Tate, praising his work and finding in it the only major poetry by a contemporary other than Crane. Shortly after receiving Crane's letter he wrote on September 15 to Tate, acting as a conciliator between the two men, having found Crane's isolation and unhappiness painful. He asked Tate not to be irritated by Crane, who had told him at their meeting in California that Tate was annoyed with him. Winters conceded that Crane might be hard to take in personal association but because of the quality of his mind and work, he was one of very few people who should be accepted and tolerated, whatever just occasion for irritation his disorderly conduct might create. Tate found the moral advice impertinent, and he did not write to Winters again until December when he was on his way to Europe. Winters' assurance that Crane admired Tate immensely did not move him. Crane in this difficult period of his life had become a trial to his friends. Tate's patience and generosity had been called on too often, and Winters had seen Crane only at his most engaging and sober moments.

After his grandmother's death, Crane's troubles with his mother increased. She refused to sign the papers that would permit him to receive his legacy from his grandmother's estate, and she kept urging him to join her in California. That was the last intent in Crane's mind; his main desire was to keep as far from his mother as possible, and he intended to use his share of his grandmother's estate to keep, as Unterecker puts it, not only a continent between them but an ocean as well. Europe was his destination. With all his confusing and embittering problems, attention to purely literary matters was impossible, so that some six weeks lapsed before he wrote again to Winters. The occasion was Winters' review of Tate, appearing in the *New Republic* for October 17.

110 Columbia Heights
Brooklyn, N.Y.
Oct. 23 '28

Dear Winters:

I won't enumerate all the excuses I've had for my negligence of you. They wouldn't seem valid to you without inexcusable details on my part, and perhaps even then you'd need a slice of Babylonian routine yourself, directly experienced, before you'd be able to summon the necessary charity.

I've started two or three letters, been interrupted or obliged to complete some office work at home, etc. etc. But I have wanted to say something about the three sonnets you sent, long before this, and even now they aren't with me. So I can only give you my preferences: the Emily one first, the one ending—"I'm dead, I'm dead" next. But the other one, though ambitious and solid emotionally, somehow falls short of a sufficiently rich intonation. Allen Tate is more successful sometimes at expressing something of the same feeling of cerebral thunder in a vacuum, "invisible lyric seeds the mind," etc. But I think this group is superior, less strained than the sonnets in the Caravan.

Your review of Tate in the N.R. strikes me as nothing less than noble. Of course I resent being posed in a kind of All American Lyric Sprint with anyone, as the competitive idea seems foreign to my idea of creation. But that is probably too personal a reaction to have any pertinence to the major critical issues of the review. I also think that while Tate has a very complex mind and possibly a wider grasp of ideas than I do—he nevertheless has not come to any closer grips with his world than to simply state the dilemma in a highly inferential manner, which we're all obliged to do most of the time. Tate's greatest rage against me at times has been on account of my avowed (and defended) effort to transcend these Eliotish sighs and tribulations, and to reach some kind of positive synthesis.

Tate faces the issue more squarely than the later Eliot. I like your appreciation of his really unflinching valor. But when you speak of my "illusions" you convince me that you surely are mistaken in a number of my intentions. I am not content with being an absolute Stoic. I mean, stoicism isn't my goal, even though I'm convinced as much as you and Tate are, of the essentially tragic background of existence. There's something entirely too passive about stopping there (I don't care if even so great a poet as Hardy did!) and counting out, like the beating of a clock, the "preconceived" details of disappointment. For that is the stoic's pride—that all will pass but his endurance. It seems to me that Aeschylus, assuming the same materials, does a lot more with them. At least he makes something out of them, call it all illusion or not.

After many inquiries and some intrigue, even, I'm back in the old house where I have a view of the harbor again. Rooming houses depress me terribly, and this is about the only one that sets me reading and writing a little, though I actually haven't had time, with the rush at the office, to read more than the usual reviews on the can or in the subway. I suspect I'll soon be off your list if I don't do better.

Yours,

Crane

This was to be the last substantial letter in their correspondence for more than a year. One short letter refers briefly to the problems with his mother and gives a forwarding address in London.

110 Columbia Heights
Brooklyn, N.Y.
Nov. 29th, '28

Dear Winters:

I've been encircled too much by the whirlwind hysterics of—well, Fate (if one may allude to one's family in that way) to answer your last. And it isn't possible now, either.

I am hoping to get off to London on the 8th of next month, if the feat can be managed. May stay in Europe a couple of years, some quiet and secluded working hours on the island of Majorca being my objective.

At any rate, the best address I can give for the next month is c/o The Guaranty Trust Co., 50 Pall Mall. S. W. 1, London. I'm sorry to be so limited right now in my responses, but it may be that distance will lend me a part of my thinking and speaking apparatus again.

> *Best wishes, as ever,*
> *Hart Crane*

A final postcard promises letters after arrival in London.

Am on my way as per schedule. I'll be able to write after I get to London—or later on the way. Please excuse delay.

> *Hart*

The letters would not be forthcoming, so that from the period between December of 1928 and December of 1929, the relations between the two men broke off, not because of any dispute or rancor but because of Crane's reluctance to continue the kind of serious literary discussions and considerations that mark his correspondence with Winters. The correspondence might have become less sympathetic, for Winters was consolidating his sense of poetics and establishing new directions for his work and thought. In his freshly developed optique, his admiration for Crane's work diminished, so that Crane became the object of probing analytical judgment rather than the occasion for appreciative reviews, essays, and letters.

The silence that fell over the correspondence of Crane and Winters between December 1928 and January 1930 was matched, in Crane's career, by a year of relative public silence. During 1929 Crane published in magazines only three poems, two of them written much earlier, the third—"A Name for All"—a poem so dull that it is hard to believe Crane could have written it and astonishing that he should have published it. It almost seems that he had ceased to take poetry seriously, and if it had not been for the enthusiasm of Harry and Caresse Crosby, he would quite probably never have written the three sections of *The Bridge*—"Indiana," "Cape Hatteras," "Quaker Hill"—that marked his only significant productivity after the completion of "The River." And those three sections have been seriously questioned by the bulk of students of Crane's work; they are among the weakest segments of the poem. The Crosbys were so taken by the work completed before Crane's arrival in Paris in January of 1929 that they did not feel it necessary for Crane to write any more of the poem. Crane still felt committed to the design that he had described to Otto Kahn, Winters, and others, and one of the terrible agonies he underwent during that period grew from his dissatisfaction with his new work and the doubts this cast on the entire project. The excitement of life in Paris was no compensation for the frustrations that overwhelmed him as he contemplated the ruins of his poetic enterprise. Solitude in southwest France and a visit to Robert Graves in the Camargue were no help, and dissipation in Marseilles gave temporary satisfaction but left him with his overwhelming problem. In addition to his troubles with his writing, and growing from them, his sexual excesses became more flagrant, his drinking uncontrollable, and his violence so spectacular that his brawling in the Café Select led to arrest, imprisonment, a brutal beating by the police, a fine, and a very stern judicial warning.

He managed to get some work done on "Cape Hatteras" in France, but when he left for the United States in July, the months in Europe had been largely wasteful. Two years had passed since the brief period of happiness and productivity that resulted in "The River." His morale was destroyed, and as his drinking continued he was afflicted with hallucinations and nightmares. Only the loyalty of a few friends remained and helped him to do what he could on *The Bridge*, until in December he gave the poem over to the Crosbys for publication by the Black Sun Press. He had concluded, as best he could, the labor of years. On December 26 he sent a final revised version of "Quaker Hill" to Caresse Crosby with a postscript asking her to send a review copy to Yvor Winters.[12] So that year ended, with the suicide of Harry Crosby, the unsatisfactory completion of his ambitious project, and prospects that were unclear.

For Winters the year had been very different. While Crane was living an extreme version of the image of the bohemian poet, Winters was living a quiet and productive life as a happily married literary student, with the satisfactions of a rural setting and the pleasures of systematic academic study. Poetry continued to come, though in traditional measures rather than free verse, and under the tutelage of William

Dinsmore Briggs and in company with new and admiring friends, neighbors, and fellow graduate students he explored the range of verse in English from Chaucer on, while maintaining and extending his interest in French verse from Baudelaire through Valéry. He also began writing his first extended critical prose since his master's thesis at Colorado in 1925, in preparation for his doctoral dissertation and to define his own poetics. That enterprise began in 1928, and by August 20 of that year, he had completed the important and incisive essay that formulated the intent and design of his doctoral thesis and his eventual first critical book, *Primitivism and Decadence*. The essay was published in *American Caravan* for 1929 under the title "The Extension and Reintegration of the Human Spirit, Through the Poetry Mainly French and American Since Poe and Baudelaire."[13] He continued shuffling the poems in *Fire Sequence* and adding new poems. Early in 1929 he began publishing in mimeographed form *The Gyroscope*, including new work by himself and others and severe commentaries on current literary practice. Winters was active in all aspects of the poetic enterprise. He went on writing brief reviews and fresh poems as well as his extensive critical work and his editing. He was busy, happy, and productive. He continued raising Airedales, and at the instigation of Janet Lewis Winters—who was tired of making drawings of dogs—acquired goats and other animals. They maintained an extensive vegetable garden that would ease the economic troubles of life during the Great Depression. The antithesis to Crane is striking.

At this point the two men seem to be living out the allegorical types with which they have been associated, antithetical in social and inner life. Winters profited from his stability by maintaining a continuous flow of verse and criticism, and he also used his relative freedom to articulate the basis of his thought about life and art. In the academic year 1928–29, he was supported by his father, so that his life was set in a frugal design but he was free of the interruptions of teaching. What emerged from his investigations and meditations was the rational stoicism that would mark his basic point of view from that time onward. It had always been in the background of his thought; now it became systematic and primary. Basically, Winters accepted the view of science that dominated Hardy's thought and was evident in coarser terms in Jacques Loeb. The escape to mysticism, which he associated with Crane, he found evasive and untrue. When Yeats' *The Tower* appeared in 1928 he thought it the only Yeats that was genuinely major, but he despised what he took to be the charlatanry of "The Gift of Harun Al-Rashid." His dislike of mysticism and especially of spiritualism came from his childhood experience. His mother correctly predicted the death of some twenty people, and when he was very young dragged him off to séances; his reaction drove him to his youthful interest in the sciences, and it was one of the formative forces in his life. His experience in the tuberculosis sanatorium reinforced his inclination toward stoicism.

I do not mean that Winters in his later work accepted completely and without qualification the mechanistic structure of the world. His sonnet "The Invaders" is eloquent testimony to the limits of the scientific view, but it is ambivalent. What the invaders have done is, in a phrase that echoes through his thought, to strip life bare, and in the process to dissolve "our heritage of earth and air!" The color of the earth has been stripped, leaving "The naked passion of the human mind." This mental passion is demonic, and as Grosvenor E. Powell has argued, Winters took the concept of the demon very seriously:

> Aquinas tells us that a demon may be said to be good in so far as he may be said to exist; that he is a demon in so far as his existence is incomplete. This statement is a necessary part of the doctrine of evil as deprivation. But a demon, or a genius, may be almost wholly deprived of being in large areas in which theoretically he ought to exist, and at the same time may have achieved an extraordinary degree of actuality in the regions in which he does exist; and when this happens, his persuasive power, his possessive power, is enormous, and if we fail to understand his limitations he is one of the most dangerous forces in the universe. Our only protection against him is the critical faculty, of which, I fear, we have far too little.[14]

What matters in the scientific view of the universe is its "extraordinary degree of actuality," and its incompleteness is one compelling argument for the imaginative force of art, which can restore to experience those qualities that the demon of "The naked passion of the human mind" cannot realize or entertain. In the period from 1928 through 1929, Winters developed in the fullest form those ideas that would characterize his mind thenceforward. What was lacking in the modern view of the world was any justification of a moral point of view. The horror of the human condition was so great that only the great artist could face and control it:

> The facts of life at best are disheartening; the vision of life which man has little by little constructed (or perhaps one should say stripped bare) is all but crushing. . . . The artist who is actually ignorant of the metaphysical horror of modern thought or who cannot feel it imaginatively—and there are many such—is of only a limited, a more or less decorative, value. But the artist who can feel the full horror, organize it into a dynamic attitude or state of mind, asserting by that very act his own life and the strength and value of his own life, and who can leave that state of mind completed behind him for others to enter, has performed the greatest spiritual service that can be performed.[15]

In contrast with this noble stance, Winters derided the mystic and the nihilist for their evasions and their lack of courage. He never explicitly defines the "metaphysical horror of modern thought," though he seems at one point to identify it with a "sense of time in an incomprehensible universe." The horror is also associated with that solipsistic mysticism that Winters was convinced led to self-annihilation. Mysticism, nihilism, or the scientific view "stripped bare" by years of study and experiment—these alternatives were inferior to what should best be called a kind of "moral aestheticism." Winters writes that

> Art is the most intense moment of consciousness: the intensity of the moment of fusion is the final moral assertion of the artist, who by that act *makes an integral part of his own dynamic existence* the fact that he has met [life], no matter how terrible it may be. It is the final proof that he, as a self-directed integer, is morally superior to the facts of life. A successful poem, then, may be, as an experience and a moral evaluation, a negation of the ideational material that it contains. This fact alone can explain the spiritual security to be found in the most terrible of the tragic poets.[16]

This passage presents certain difficulties, though I am at a loss to think of a way that the difficulties could be avoided. Art differs from experience; the moment of fusion is the total imaginative and moral understanding of the data of experience and is not to be confused with mere intensity of emotion or perception. Unlike the metaphysical pantheist, the artist is superior to the aggregate of data; unlike the nihilist, he asserts as a high value his own capacity to achieve through his dynamic existence a moral superiority to meaningless data; unlike the scientist, he creates a moral and aesthetic entity that transcends the merely mechanistic and abstract. Art thus becomes the basis rather than the expression of meaningful experience. Winters makes the highest possible claim for the importance of art, but he cannot demonstrate its legitimacy; he makes an assertion, an act of faith.

And that is what the preliminary sections of the essay on "The Extension and Reintegration of the Human Spirit" compose, an assertion of passionate belief. With variations and extensions, it would remain the center of Winters' thought about art and letters.

The remainder of the essay goes over ground that Winters would cover more fully in *Primitivism and Decadence*, notably his taxonomy of poetic methods, and material discussed in earlier work on Imagism and in his correspondence with Crane and Tate. Winters continues to treat Crane's work with great respect, and he adduces him as an example of a poet whose verse embodies a fusion of allegorical with imagistic qualities:

Such things as *Serenade at the Villa*, for instance, or most of Hart Crane, implicate entire ranges of ideation and feeling that cannot be reduced to any formula save the poem itself. . . . Hart Crane, by means of his semi-allegorical method, continually and most often successfully attempts to evade an unequivocal statement . . . by constantly running his allegory ashore on the specific. He is an example of a soul with a natural taste for the schematized and abstract being forced by his milieu toward the specific; and it is on the specific that by far the greater part of the important poetry of the last eighty years has been based in the main.[17]

Crane's merits are illustrated by comments on "Repose of Rivers":

We have here an obvious and commonplace symbol—the course of a river standing for the life of man—and the monologue is presumably spoken by the river itself. The symbolic value of the details, however, is not so precisely determinable—they are details not of the life of man nor even directly referable to the life of man, but are living and marvelous details of a river's course, with strange intellectual and emotional overtones of their own. Mr. Robert Penn Warren has remarked that the life of an allegorical poem resides precisely in that margin of meaning that cannot be interpreted allegorically. . . . the words are constantly balancing on, almost slipping from, the outermost edge of their possible meaning. Their meaning is defined frequently not by the dictionary, but by their relation to other words about them in the same predicament.[18]

Crane read the essay and was pleased by it; it was one of the few critical works that he read seriously during 1929. The sympathetic treatment of his poetry he appreciated and had come to expect. Winters was placing him in the company of Baudelaire and Mallarmé, and in his conclusion described Crane's poetry as among the major efforts and great achievements of the century.

After the break in his correspondence with Crane, Winters continued writing to Tate. His interests in traditional form increased, and his respect for Tate's verse mounted. He preferred Tate's new work to Crane's and saw Tate as Baudelaire to Crane's Rimbaud. In a long letter written on Christmas night of 1928, on the verge of Tate's departure for Europe, he apologized for having tried to intervene in Tate's relation with Crane, expressing his continued regrets that the two most intelligent men in New York should have quarreled. Under the tutelage of William Dinsmore Briggs he read Thomas Aquinas and widened and deepened his knowledge of the traditions of English poetry, comparing the cadences of Crashaw with the definitions of Aquinas. After Tate's arrival in Europe, Winters maintained the correspondence. His opinions had not yet settled, and when he reread Emerson he compared him favorably with Valéry and set him a little lower than Dickinson. Tate received a copy of *The Gyroscope*, and as the year progressed Winters found more and more merit in Tate's new verse, suggesting that only the late work of Hardy was better. He continued writing sonnets and experimented with heroic couplets. He sought in his own work and found in Tate's the intellectual discipline and definition that he believed to be the only true bases for meaningful development.

The essays that Winters wrote for *The Gyroscope* established a tone and point of view that were austere and in Winters' sense of the term classical. Crane could not have read them carefully; otherwise he would not have been surprised at Winters' review of *The Bridge*. In his "Statement of Purpose" for the magazine, Winters specifically opposed "all doctrines of liberation and emotional expansionism" and "religious expansionism," including all forms of mysticism. He opposed all "doctrines which advocate that the poet 'express' his country (Whitmanian Rousseauism) or his time."[19] He had other animadversions, but these would be enough to condemn Crane's effort. In the third issue of *The Gyroscope*, Winters made some notes on contemporary criticism that reveal some of the arbitrary dogmatism that is familiar to readers of his later work. The occasion for the notes is essays by Tate and Eliot that Winters interprets as asserting that there is no adequate rational basis for ethics. Eliot's famous essay in his homage to Lancelot Andrewes announced his embracing of the Anglican faith; Tate's essay on the fallacy of Humanism left him, as Winters saw the matter, in a very ambiguous position. Winters scorns ambiguities, and he needs no basis for an ethical position—without faith and revelation, and modern man cannot accept either, the best choice is simply the least comforting of the various ethical possibilities. The source of evil is in emotion, and the reduction of emotion to a minimum is the only way to a controlled and harmonious life. As far as belief is concerned, the only necessity is a belief in existence. The ideal point of view is that of the distinterested observer.

Winters seems in this essay to go beyond stoicism to a kind of emotional masochism, but he thought of himself as redressing a balance. To his mind the Stoics failed because they refused to take the emotions into account at all and looked to a pure order of the intellect. He was willing to admit what he called the "irreducible emotion" and thought that emotion so revealed by disciplined moral evaluation might then be a source of good rather than evil. Such an emotion would be the substance of a work of art. Unlike the Stoic collapse, the modern point of view originated in "an orgy of emotionalism (over a century long) at the expense of intellect." Aristotle, he conceded, saw the feelings rather than reason as "the principle of and guide to virtue," but he affirms that Aristotle "provides the feelings, however, with a very powerful intellectual substructure and a profoundly difficult emotional discipline, of which the arts are an important part. These notes, then, are basically Aristotelian."[20] As so often with the criticism of the later Winters, one has to look beyond the dogmatic assertion to the motive force. The main motive is isolating and purifying the fundamental nature of art and, more specifically, poetry. He would take a man's poetry as a better guide to his ethics than any purely ethical statement. The notes were extensions of earlier work, and what is new in them is the brusqueness and bluntness of their tone.

Crane could not have read carefully Winters' essays written during the break in their correspondence, though he laid claim to having at least seen them. Over a year since his departure for Europe, he sent Winters a carbon copy of *The Bridge* in its final form, assuming that Winters would be willing to write a review. He had already asked Caresse Crosby to send a copy of the final printed version to Winters for that purpose. The letter is a curious one; after all, the two men had written steadily to each other for more than two years, and forty-four of Crane's communications are extant, only to have the correspondence broken without explanation. Crane is reasonable to assume that Winters would take the resumption of the relationship with some surprise, but he is truthful when he asserts that he had written to very few people, and then briefly, during the period. The letter is candid, and it is a saddening revelation of Crane's insecurity with his work which simply would not permit the intrusion of another sensibility that could increase his doubts and worries. He might have profited from the criticism, but it would certainly have slowed him down, and that was the last thing he wanted.

> 190 *Columbia Heights*
> *Brooklyn, N.Y.*
> *January 14th, 1930*

Dear Winters:

In this same mail I'm sending a complete copy of the Bridge—as it is being set up for the Black Sun Edition in Paris now. This edition will be ready about a month from now, the Liveright edition on April 1st.

"A fine time to be writing me!"—you may rightfully observe. But I am hoping that you haven't totally misunderstood my lengthy silence. To begin with, I haven't been in a mood for any sort of correspondence with anyone for a considerable time; and secondly, though you may not consider the statement as complimentary to your power as I do,—I have not wanted, for the time being, to engage myself in any further controversies, metrical, theoretical, ethical or what not, which letters (especially from you) frequently occasion. That kind of stimulus is apt to be dangerous at the time when one is desperately trying to complete any preconceived conception like my Bridge project. But here it is, now—very much larger than I had originally planned it, and at long last, something of a satisfaction, at least to me.

I have asked Mrs. Crosby to send you a copy of the Paris edition for review—not that you actually need review it, but that I want you to have a copy of what is physically one of the most beautiful libros I know of. You ought especially to appreciate the three photographs therein, taken by Walker Evans, a young fellow here in Brooklyn who is doing amazing things.

There is much on which to congratulate you,—especially the superb essay in the Caravan. I have seen a couple of issues of the Gyroscope which were certainly not to be sneezed at. You may put me down as one of your subscribers—with as many of the earlier issues as are available. Also I hope I may hear from you sometime soon, however little I may deserve to.

> *Best wishes, as always,*
> *Hart Crane*

Winters replied that he would review *The Bridge*, and Crane was delighted. Reviews from Tate, Cowley, Schneider, and Winters would assure a good press, and he assumed that Winters would use his contacts at *Poetry* to place the review. Their relationship was reestablishing itself at the old comradely level, or so Crane believed.

> *190 Columbia Heights*
> *January 27th*

Dear Winters:

I'm glad to hear that you feel like commenting on the Bridge. Tate has made arrangements to review it for the Hound & Horn, Cowley for the New Republic, and Schneider for the Chicago Eve. Post. I don't know who has taken it for the Herald-Tribune, but out of the list for the Paris edition only two choices remain: Poetry and the Nation.

I recently sent the *Indiana* section to H. M. [Harriet Monroe]. . . . Zabel replied that she was in the east and he was unable to accept it without her consent, however much he wanted to. His attitude was so complimentary and friendly that I judge there may have been some change of mind around their office. At any rate it offers a parallel to their recent invitation to you as described in your letter. I'm glad you're writing for them again. There aren't too many openings for any of us. I'm eager to read your exposé of Jeffers. I've always felt that Jeffers was sincere—but that doesn't quite suffice,—and somewhat "gifted"—to use a horrible word. But everything he has ever written, of any length, at least, excepting The Tower Beyond Tragedy, has given me a vague nausea. He really is a highstepping hysteric, I'm afraid.

You couldn't be expected to like Crosby's work. I find only a little pure ore here and there. I liked him personally, however, and was very disturbed at his death. . . . But since it is quite probable that he desired it as one more "experiment," I've reserved most of my sympathy for his wife.

Thank you for the promised Gyroscopes, though I'm sorry that there won't be any more. It won considerable and respectful notice, but I imagine took too much of your time.

Isn't there some chance of your coming east this spring?

Yours,
Hart Crane

P.S.—The Paris edition will be about the 1st of March. The Liveright edition will be ready on April 1st. The two might as well be reviewed together. Here are the proper headings for your review:
THE BRIDGE.   by Hart Crane.   Paris.   The Black Sun Press. $10.00.
THE BRIDGE.   by Hart Crane.   New York.   Horace Liveright. $2.50.

Paris edition is limited to 200 copies on Holland Van Gelder, at $10.00. 50 copies on vellum (autographed) at $25.00. If you know of anyone interested in getting the Paris edition refer him to Harry F. Marks, Bookseller, 31 West 47th St. N.Y. who is the agent here for all Black Sun publications.

Crane might have had some hesitations if he had read Winters' letter to Tate with serious reservations about the three added sections. Winters wanted time to read and reread the whole before making up his mind.

Winters did not send an advance copy of the review to Crane, and the letter previously quoted was the last from Crane which he preserved. When the review appeared in the June issue of *Poetry*, Crane was shocked to the point of outrage. The review has excited a great deal of comment in studies of Crane, most of it sharing Crane's indignation. Crane wrote Winters a diatribe against it, and he summarized his arguments in a letter to Isidor Schneider:

If you have read Winters' attack in the June issue of *Poetry* you cannot have been more astonished than I was to note the many reversals of opinion he has undergone since reading my acknowledgment to Whitman in the later "Cape Hatteras" section.

Had it not been for our previous extended correspondence I would not, of course, have written him about it. But as things stood I could hardly let silence infer an acceptance on my part of all the wilful distortions of meaning, misappropriations of opinion, pedantry and pretentious classification—besides illogic— which his review presents par excellence. I must read what prejudices he defends, I understand, against writing about subways, in the anti-humanist symposium. Poets should defer alluding to the sea, also, I presume, until Mr. Winters has got an invitation for a cruise![21]

The review is not one of Winters' best critical commentaries, and it has an unpleasantly pompous tone, particularly in its opening definitions. Crane's disappointment is understandable and justified, especially in view of Winters' encouragement and his high opinion of those segments of *The Bridge* finished by summer of 1928. But the review itself is oddly divided between appreciative comments on lines, passages, and entire sections of the book and a harsh unyielding dislike of the basic motivations. The charges made are the classic ones directed against *The Bridge*, that it lacks structure and coherence, that there is no genuine controlling complex of ideas, that individual sections have limited poetic merit, that although the local texture is often obscure to the point of being impenetrable, only isolated brilliance rescues the book from total failure. From another source, these indictments could have been brushed aside as instances of faulty comprehension and judgment, but Crane prized Winters' opinions and had anticipated a review closer in tone to that of *White Buildings*. Crane's rage came from more than disappointment; Winters was striking at his own feelings of insecurity about the outcome of more than five years of work. In a real sense, Crane's entire career was called into question.

It would have done little good to argue with Winters that *The Bridge* expressed Crane's country, for that was an argument for "Whitmanian Rousseauism," already condemned in his "Statement of Purpose" for *The Gyroscope*. The same statement of principles condemned the attempt of the poet to express his time, all forms of mysticism and religious expansionism, and all doctrines of "liberation and emotional expansionism," anything that subordinated the intellect.[22] Winters' review starts with an attempt to classify *The Bridge*, and he finds it neither epic, didactic, nor a lyric. If anything it is a collection of lyrics in the Whitmanian manner, and that limits the book severely. After a brief outline of the eight sections of the poem, Winters turned to a direct attack on the fallacy of attempting an epic in the Whitmanian manner. The comparison with Vergil shows the limitations of Whitman's point of view, for Vergil had at the background of his work a hierarchy of human values whereas Whitman had no way of discriminating between one type and quality of human experience and another. Hence the Whitmanian tradition permitted either an indiscriminate celebration of energy or, and Winters here cites the example of Jeffers, nihilism. All values being equal, there were none. Whitman, Crane, and Jeffers were capable only of occasional excellences: "Mr. Crane, since he possesses the greatest genius in the Whitmanian tradition, and since, strangely enough, he grafts onto the Whitmanian tradition something of the stylistic discipline of the Symbolists, most often exceeds himself in this manner."[23] Winters exemplifies Crane's transcendence of the limits of his tradition by citing the last eight stanzas of "The River" and quoting three, and he so admires the entire passage that he admits "I cannot read it—much less read it aloud—without being profoundly moved."[24]

Winters makes it clear that in pointing out defects in *The Bridge* he is "analyzing the flaws in a genius of a high order."[25] This judgment is crucial to any understanding of Winters' later criticism, of Crane particularly but of Yeats, Frost, Hopkins, and Eliot as well. He took poetry with an abiding seriousness, so that it became a matter of life and death. The more attractive and beguiling the effects of a poet, the more searching the analysis. What troubled Winters as he contemplated the completed form of *The Bridge* was the lack of any "adequate ideational background" in which the perceptions could find something more than the temporary magic of excitement to the point of frenzy.

The brilliance of Crane is not denied in the review, and he concedes that individual lines and passages are superb poetry, that "Cutty Sark" is a perpetual delight, that in fact all the segments of the poem contain fine things. It would be possible to abstract sentences and paragraphs of the review which would look very good on a dust jacket of the book. But Winters, as in his earlier review of *The Fugitive*, was using *The Bridge* as a means of illustrating the perils of anti-intellectualism. Crane exemplifies, as does the later work of James Joyce, Elizabeth Madox Roberts, and William Carlos Williams, the disintegration of genius in a stylistic automatism, the failure of the understanding to control, order, and fuse perception. Winters was not the same critic who had received the several segments of *The Bridge* between 1926 and 1928. He was no longer appreciative, no longer concerned with felicities rather than with general informing principles that would place all the elements of the poem in an integrated harmonious set of relations. His historical judgment and his moral judgment intervened, so that Crane became exemplary of processes in the history of ideas and of ethics that were deleterious to the total imaginative and intellec-

tual life of poetry. It may seem curious that even in writing the review
Winters should have thought of Crane as one of the four or five most
important poets of the era,[26] but it was exactly the genius displayed by
Crane that led Winters to make him an example; a lesser poet would
not bear the burden:

> It is possible that Mr. Crane may recover himself. In any event, he has given us,
> in his first book, several lyrics that one is tempted to call great, and in both books
> several charming minor lyrics and many magnificent fragments. And one thing he
> has demonstrated, the impossibility of getting anywhere with the Whitmanian in-
> spiration. No writer of comparable ability has struggled with it before, and, with
> Mr. Crane's wreckage in view, it seems highly unlikely that any writer of compar-
> able genius will struggle with it again.[27]

In spite of the qualifications and implied defenses of the review that I
have made, it is by no means pleasant reading. Its praise is grudging
and very qualified; its tone is at times pedantic, at others surly; and the
tone overrides any praise. It is no wonder that Crane found it offensive, and with the background of past praise and admiration from Winters, Crane had every reason to be shocked. Several other reviews by
friends were at best qualified in their praise, and Allen Tate came very
close to Winters' judgment. But Crane already knew of Tate's reservations about *The Bridge*, and the review was in tone as friendly as its
title, "A Distinguished Poet."[28]

Although the correspondence ended with the review, Crane remained at the forefront of Winters' mind for many years. In *Primitivism
and Decadence* (1937) Crane is mentioned some twenty-four times; only
Williams and Eliot were so frequently cited, and not even Stevens came
close to such frequency. Winters wrote two poems on Crane's death,
and eventually in 1947 put an end to his long reflections on Crane with
"The Significance of *The Bridge* by Hart Crane, or What Are We to
Think of Professor X?" All this is an epilogue to the correspondence.

Epilogue

Between 1930 and 1934, Crane remained central to Winters' thought
and poetic concerns. When his doctoral dissertation was completed
(1934) the text was in most respects identical with the ultimate book
Primitivism and Decadence (1937), and Crane figures largely in his arguments. When he received the news four days after Crane jumped from
the poop of the *Orizaba* on April 27, 1932, he was deeply saddened at
the death of this very great poet and wrote to Allen Tate with a peculiar blend of loss and self-vindication. He had been reading Crane carefully and had concluded that suicide was the inevitable way out for

him, the final result of a century of easily accepted pantheistic mysticism. And the death paralleled Crane's casual acceptance of Harry Crosby's suicide. During the two following years he wrote two poems that pivoted on Crane's death, "The Anniversary, To Achilles Holt," and "Orpheus, In Memory of Hart Crane."[29] The first of these may celebrate an anniversary shared by Holt and Winters; it may refer to the first anniversary of Crane's death, loosely identified with summer. A quart of wine is shared for the parting of two friends; the season momentarily confuses motivation. Earth follows the sun toward its own ultimate dissolution, propelled by forces it cannot control, but in the confusion and the mechanical movement of the earth, man maintains his obligation of free will. Crane's death intervenes and guides the mind to the terrible reminder of human mortality and the possible breakdown of the will:

> Crane is dead at sea. The year
> Dwindles to a purer fear.

"Orpheus, In Memory of Hart Crane" is one of Winters' several classical allegories, and in it he plays rather loosely with the myth. His interest is in the poetic dilemma rather than in decoration. The association of Crane with Orpheus may have come from the presence of Crane's collage of the "Musician Apostolic" in Winters' study, framed and carefully preserved. The poem divides exactly in two, nine lines devoted primarily to the partial resurrection of Eurydice, nine treating the death of Orpheus. In the opening stanza the reference to Zeus' shrine at Dodona is justified only by the legendary antiquity of Orpheus. The line "Wisdom never understood" is cryptic—did the music of Orpheus render wisdom that was not understood or did Orpheus fail to understand a greater wisdom? Or is it impossible for tree, flesh, and stone to comprehend what charms them? Wisdom is at any event a failure, and the song itself seems to be merely illusory, working only while its tones continue. In this version it is not Orpheus' backward glance that reconsigns Eurydice to the underworld but a break in his singing.

> Climbing from the Lethal dead,
> Past the ruined waters' bed,
> In the sleep his music cast
> Tree and flesh and stone were fast—
> As amid Dodona's wood
> Wisdom never understood.
>
> Till the shade his music won
> Shuddered, by a pause undone—
> Silence would not let her stay.

The second section of the poem turns directly to the death of Orpheus, which seems to be willed, a matter of choice rather than victimization. Orpheus gives his flesh in a terrible act. The tongue remains immortal; but the song is unmeaning.

> He could go one only way:
> By the river, strong with grief,
> Gave his flesh beyond belief.
>
> Yet the fingers on the lyre
> Spread like an avenging fire.
> Crying loud, the immortal tongue,
> From the empty body wrung,
> Broken in a bloody dream,
> Sang unmeaning down the stream.

The poem has admirable things in it, but the collocation of Orpheus with Crane does not seem to add much to either figure—the poem breaks in two. What might serve to unify the two halves of the poem is the sense of the failure, the inutility, of prophecy. There is a kind of glory and a kind of waste. Crane, to Winters' mind, could have been four times the poet he was, great though he was. Taken in those terms, there is a deep sadness in the poem and a relentless judgment. Winters advises that readers of poetry trust the poem rather than the author's ethics, and if one does so, the split in this poem indicates unresolved experience, not fully mastered and comprehended. There is a multiplicity of themes and uncontrolled ambiguity. Does "Wisdom never understood" mean that wisdom never did understand or wisdom never was understood? Is the "as" in the preceding line to be taken as adverb or conjunction? Why is the song "unmeaning" in the closing line? Because of the separation of head from body, the disintegration of perception and meaning? Whose dream is treated in the next to last line? That of Orpheus or that of the Maenads? The split and tension in the poem seem to indicate ambivalence toward the poetic enterprise, and particular trouble when contemplating the work of Crane.

The poem was written while Winters was completing his doctoral dissertation, the core of which is contained in *Primitivism and Decadence*. In that book, Crane is a major figure, and the references to him involve problems of symbolic and structural meaning. Those to Williams, who serves as his counterpart, more frequently concern metrical problems. In this poem Winters faces the emotional rather than theoretical and taxonomic problems raised by the figure of Crane. There is a deeply felt emotional quality to the poem that is, to use a term dear to Winters, untranslatable. The difficulties noted above are not insuperable. There are many better poems by Winters, but this is a remarkable piece of work.

Winters, in the period after Crane's death, could not reject or accept this great and disturbed spirit. He was at the center of the critical and poetic problem, and that problem was at the center of life. Crane was the ultimate outcome of the Romantic tradition in general and the tradition of American transcendentalism in particular. His work was a prime example of "pseudo-reference" because Crane was required to speak of the unknowable in the terms of the knowable. Further, Crane was extremely limited in his possible subject matter; his point of view did not permit exact moral discriminations and made his perception of human experience vague or, in a poem like "Indiana," sentimental and weak. His best work exhibited a fragile relation between the isolated poet and some undetermined reality, identified as Eternity:

> Crane's attitude . . . often suggests a kind of theoretic rejection of all human endeavor in favor of some vaguely apprehended but ecstatically asserted existence of a superior sort. As the exact nature of the superior experience is uncertain, it forms a rather uncertain and infertile source of material for exact poetry; one can write poetry about it only by utilizing in some way more or less metaphorical the realm of experience from which one is trying to escape; but as one *is* endeavoring to escape from this realm, not to master it and understand it, one's feelings about it are certain to be confused, and one's imagery drawn from it is bound to be largely formulary and devoid of meaning. That is, in so far as one endeavors to deal with the Absolute, not as a means of ordering one's moral perception but as the subject itself of perception, one will tend to say nothing, despite the multiplication of words. In *The Dance* there seems to be an effort to apply to each of two mutually exclusive fields the terms of the other. . . .
>
> Crane's best work, such as *Repose of Rivers* and *Voyages II*, is not confused, but one feels that the experience is curiously limited and uncomplicated: it is between the author, isolated from most human complications, and Eternity. Crane becomes in such poems a universal symbol of the human mind in a particular situation, a fact which is the source of his power, but of the human mind in very nearly the simplest form of that situation, a fact which is the source of his limitation.[30]

These poetic powers and limitations were further to be seen as the necessary outgrowth of Crane's Whitmanian point of view. Crane's suicide both troubled and vindicated Winters—troubled him because he liked Crane and admired much of his work; vindicated him because so far as Winters was concerned a world without some moral base for discrimination of value was not humanly habitable. As early as 1929 he had suggested to Eugene Jolas that his surrender to the unconscious left him with only two alternatives, the abandonment of that surrender or "the suicide of a gentleman."[31] Jeffers' sense of the meaninglessness of human life, taken literally, would also lead to suicide.[32] Crane, unlike Jolas and Jeffers, had taken his position to its ultimate necessary conclusion:

It may seem a hard thing to say of that troubled and magnificent spirit, Hart Crane, that we shall remember him chiefly for his having shown us a new mode of damnation, yet it is for this that we remember Orestes, and Crane has in addition the glory of being, if not his own Aeschylus, perhaps, in some fragmentary manner, his own Euripides.[33]

Crane was a tragic figure and his own tragedian.

After the publication of *Primitivism and Decadence,* Crane held a less prominent place in Winters' criticism and was very infrequently mentioned. When he collected his three critical books under the title *In Defense of Reason,* however, Crane reappeared, and in the concluding essay became Winters' chief example of the dangers and follies of the tradition flowing from Emerson through Whitman. The essay "The Significance of *The Bridge* by Hart Crane, or What Are We to Think of Professor X?" summarizes and extends the point of view already developed in less systematic form in Winters' earlier work. The essay is well known and is sometimes adduced as final proof of Winters' wrong-headedness and heartlessness. To anyone who has followed the present text, the essay should come as no surprise. In it Winters decries Emerson for placing impulse above reason and constructing an optique that makes the discrimination of values impossible. Whitman comes under the same condemnation and Crane is given as the disastrous end product of mystical pantheism. Professor X represents those genteel scholars who simply do not take thought or literature seriously. Crane is the serious poet who lives out in his work, life, and death the ideas that are at the heart of American transcendentalism and of the Romantic movement generally.

The essay is extremely personal, and in it Winters makes use of his correspondence with Crane and talks in moving terms of his four evenings of conversation with Crane. Primarily, however, he is concerned with Crane as example rather than friend, and it should be remembered that Crane and Winters were never genuinely close friends in the sense that Tate and Crane were, or Waldo Frank and Crane or Malcolm Cowley and Crane. Winters never had to put up with the drunkenness, the furniture smashing, or the telephoned apologies at four o'clock in the morning. He knew neither the full rewards nor the vicissitudes of friendship with Crane which such people as Tate, Cowley, and Josephson knew only too well. There were for Winters no softening forces such as arise from shared pleasures and exasperated forgiveness; Crane could remain a literary type without the full features of a complex remembered human figure. Nothing like Malcolm Cowley's reminiscences clouded the generalized idea with affectionate trivia:

Crane . . . had the absolute seriousness which goes with genius and sanctity; one might describe him as a saint of the wrong religion. He had not the critical intelligence to see what was wrong with his doctrine, but he had the courage of his convictions, the virtue of integrity, and he deserves our respect. He has the value of a thoroughgoing demonstration. He embodies perfectly the concepts which for nearly a century have been generating some of the most cherished principles of our literature, our education, our politics, and our personal morals. If Crane is too strong a dose for us, and we must yet retain the principles which he represents, we may still, of course, look to Professor X as a model. But we shall scarcely get anything better unless we change our principles.[40]

Two decades had by now passed since Crane wrote first to Winters and asserted their common ground in the work of Whitman. Whether Winters objected at the time we do not know; by 1947 the Whitman tradition was anathema to Winters, and he saw in it the cause of Crane's deterioration and death. From this point on, Winters hardly refers to Crane. In his last critical work, *Forms of Discovery*, Crane is mentioned only twice; none of Crane's poems is included in his final anthology, *Quest for Reality*. There is nothing more to say. For twenty years Crane was central to Winters' poetics, and this essay is Winters' final farewell; it is close to being a rite of exorcism.

Reprinted from Thomas Parkinson, *Hart Crane and Yvor Winters, Their Literary Correspondence* (Berkeley: University of California Press, 1978).

Notes

1. Malcolm Cowley, *A Second Flowering: Works and Days of the Lost Generation* (New York, 1973), p. 210.

2. Yvor Winters, *Early Poems, 1920–28* (Chicago, 1966), p. 13.

3. John Unterecker, *Voyager: A Life of Hart Crane* (New York, 1969), p. 574.

4. Yvor Winters, *In Defense of Reason* (New York, 1947), pp. 599–600.

5. From "On a View of Pasadena from the Hills," *Collected Poems*, p. 64.

6. Winters, *In Defense of Reason*, pp. 589–90.

7. See "The Realization," *Collected Poems*, p. 46, lines 10–11.

8. *Poetry* (April 1928), pp. 46–47.

9. *The New Republic* (March 21, 1928), p. 165.

10. "Mr. Moon's Notebook," *The Saturday Review of Literature* (March 10, 1928), p. 665. Winters' reply was not printed.

11. "Fugitives," *The Uncollected Essays and Reviews of Yvor Winters* (Chicago, 1973), p. 55. Originally in *Poetry* (February 1928), pp. 102–7.

12. *The Letters of Hart Crane*, ed. Brom Weber (Berkeley and Los Angeles, 1965), pp. 347–48.

13. Yvor Winters, *The Uncollected Essays and Reviews*, ed. Francis Murphy (Chicago, 1973), pp. 255–70.

14. Yvor Winters, *In Defense of Reason* (New York, 1947), p. 601. See also Grosvenor E. Powell, "Mythical and Smoky Soil: Imagism and the Aboriginal in the Early Poetry of Yvor Winters," *The Southern Review* (Spring 1975), especially pp. 310–15.

15. Winters, *The Uncollected Essays and Reviews*, pp. 226–27.

16. Ibid., pp. 227–28.

17. Ibid., p. 266.

18. Ibid., p. 247.

19. Ibid., p. 216.

20. Ibid., p. 222.

21. *The Letters of Hart Crane*, p. 352.

22. Winters, *The Uncollected Essays and Reviews*, pp. 216–17.

23. Ibid., p. 76.

24. Ibid., p. 77.

25. Ibid.

26. Yvor Winters, "Poetry, Morality and Criticism," *The Critique of Humanism*, ed. C. Hartley Grattan (New York, 1930), p. 316.

27. *The Uncollected Essays and Reviews*, p. 82.

28. *The Hound and Horn* (July-Summer 1930), pp. 580–85.

29. Yvor Winters, *Collected Poems* (Denver, 1960), pp. 81, 85.

30. Yvor Winters, *In Defense of Reason* (New York, 1947), pp. 27–28.

31. Yvor Winters, *Uncollected Essays and Reviews*, ed. Francis Murphy (Chicago, 1973), p. 250.

32. Winters, *In Defense of Reason*, p. 32.

33. Ibid., p. 101.

34. Malcolm Cowley, *A Second Flowering: Works and Days of the Lost Generation* (New York, 1973), pp. 204–5.

35. Ibid., p. 211.

36. Winters, *In Defense of Reason*, p. 590.

37. John Unterecker, *Voyager: A Life of Hart Crane* (New York, 1969), p. 610.

38. Winters, *In Defense of Reason*, p. 599.

39. Ibid., pp. 599–600.

40. Ibid., pp. 602–3.

Some Grand Poems

5

Whitman's "When Lilacs Last in the Door-Yard Bloom'd" and the American Civil Religion

Whitman's great poem, so often thought of as his elegy for President Lincoln, is better considered as one more document in what Robert Bellah calls, in his *Beyond Belief*, the American Civil Religion. Especially when read in its first printed version, the poem belongs with such non-sectarian but deeply religious works as the Declaration of Independence, Washington's Inaugural Address, Lincoln's Gettysburg Address and his Second Inaugural Address. In that religion, which has its own heroes and martyrs, holy places and rituals of observance, the figure of Lincoln has symbolic stature that extends beyond the merely personal, and it is so that Whitman sees his death, not that of one alone but that of the sacrificial participants in the Civil War. Bellah notes that "With the Christian archetype in the background, Lincoln, 'our martyred president,' was linked to the war dead, those who 'gave the last full measure of devotion.' The theme of sacrifice was indelibly written into the civil religion." It is surprising that the Christian archetype remained so far in the background that Whitman mentions it nowhere in "When Lilacs Last in the Door-Yard Bloom'd." Lincoln was shot on Good Friday and died on Holy Saturday, and that should warn critics who give Whitman no credit for decorum or tact. His great poem on the war dead is one of the most tactful poems in English.

For lovers of books, those who have a passion for editions of singular importance, who love to hold in their hands a book that a great man not only wrote but touched—there is one American book that is the most adored. It is not Walt Whitman's *Sequel to Drum-Taps* but his famous blue book, now in the New York Public Library, the basis for the "workshop edition" of *Leaves of Grass* that appeared in 1867. That book is very much in the background of "When Lilacs Last in the Door-Yard Bloom'd," as is the entire history of *Leaves of Grass*. I am now going to embark on a long preamble to the tale of "When Lilacs Last in the Door-Yard Bloom'd," taking a course that will be entirely too simple for scholars but novel to many readers of *Leaves of Grass*.

Most readers of the deathbed edition of *Leaves of Grass,* the basis of such fine texts as the New York University Press's Reader's Edition of *Leaves of Grass,* have had a mild hoax played upon them by Whitman and his subsequent editors. To read *Leaves of Grass* they would have to turn to the 1860 edition, edited in facsimile with an introduction by Roy Harvey Pearce. That is the book of the democratic individual and of the body that is *Leaves of Grass.* In subsequent editions, in 1867, 1871, and 1876, the material of the 1860 volume is printed under the title *Leaves of Grass;* the remaining material is variously called "Drum-Taps and Memories of President Lincoln" (1867); "Passage to India and Other Poems" (1871); "Two Rivulets" (1876). Only in 1881 did Whitman give up his projected second book, which was to celebrate the democratic nation and the spirit. One title he had in mind for it was "Airs of Lilac Time," used in variant form as title for his last poetic memories of the Civil War, "Ashes of Lilac Time." Even after his stroke in 1873 he did not give up his project, as the centennial edition of 1876 shows. But in 1881 he decided to set matters in such order as he could, make the best arrangement possible of all his poems to date, rewrite and radically re-punctuate the poems, and call the whole *Leaves of Grass.* Poems written later were, in an odd metaphor, considered annexes.

There are two books of Whitman's poetry, then, one completed in 1860, the other existing only in fragmentary form. Walt Whitman's unfinished book—the history of American poetry since 1860 could be written under that rubric. A central document would be "When Lilacs Last in the Door-Yard Bloom'd." It is not part of *Leaves of Grass,* and it may well have occasioned his decision to make a separate book.

> Leaves of Grass, already published, is, in its intentions, the song of a great composite *Democratic Individual,* male or female. And following on and amplifying the same purpose, I suppose I have in my mind to run through the chants of this Volume, (if ever completed,) the thread-voice, more or less audible, of an aggregated, unprecedented, vast, composite, electric *Democratic Nationality.*

Thus, in almost bibliographical fashion, Whitman in 1872. Preparing the centennial edition of his work in 1876, he extended his meaning and clarified it:

> It was originally my intention, after chanting in Leaves of Grass the songs of the Body and Existence, to then compose a further equally needed Volume, based on those convictions of perpetuity and conservation which, enveloping all precedents, make the unseen Soul triumph absolutely at last. I meant, while in a sort continuing the theme of my first chants, to shift the slides, and exhibit the problem and paradox of the same ardent and fully appointed Personality entering the sphere of the resistless gravitation of Spiritual Law, and with cheerful face estimating Death, not at all as the cessation, but as somehow what I feel it must be, the entrance upon

by far the greatest part of existence, and something that Life is at least as much for, as it is for myself.

But the full construction of such a work (even if I lay the foundation, or give impetus to it) is beyond my powers, and must remain for some bard in the future.

Later, Whitman would insist on the unity of the 1881 and succeeding editions of the book called *Leaves of Grass*. Here in his grief and hope on contemplating his beloved country at its centennial and in his realization of what the stroke of 1873 had done to his powers, he gives a different legacy. Near death in 1891, he would define his work in other terms: "In the long run the world will do as it pleases with the book. I am determined to have the world know what I was pleased to do." What he was pleased to do in 1891 has been universally respected; yet there is a wonderful poignancy in his earlier sense that he was not to create a monument but a charge to his poetic godchildren. Fortunately, they have recognized that charge, so that from Pound through Duncan poets have built upon the foundations of the unfinished book. *Leaves of Grass*, however defined, however edited, is the American equivalent of Spenser's *Faerie Queene*, an unfinished cathedral that only centuries of work can bring to perfection.

Whitman in 1865 was busy in rewriting the 1860 *Leaves of Grass* for a fresh edition to include *Drum-Taps* and, eventually, the *Memories of President Lincoln*, notably "When Lilacs Last in the Door-Yard Bloom'd." Supporting his mother and his feebleminded brother, he was working with evident success as a clerk in the Department of the Interior. Six weeks after Lincoln's death, a new Secretary was appointed, and a forbidding circular was issued by him to the heads of the several offices in the department, asking those officials "to report as to the loyalty of each of the employees under him, and also whether there are any whose fidelity to duty or moral character is such as to justify an immediate dispensation of their services." A month later, Whitman received an official note that his services would be "dispensed with from and after this date." The occasion, Whitman was always convinced, was the presence in his office of the famous blue book of *Leaves of Grass*. The testimony of his friend J. Hubley Ashton, then Assistant Attorney General of the United States, verified Whitman's suspicions, and Ashton had the good sense and courage to grant Whitman a parallel position in his own office. He was among friends, he was respected, his economic anxieties were diminished. During the summer of 1865 he finished the *Sequel to Drum-Taps*, and in October "When Lilacs Last in the Door-Yard Bloom'd" was printed, at Whitman's expense.

Did Lincoln read Whitman? Did he really say, if and when Whitman was pointed out to him as the poet, that he was a man? Whitman certainly saw Lincoln on several occasions, though at a distance. Lincoln's supposed reading of Whitman and his reported comment on his appearance are unverifiable anecdotes. We know from the poem and from Whitman's repeated lecture on Lincoln, that Whitman loved Lincoln, but what, when he loved Lincoln, did he love?

I think that returning to the blue book and bearing in mind Whitman's projected second book will clarify matters. The 1867 edition of *Leaves of Grass* caused Whitman more than administrative troubles—it brought his poetics to a critical point. Many poets pay close attention to their early work and revise and re-arrange it almost compulsively, and Whitman was of that company. The early work is the determinant, the creator of possibilities and of boundaries. Poets rewrite and edit their early work not out of perversity or any desire for perfection but because they are effectively remaking themselves as they remake the work. Tennyson in his famous ten years of silence was not simply rewriting to satisfy his surly critics; he was establishing the shape of his future as well as past poetic career. Coleridge's multiple versions of "The Ancient Mariner" were compelled by moral and religious demands as much as by aesthetic. The variants of Pound's first three *Cantos* exist because he knew that what was done there would move not only the poem but him into an inevitable design. Arnold's excision of "Empedocles on Etna" from the 1853 edition of his work was, as he overtly states, a moral as well as aesthetic act. Whitman's workshop edition of 1867 exhibits parallel motives.

The five years of the war culminating in the death of Lincoln gave him a new perspective on his early work. He attempted by rewriting and re-ordering to incorporate some of the wisdom and even some of the experience gained during the war. But when it came to *Drum-Taps* and the *Sequel,* he could not integrate them with the revised *Leaves of Grass.* They appear, as Allen says, as separate entities which, "with consequent separate pagination, were simply bound in with *Leaves of Grass:* they had not yet been truly integrated into it." Allen is committed to the idea that the deathbed edition is an integrated work of art, and he is committed to Whitman's own late definition of what his work came to:

> "Leaves of Grass" indeed (I cannot too often reiterate) has mainly been the outcropping of my own emotional and other personal nature—an attempt, from first to last, to put a *Person,* a human being (myself, in the latter half of the Nineteenth Century, in America,) freely, fully and truly on record. I could not find any similar personal record in current literature that satisfied me. But it is not on "Leaves of Grass" distinctively as *literature,* or a specimen thereof, that I feel to dwell, or advance claims. No one will get at my verses who insists upon viewing them as a literary performance, or attempt at such performance, or as aiming mainly toward art or aestheticism.

This comment is from "A Backward Glance O'er Travel'd Roads," the preface to the *November Boughs* of 1888. It has, or the point of view it embodies has, caused considerable mischief, and it has also made Whitman seem less a poet than in fact he was. Part of the reason for this diminishing of his stature by the statement comes not from him but from fuzzy ideas of what the "personality" or "self" is.

The self or personality—I shall use the term "identity" to limit the complexities that would come from such historical movements as Transcendentalism—can be defined as a primarily social reality. An identity would then be the sum of its associations, additive and with its center to be found in its function. It would be determined, genetically, familially, conventionally by the rituals and sacraments of its society and religion, professionally by the code of its function, as part of a hierarchy of actions necessary to the culture in which it participated, and ideologically by the entire complex of being in which it took its place. It might be granted liberty in a social frame or it might passively exist in a despotism.

Such a generic type is a schema, not necessarily ever existent in nature, and even in a fixed society conflict at any point in the movement toward function or identity leads toward individuation. But there is another sense of identity that looks on the person as pre-existent, as a unique soul that can be discovered or revealed through experience. The value of this identity does not exist in its function but in its existence, given and potentially active. Liberty may be granted to it, but it has something more important than civil permissions—it has inherent freedom. It pre-dates and has primacy over any social contract. Its primary obligation is not to the culture into which it is born but to the expression and revelation of the nature which is its own and which is in conformity with some nature external to the social. This identity in a rigid society is frequently in a state of unending conflict and because it is a law unto itself may become anomic and destructive to others and to its own social being. Martyrs and fools and saints and bums share this quality. Sometimes the society may declare one of its martyrs or saints a bum, as the Soviet Union declared Solzhenitsyn a "parasite."

Solzhenitsyn places the entire question of the "self" or "personality" on a different plane, one more appropriate to discussion of genuinely creative literature. For he is neither a man who accepts the social role offered to him nor one who simply denies the social contract. He offers instead a set of cultural possibilities that grow from what he takes to be the best of the several directions and qualities of life within his culture. And he condemns what he takes to be the worst. Solzhenitsyn would never deny his function; he merely conceives his function to be different from what is imposed upon him. He asserts his freedom because liberty has been denied him. He suffers because he insists on being a Russian Christian Socialist man—and this may be why he seems so alien even to someone who admires him as devoutly as I do. It may also account for what seem to be confusions or simplifications in his thought. And it accounts for his enormous achievement and courage.

I am not comparing Whitman directly with Solzhenitsyn. The abuse suffered by Whitman in his lifetime was painful but relatively mild. He lost one job and got another from an unfeeling but not hostile government; his books had to struggle for their audience, but he did not risk his life and his family's well-being in the process. What the two writers share is their creation of a cultural complex with legitimacy beyond the individual. It is hard to think of Solzhenitsyn saying to himself that he was expressing his personality; the very idea would be hopelessly distant from his motives. He would be more likely to appeal to the concept of objective truth. What he is placing "freely, fully and truly on record" is the shared experience, the love and suffering, of the insulted and injured and murdered, with whom he participates, personally, but always as part of a larger truth. Whitman falls into the same category. There were distinct limits to his freedom, growing not from political terror but genteel conventions. The person he exhibits in his poems is a creation: "a great composite *Democratic Individual*," and "an aggregated, unprecedented, vast, composite, electric *Democratic Nationality*." The key terms are *composite* (repeated) and *aggregated*.

Whitman resorted in 1888 to the notion of self-expression, "the outcropping of my own emotional and other personal nature—an attempt, from first to last, to put *a Person*, a human being (myself, in the latter half of the Nineteenth Century, in America,) freely, fully and truly on record." He did so because his grand design could not, for medical reasons, be brought to fulfillment. What he declares, however, is not what the poems do, unless one accepts the notion of the person or self as being a cultural complex, individuated but gaining its major form in its associations. Modern people have the further problem of choosing from a wide variety of options their ultimate cultural complex. They have the further obligation to choose and even, in a real sense, create symbols that stabilize their being and communicate to others their exact feelings. In writing "When Lilacs Last in the Door-Yard Bloom'd" Whitman refused one cultural option—the Christian analogy—and shaped three symbols that were in effect fresh creations. He also selected not from "personal" experience but from national experience, as reported in the press, much of the data in the poem. It is the expression of a composite aggregated Democratic Nationality and a composite Democratic Individual.

The contexts of Whitman's three major symbols in the poem clarify their origin and weight. The scent of the lilacs haunted him years after the event:

> I remember where I was stopping at the time, the season being advanced, there were many lilacs in full bloom. By one of those caprices that enter and give tinge to events without being at all a part of them, I find myself reminded of the great tragedy of that day by the sight and odor of these blossoms. It never fails.

In the months preceding the death of Lincoln, the very heavens were portentous, as Whitman described them early in March of 1865:

> Indeed, the heavens, the elements, all the meteorological influences, have run riot for weeks past. Such caprices, abruptest alternations of frowns and beauty, I never knew. It is a common remark that (as last summer was different in its smells of intense heat from any preceding it) the winter just completed has been without parallel. It has remain'd so down to the hour I am writing. Much of the daytime of the past month was sulky, with leaden heaviness, fog, interstices of bitter cold, and some insane storms. But there have been samples of another description. Nor earth nor sky ever knew spectacles of superber beauty than some of the nights lately here. The western star, Venus, in the earlier hours of evening, has never been so large, so clear; it seems as if it told something, as if it held rapport indulgent with humanity, with us Americans. Five or six nights since it hung close by the moon, then a little past its first quarter. The star was wonderful, the moon like a young mother. The sky, dark blue, the transparent night, the planets, the moderate west wind, the elastic temperature, the miracle of that great star, and the young and swelling moon swimming in the west, suffused the soul.

Shortly after the death of Lincoln, Whitman and his friend John Burroughs took many long walks in which Burroughs, then gaining fresh knowledge of the birds he loved and of which he would later write with surpassing skill, expostulated on the song of the hermit thrush. Whitman took notes:

> *Hermit* Thrush
> Solitary Thrush
> moderate sized
> grayish brown bird
>
> ———————
>
> Sings often
> after sundown
> sometimes quite
> in the night

is very seclusive
likes shaded
dark places
in swamps

---

is very shy

Sings in May
& June

---

not much after
June

---

is our best
songster
song clear &
deliberate—has
a solemn effect

—It is perhaps
all the more
precious, because
it is only seen
in secluded
places—he
never sings
near the farm
houses—never

in the settlement
—is the bird
of the solemn
primal woods
& of
Nature pure
and holy—

These notes were taken down during a conversation with John Burroughs, though the hermit thrush is so widely distributed a bird that Whitman had certainly heard its unforgettable song from his childhood on Long Island. The extraordinary weather he read as ominous, noting that every battle was succeeded by a storm. The lilacs were growing by his mother's home. Whitman was not in Washington that Easter weekend, and there is reason to doubt that he returned to the capital until after the public obsequies for Lincoln, and further reason to doubt that he saw the funeral train. On Holy Saturday the family prepared all meals but ate nothing, their chief concern being the newspaper reports, which they read with absorption, all the morning and evening editions. The matter for "When Lilacs Last in the Door-Yard Bloom'd" was secondhand, taken from public accounts and the reports of his Washington friends O'Connor, Burroughs, Lamson, others. All the matter, that is, except the scent of the lilac, the song of the bird, the luminous western star.

The manuscript of the poem has evidently disappeared. Except for the brief notes on Burroughs' description of the bird, there survive a thesaurus of phrases suggesting mourning and grief and two fragments of early drafts. There is no definite proof that that catalogue is pertinent to this particular poem. When it first appeared, the poem was divided into twenty-one (not, as in later versions, seventeen) sections and further subdivided into forty-three phrasal units that might be called free verse stanzas. The song of the bird was not distinguished by italics until 1871. The punctuation was heavier, indicating pause, measure, and weight of greater gravity than the later punctuation would suggest. One reason for the sense of fluent rush in 1881 and later editions of Whitman is that he radically changed the punctuation, as witness the opening stanza of "When Lilacs Last in the Door-Yard Bloom'd":

1 When lilacs last in the door-yard bloom'd,
And the great star early droop'd in the western sky
   in the night,
I mourn'd . . . and yet shall mourn with ever-returning spring.

Stanza two of the first section shows almost a mathematical deviation in the punctuation:

2 O ever-returning spring! trinity sure to me you bring;
Lilac blooming perennial, and drooping star in the west,
And thought of him I love.

And in the first line of the third stanza of the poem (beginning the second section), Whitman ultimately deleted all the commas that appeared in the first version: "O powerful, western, fallen star!"

I stress the notation of the poem because it was, in its original version, much more stately, more clearly distinct in its movement—more deliberated and less rhapsodic. It is, even in the first version, rhapsodic enough.

So the poem begins with the line that has echoed through our poetic history. Whitman was not the only one to note the lilacs; the physician who attended the dying president, Colonel Charles S. Taft, never forgot them: "The yard of the house was full of blossoming lilacs, and as long as Charlie Taft lived the scent of lilacs . . . brought back the black horror of that dreadful night." Lincoln's coffin was banked with lilacs as well as roses and lilies. Funeral customs being what they are, each stop of the train in its seventeen hundred mile progress to Springfield found crowds waiting with various blossoms to deck the coffin. A spontaneous ritual was enacted within the country, a ritual that restored the continuity of birth and death in the form of flowers. From this outpouring, Whitman created a symbol. He and Colonel Taft were not the only Americans who are stirred into a muse on contemplating a flowering lilac. Even Californians like myself who in their youth thought that the mountain ceanothus was the flower Whitman had in mind have had their awareness altered by the poem.

Whitman created a symbol. That is no small thing to effect. It seems to me the primary datum and triumph of the poem; it rests at the core of the poetic enterprise. But he had collaborators, all those humble men and women standing at railroad stations with camellias, roses, lilies-of-the-valley, one woman by the railroad track the train passed with a bunch of wild flowers, official commissions with elaborate floral pieces. Sandburg's account of the funeral and the train trip is more florid than the contemporary account of Coggeshall, but Whitman with his sprig of lilac broken off for the memory of the death was participating in a composite action.

At first he merely holds that broken branch. Perhaps it is to be construed as spiteful or destructive, a revenge against flourishing nature, a siding with death? It is surely gratuitous, and the poem's resolution, the song of the remote bird, calls for lovely and soothing death. Whitman is not cunningly contriving a symbolic overtone; the action of the poem itself forces him to it. An idle act, thoughtless, abstracted: "A sprig, with its flower, I break."

The poem begins with a trinity, not the symbolic one of lilac, star, and bird, but a trinity that should warn us that no one of those symbols "represents" Lincoln. Ever-returning spring will always bring a trinity with it, but it will be composed of lilac, star, "And thought of him I love."

The poem never identifies Lincoln, any more than it mentions slavery. The person lamented in the poem might be any of numerous young men for whom Whitman did personal services in the terrible hospitals of the Civil War. But it seems to me that the person is collective, is a composite of all those whose death sanctified the soil of these states and whose blood was the binding element of the Union, Lincoln's being only the last of these many deaths. The real subject of the poem is not its occasion. Lincoln's death was a public matter; the obscure and in many instances forgotten deaths of the Civil War were private; the occasion of Lincoln's death permitted Whitman to make those deaths public and part of the American conscience and consciousness. Swinburne was right to identify the poem as a nocturne, for the term elegy places it in an improper genre.

I have already noted the deliberateness of movement of the poem, the heavy pointing of individual lines, the numerical setting of each stanza as a separate building block, and the more numerous sections than those in the most commonly known version. It might help to see the divisions of the poem as originally intended.

The first four sections compose an overture, beginning with a non-Christian trinity that will recur as surely as Easter with spring: lilacs, the great star, and thoughts of him I love. As I said earlier, "he" is not identified. The second section turns more fully to the beautiful ominous star, in the third the poet breaks a sprig of lilac, and in the fourth the hermit thrush sings in his solitude "Death's outlet song of life. . . ." Hence in the overture the dominant metaphors of the poem are established, lilacs, evening star and approaching night, the lilac with every leaf a miracle, the shy and hidden bird with bleeding throat.

Sections five through seven then turn to the land shattered by death and sanctified and healed and united by death, that dark democracy, the land as a whole, the mourning female figures of the several united states, and the sprig of lilac imaginarily deposited not for one alone but for all coffins. Not for one alone: the basic quality of the poem.

In sections eight and nine, the chanter descries the meaning of the western orb, and he then turns again (section ten) to the land as a whole, asking how he will sing, and his song will be like that of the sea-winds from Atlantic and Pacific mingling over the central prairies. Section eleven then takes a rural and pastoral vision with which he can adorn the "burial house of him I love." The dead of the war will be accompanied by visions of the glorious light of late April, with wild sweet herbage, prolific forests, flowing rivers, and ranging hills. They will know of the city and the hard work and the night's rest. In section twelve, body, the democratic individual, and soul, the democratic nation, will be this land, the great cities, the abundant farms, and always the glorious sun bathing and illuminating the entire country, the nation. In section thirteen he returns to the symbolic centers of the poem: star, lilac, but above all the bird who will sing the chant of death.

The next three sections became one in 1881, and the poem suffered from their blending. The contrast between the original sections fourteen and fifteen thus gets lost. We do not see the development from day to night and from the sun to the dark cloud as clearly as we should, so that the knowledge of death that begins section fifteen merely blurs into the preceding section. Worse than that, the lack of any break between section fifteen and section sixteen, combined with italicizing section sixteen, places the reader in the awkward position of believing that hermit thrushes are opera singers with a pretty good control of English. In the original ordering, the voice of section sixteen was clearly the voice of the spirit of the chanter which *tallied*—paralleled, equalled—the song of the bird. Telescoping the three sections denies each of them its proper gravity, destroys the clarity of the poem's dramatic movement, and places us in an absurd position. The good sense that marked the original poem suffers a serious blow. The paean to Death, strong Deliveress, is not romantic nonsense; the attitude toward death, one's capacity for welcoming its reality, is the measure of one's receptivity toward life and Whitman's capacity for acceptance was absolute. After all, for the years of the Civil War, Whitman deliberately placed himself in the presence of death and ministered to the dying young men of the armies. In the song of his spirit, death suffuses the land he loves and ultimately heals and binds.

The same telescoping motive brings sections seventeen and eighteen into a single section fifteen in the 1881 version. They should be kept distinct. Seventeen is a preparation for the vision of the armies which is in many ways the raison d'être of the poem. It also brings us from the spirit's song to the body's sight, and the counterpointing of song and sight and body and spirit throughout the poem is one of its most notable achievements. Having no break between seventeen and eighteen blurs the perception of the dramatic movement of the poem, as did every detail of the 1881 changes.

The last three sections are also victims of this telescoping motive. Section nineteen serves to lead away from the terrible sadness of the vision of armies. He must pass those visions, unloose the hold of his comrades' hands at least for the moment while he affirms once again the song of the spirit, "Death's outlet song of life." Then in section twenty he must consider the possibility of leaving lilac, song, and star, who are and represent his comrades, his dead and dying soldiers and their bereaved comrades.

Finally, in the twenty-first and last section, he reclaims them, and he reclaims the knowledge and thought of death, "for the dead I loved so well." He can, at the end of the poem, speak of one soul, "the sweetest, wisest soul of all my days and lands . . ." because that one soul is now identified with the land, with the dead and grieving, with the ultimate triumph of the soul, the Democratic Nation.

Lilac and star and bird, twined with the chant
of my soul,
With the holders holding my hand, nearing the call
of the bird,
There in the fragrant pines, and the cedars
dusk and dim.

This is what Stevens, in quite another context (and ironically) would call "The holy hush of ancient sacrifice."

What I have tried to do, lacking the manuscripts, is to get as close as possible to the original motive of "When Lilacs Last in the Door-Yard Bloom'd," to see as fully as possible its deliberateness, its specific poetic gravity, as evident in the original printing, the heavy pointing, the sense of each paragraph within each section as a building block for the entire architecture, and the function of each section in the dramatic whole. The standard printing, first made in 1881 and maintained through the authorized deathbed edition, does not let readers appreciate the poem to the fullest.

It may seem pedantry to stress so pedestrian a matter as textual problems. But it is thoroughly clear to me that Whitman's revisions, especially those made for the 1881 edition, are not always beneficial. The revisions of Yeats and Goethe, those made by Tennyson of his first book, are always in some sense aesthetic improvements. Whitman was ailing and had lost much of his poetic gift and sense after his stroke in 1873. Reading any of his major poems, we should always return to the original printing at least and at times to the original manuscripts, for he sometimes censored his manuscripts to conform to genteel standards. "When Lilacs Last in the Door-Yard Bloom'd" is the most egregious example of a great poem tampered with to its detriment. The fact that the standard printing still allows readers to experience a great poem is no tribute to the revisions but to the overwhelming strength and beauty of the original.

I have tried to stress what has always struck me, that the poem is not an elegy but a nocturne for the nation. It is part, now, of what Robert Bellah calls the American Civil Religion, with no reference to any specifically Christian ritual or dogma, in the category of the Declaration of Independence, the Constitution of the United States, some of the inaugural addresses of our thirty-nine presidents, always excepting the last four, and Lincoln's Gettysburg Address. There are other documents central to our civil religion, though none so sonorous and lovely as Whitman's greatest single poem.

Early I remarked on the tact that kept Whitman from making a facile and possibly fatal identification of Lincoln with Christ. This is one reason for my thinking that the stress on Lincoln is so minor as to suggest a motive different from that of the conventional elegy, and Swinburne's description of the poem as "the most sweet sonorous nocturne" grants us a phrase that more clearly evokes the quality of the poem, its musical organization, what Eliot would call in his "The Music of Poetry" a contrapuntal arrangement of subject matter, its nocturnal emphasis on the terror and beauty of the darkness in which we so often live and toward which we are dying, and its operatic rhetoric and poetic. The refusal to use the Christian parallel also places the poem in that very special American Civil Religion that is the unconscious doctrine that Americans live by. None of us can really escape early religious training, the Episcopalianism of Eliot, Wilder's Presbyterianism, the Puritanism of Dickinson; the Quaker background of Whitman appears very briefly in his habit of designating months by their number (the fourth month). Although Thornton Wilder has been called the last Presbyterian, at the close of his *The Cabala*, he conjures the shade of Virgil, as so many American writers are fond of doing, and his anonymous hero asks

> Master, I have just spent a year in the city that was your whole life. Am I wrong to leave it?
>
> Let us be brief. This world where Time is, troubles me. My heart has almost started beating again,—what horror! Know, importunate barbarian, that I spent my whole lifetime under a great delusion,—that Rome and the house of Augustus were eternal. Nothing is eternal save Heaven. Romes existed before Rome and when Rome will be a waste there will be Romes after her. Seek out some city that is young. The secret is to make a city, not to rest in it. When you have found one, drink in the illusion that she too is eternal. Nay, I have heard of your city. Its foundations have knocked upon our roof and the towers have cast a shadow across the sandals of the angels. Rome too was great. Oh, in the pride of your city, and when she too begins to produce great men, do not forget mine. When shall I erase from my heart this love of her. I cannot enter Zion until I have forgotten Rome.

Virgil urges Wilder's narrator to abandon his passion for created things, but when the Mantuan ghost disappears, the narrator's ship carries him to his own destiny, to make a city, not to rest in it. "The shimmering ghost faded before the stars, and the engines beneath me pounded eagerly toward the new world and the last and greatest of cities." So Whitman's poem is one of those contributions toward our common civil religion that urges us to make a city, not to rest in one. We are fortunate in the size and diversity of our continent. And for those of us who have chosen to make our city in northern California, there is plainly no time to rest. Whitman was attempting to create a culture, and his most sweet and sonorous nocturne has given his fellow citizens both a place to rest briefly and an emblem of what we might accomplish.

Reprinted from *Southern Review*, Winter 1983.

> Jove in the clouds had his inhuman birth.
> No mother suckled him, no sweet land gave
> Large-mannered motions to his mythy mind . . .

The pleasures of that last line are so intense that it always comes to me as a delightful surprise. No other words in any other order could say in so brief a compass all that those words exactly do. I am paraphrasing Coleridge's definition of a blameless style. It is a shame that he never saw this poem.

Against this "mythy mind," which Stevens accepts with amused fondness, he proposes an earthly paradise. He has already affirmed that "Divinity must live within herself," and he now affirms that it is our blood, "commingling, virginal / With heaven . . ." that "brought such requital to desire / The very hinds discerned it, in a star." The syntax is ambiguous at first glance, but clearly what the hinds discerned in the Star of Bethlehem was "requital," the requited love of human desire and heaven. Yet heaven is a human invention, and the comical Jove and the tragic Christ are also human inventions.

They are human inventions that diminish human reality and external nature, that alienate human beings from themselves and from the earth and sky. Gods should not promote such rituals—they should grant us our brief human dignity, especially since they exist only at our sufferance. This is an impish religious sense, and a refreshing one. It does not satisfy the lady. She sees the limits of a world where the earth should seem the only paradise knowable to man. She is not satisfied with that prospect, even though it has its rewards:

> The sky will be much friendlier then than now,
> A part of labor and a part of pain,
> And next in glory to enduring love,
> Not this dividing and indifferent blue.

The argument does not persuade her. She becomes petulant. She likes the summer bough but she does not want the winter branch.

> She says, "I am content when wakened birds
> Before they fly, test the reality
> Of misty fields, by their sweet questionings;
> But when the birds are gone, and their warm fields
> Return no more, where, then, is paradise?"

Alas, the measures destined for her soul do not suffice.

This is enough to make the thinker a little cross. Having the last word, as the poet always does, he crushes her with an unanswerable argument. At least, she has only a feeble answer permitted to her. Up to this fourth stanza, the poem has been gentle, serious and playful by turn, speculative, questioning. Its strongest rhetoric has been the rhetorical question, unanswerable but still a question. The lady's question is not rhetorical; the thinker's answer is:

> There is not any haunt of prophecy,
> Nor any old chimera of the grave,
> Neither the golden underground, nor isle
> Melodious, where spirits gat them home,
> Nor visionary south, nor cloudy palm
> Remote on heaven's hill, that has endured
> As April's green endures; or will endure
> Like her remembrance of awakened birds,
> Or her desire for June and evening, tipped
> By the consummation of the swallow's wings

Rhetoric: the Ciceronian sentence, complete only with the last brilliant phrase; not the Senecan amble with its brief sorties into rhetoric. The very phrasing of this single long sentence (and the semi-colon is not merely a way of keeping it a single sentence, it is instead an essential balancer): not, nor, neither, nor, nor, nor; or, or. The effect is cumulative and overwhelming. No poet could read the last phrase (tipped / By the consummation of the swallow's wings) without low feelings of frustration and envy. It is the consummation of the argument, the consummation of the sentence, and it is consummate poetry. There is a bravura of beauty in it. For it evokes those grand June evenings when the swallow's last flight of the long nest-building and food-seeking day occurs, when the swallow's work is consummated and the day achieves its fullness and end: consummation. Other beauties will replace the swallow, in some areas night-hawks, in others bats, but it will remain as part of memory and desire. Yes, I have made a *bêtise*— bringing my experience into the poem. But the poem forces precisely that upon its reader, that he bring his own experience into the poem. Are there to be no natural swallows and June evenings in the reader's experience when he adds to that experience the experience of the poem? The poem requires our memory and desire to enter and complete its world.

The intimacy of the poem is reciprocal. Yeats liked to quote John Stuart Mill to the effect that rhetoric is heard, poetry is overheard. Great rhetorician that he was, he could, like Stevens, make rhetoric as intimate as revery. We are, with Whitman, Yeats, Wordsworth, Donne, and Stevens made accomplices in the rhetorical as well as the poetical design. The intimacy and cogency make rhetoric and poetic coterminous, and unite reader and poet in a single action.

The lady, however, does not concur, and by now both the thinker and the reader are becoming impatient with her unwillingness to see the truth. Because the poem is true. It is also beautiful. And, as a poem, it is good. Hence the thinker allows her only the briefest querulous statement:

> She says, "But in contentment I still feel
> The need of some imperishable bliss."

That is quite enough. How could she be so greedy? She is defying natural law and must be set straight:

> Death is the mother of beauty; hence from her,
> Alone, shall come fulfilment to our dreams
> And our desires. . . .

Typing, I fell into false rhetoric and typed "fulfilment *of* our dreams. . . ." Even in the small matter of the preposition, Stevens shows how language can be made to act: fulfilment comes to our dreams, not of them. Foreign speakers of any language have their worst trouble with prepositions. I am incapable of remembering the law that determines whether *de* or *à* is to precede a French infinitive; the distinction between German *auf* and *an* often evades me. English— well, it is in worse shape than German or even French because as a non-inflected language it compels more prepositional phrases. The administration of the prepositional phrase is perhaps the most accurate index to any English writer's style—as witness the current clumsy sentence. But even in the tiny example just cited, Stevens refuses to corrupt his exact meaning.

But the grand statement that haunts all readers of the poem and puzzles many: Death is the mother of beauty. . . . It is not a puzzle. It means exactly what, on the surface, it says: Death is the mother of beauty. The human awareness of death distinguishes men from the other animals. Some animals use tools. Chimpanzees can be taught a sizable vocabulary in sign language, and if their voice boxes were higher in their throats could be taught to speak. But no animal, so far as we know, has any knowledge of death, or lays claim to any knowledge of death, except the human animal. From the awareness of death all specifically human blessings and curses flow. Pater observed that we are all under sentence of death with an indefinite reprieve. Freud based his most comprehensive psychology on the extension beyond the pleasure principle to the corollary principle of pain and death. It should be no puzzle, then, that death is the mother of beauty: it is a fact. For the knowledge of death gives to our moments of rapture and glory their greatest poignancy and forces us to their record and per-petuation. Hence the poetic enterprise at its greatest. I have already considered in Whitman yet another aspect of the knowledge of death, but in "Sunday Morning" the knowledge of death is a cause, the cause, of celebration.

Death is so great a cause of celebration that it makes Paradise seem trivial. Without death, there can be no beauty in Paradise. Ripe fruit will never fall, the boughs will never become branches, it will be a mockery of our perishing earth:

> Is there no change of death in paradise?
> Does ripe fruit never fall? Or do the boughs
> Hang always heavy in that perfect sky,
> Unchanging, yet so like our perishing earth,
> With rivers like our own that seek for seas
> They never find, the same receding shores
> That never touch with inarticulate pang?
> Why set the pear upon those river-banks
> Or spice the shores with odors of the plum?
> Alas, that that they should wear our colors there,
> The silken weavings of our afternoons,
> And pick the strings of our insipid lutes!
> Death is the mother of beauty, mystical,
> Within whose burning bosom we devise
> Our earthly mothers waiting, sleeplessly.

Here we come to the blemish: "insipid lutes." Whenever a reader genuinely loves a poem, he finds himself forced to justifications, as in the break between stanzas seven and eight of "Among School Chil-dren." In Yeat's poem the problems are structural and grow from a *pen-timento;* here the problem is one of texture and grows from diction.

Faced with this problem, the great refuge is the Oxford English Dictionary, a cloister where the worried philologist can find some use of the word at some time that will justify his beloved poem. Not this poem. The OED is emphatic in denying any meaning to the word but the most conventional: 1. Without taste, tasteless; also, having only a very slight taste; without perceptible flavour or flavour sufficient to gratify the palate. 2. *fig.* Wanting the qualities which excite interest or emotion; uninteresting, lifeless, flat, dull. 3. Devoid of taste, intelli-gence, or judgment; stupid, foolish, dull.

Even the etymology doesn't rescue the line: Late Latin, *insipidus,* tasteless, f. *in-* plus *sapidus,* well-tasted, wise, prudent, sapid: cf. F. *insipide.* The most contorting lover of the poem would have trouble in arguing that the lute was "imprudent," showing a fine disregard for proprieties, therefore a splendid instrument. Should the lover now have to say that, well, his beloved would be perfect if her nose were a little shorter, that his forgiveness only magnifies her other perfections? Until that line, everything was clear, granted that thought was required; here, only the blindness of love could assert perfect beauty.

Yet simply as a line, out of context, it has distinction and magic, mystery and charm: And pick the strings of our insipid lutes. Only churlish inspecting of the mouth of this incredible gift horse would check admiration—yet that is the reader's job, to collaborate, and here it is hard to say what the work is.

Any difficulties are resolved in the seventh stanza where the thinker becomes the prophet. I say "where" rather than "when," because in the poem as in Sunday mornings the matter is taken out of time into a realm of being that is continuously present: here, there, where. The celebration of death becomes a celebration of the sun, therefore of mortality. The sun is perceived by the ring of men who chant their devotion to him

> Not as a god, but as a god might be,
> Naked among them, like a savage source.

The human tribe will chant "a chant of paradise, / Out of their blood, returning to the sky. . . ." Lake, trees, and hills will enter the chant and echo it long after it is past and an indefinite "they" (men, lake, sun, trees, hills)

> shall know well the heavenly fellowship
> Of men that perish and of summer morn.

The ultimate lines of this stanza—there is one more to follow—return to humankind:

> And whence they came and whither they shall go
> The dew upon their feet shall manifest.

But humankind is transformed, now part of a unit coming from an old chaos of the sun, no longer alienated from nature and no longer alienated from the self that can become totally human.

The poem is ready for its peroration except for one final rebuff to the lady's dream:

> She hears upon that water without sound,
> A voice that cries, "The tomb in Palestine
> Is not the porch of spirits lingering.
> It is the grave of Jesus, where he lay."

The voice of the thinker, no longer simply paralleling her consciousness, now enters and reveals to it the mortality of her imagined god.
This is not Christos Pantocrator but Jesus of Nazareth. There is no Pantocrator:

> We live in an old chaos of the sun,
> Or old dependency of day and night,
> Or island solitude, unsponsored, free,
> Of that wide water, inescapable.
> Deer walk upon our mountains, and the quail
> Whistle about us their spontaneous cries;
> Sweet berries ripen in the wilderness;
> And, in the isolation of the sky,
> At evening, casual flocks of pigeons make
> Ambiguous undulations as they sink,
> Downward to darkness, on extended wings.

We are, then, human, and we are Americans, living on the vast continent that is an island extending from Alaska to Tierra del Fuego, including Whitman, Stevens, Marquez, Neruda. We are literally isolated,
but we are joined in our mortality with the sweet berries, the quail, the
deer, and finally with the casual flocks of pigeons sinking "Downward
to darkness, on extended wings."

What, then, is the greatness of this poem? Much of its greatness
comes from its truth, at once magisterial, modest, and mocking. Truth
is not a fashionable concept, and certainly it is more admired than
practiced. Truthfulness in poetry is no simple matter; Auden is right
when he says "The truest poetry is the most feigning," and it is central
to the human condition that our health can be arrived at only by medi-
cation, our naturalness only by artifice, and our truth only by fictions.
"Sunday Morning" convinces its reader that he is in the presence of
truth as majestic and final for poetic purposes as the American Constitution is for legal. Both the Constitution and "Sunday Morning" are
artifacts, products of the human imagination operating in political and
poetic arenas. They share a magisterial certainty, and the truth of
"Sunday Morning" comes in the masterful disposition of the language
toward a moral and philosophical end.

The poem presents a truth that is experiential. No matter how
many explications, no matter how many parallels in the external
world—the experience potential in the poem remains complete. T. S.
Eliot once said that it is possible to determine whether a work of literary art is literature on literary and aesthetic grounds; determining relative value after that initial decision or determining absolute value
(greatness) is a moral and religious decision. Morally, the poem presents conduct as best determined by the balances of pleasure and pain,

and acceptance of those measures. Metaphysically, it places those values in a physical and mortal world where the source of physical reality gains human devotion "Not as a god, but as a god might be." The position of the poem is one of the classic positions of mankind, and in this poem at least that classic position (the stoic hedonist) has received articulation that makes great moral and metaphysical positions accessible through passionate thought. There are other definitions of masterpieces, but here at least is one.

Must poems always think? Must they always embody some classic moral and metaphysical truth, one of those many truths that make life possible and dignified? Not necessarily, but it is true that many of the great poems in world literature are validated by their moral and religious action. The later work of Stevens has been chastised because it is not poetry but philosophy, and much recent criticism of Stevens has sought his philosophical sources or sought to justify his long thoughtful poems as if they represented some sort of odd perversion. The sources are clear enough: William James' *Radical Empiricism and A Pluralistic Universe* and the works of George Santayana *passim*. One day-dreams of Wallace Stevens receiving a copy of *Three Philosophical Poets* and saying calmly, "It is time for a fourth." And, since the appearance of Santayana's lovely book is coeval with the writing of "Sunday Morning," the day-dream continues as Stevens sits down and writes "Complacencies of the peignoir. . . ."

I find it shameful that any literary community should be flung into embarrassment by the existence of a great body of philosophical poetry by the greatest American poet who devoted practically all of his specifically literary activity to poetry. Unlike Pound, Eliot, and Williams, he wrote very little except poetry, and that poetry maintains its stature not only among his great contemporaries but also among the mighty dead. If the following passage from "Esthétique du Mal" is philosophy and not poetry, then so much the worse for poetry:

> The greatest poverty is not to live
> In a physical world, to feel that one's desire
> Is too difficult to tell from despair. Perhaps,
> After death, the non-physical people, in paradise,
> Itself non-physical, may by chance, observe
> The green corn gleaming and experience
> The minor of what we feel. The adventurer
> In humanity has not conceived of a race
> Completely physical in a physical world.
> The green corn gleams and the metaphysicals
> Lie sprawling in majors of the August heat,
> The rotund emotions, paradise unknown.

This is the thesis scrivened in delight,
The reverberating psalm, the right chorale.

One might have thought of sight, but who could think
Of what it sees, for all the ill it sees?
Speech found the ear, for all the evil sound,
But the dark italics it could not propound.
And out of what one sees and hears and out
Of what one feels, who could have thought to make
So many selves, so many sensuous worlds,
As if the air, the mid-day air, was swarming
With the metaphysical changes that occur,
Merely in living as and where we live.

It is possible to complain. Paradise is not non-physical, as doctrine makes perfectly clear. But that is to quibble, and the last thing that this glorious conclusion to a great poem should evoke is quibbling. It was good luck to be young when Stevens' poems appeared, novel and un-questionably original and profound and eloquent and stirring—as they still are.

Reprinted from *Hyperion*, March 1978.

7

Yeats' "Nineteen Hundred and Nineteen"

Of all the poems written by Yeats on the quality of life in the twentieth century, his "Nineteen Hundred and Nineteen" is the most ambitious and inclusive. This long poem in six parts is devoted to a symbolic account of the nature of the universe as it can be discerned in the intentions, failures, and achievements of the human spirit, primarily in the twentieth century but also in such analogous periods as Periclean Athens. The poem examines several possible philosophical methods of bearing such a universe and culminates in a vision of evil as the basic recurrent reality of life. It is essentially a visionary poem, and what it sees is not bounded by physical limits, is instead the ground and condition of physical life. To evaluate the qualitative limits of life, Yeats uses two basic methods, one symbolic and the other dramatic, the one establishing a series of antithetically ordered images, the other setting the human personality in relation to the order of things symbolically arranged.

The symbolic design of the poem elaborates a cluster of forces that take the forms of *antithesis* and *interpenetration* mainly and of *circularity* and *flux* secondarily, all these forces playing round the basic problem of appearance and reality. The forces thus symbolized form the basic design of the universe within which human life takes its course, and the dramatic structure of the poem presents the response of humanity to the universal design. Apart from both, contemplating the entire process, is Yeats—not Yeats the individual but Yeats the representative of his world, of his civilization in a state of crisis. He sees civilization as a struggle to keep self-control, an effort to maintain ascendancy over the forces of evil by the exertion of will, and he sees that toward the end of a civilization, when control is lost, the world falls in a last terrible surrender to the irrational outbreak. As poet and prophet he has the unsettling chore of displaying his world in the process of surrender, of dramatizing the ultimate inadequacy of the will and reason when faced with an apparent solidity that suddenly emerges as a whirling flux, only to take the form of a new circular reality, moving from pole to pole, that underlies flux and is its nonhuman motivator.

The first stanzas illustrate the intensity and compression of the whole as well as the modes of organization characteristic of the poem:

> Many ingenious lovely things are gone,
> That seemed sheer miracle to the multitude,
> Protected from the circle of the moon
> That pitches common things about. There stood
> Amid the ornamental bronze and stone
> An ancient image made of olive wood—
> And gone are Phidias' famous ivories
> And all the golden grasshoppers and bees.

The opening line introduces the conflict between appearance (lovely) and reality (flux—many), and the ambivalent "ingenious" suggests that the "things" are not only carefully wrought but somehow spurious (as "an ingenious explanation"). The very metrical pattern of the line, with its intricate complication at the start and the simple flat "are gone" at the close, asserts the mingled despair and love that motivate the entire poem. In like manner the internal assonance of "sheer miracle" at once cuts the phrase out of its surroundings and stresses the fragility and transparence of the miracle as well as its "mereness," its essential commonness. The "circle" of the third line is a recurrent image in this poem, functioning as a sign of both formality and the persistence (recurrence) of evil. The moon both moves in circles and is itself circular, and in its periodicity and its classical connotations of disorder (under the moon) it serves throughout the poem as a sign of the irrational. The moon is beyond the control of human will; it pitches (defiles, carelessly flings) both common and lovely things about. The term "things" suggests that they are fabrications, not really very important, and the reduction of the things to "ornamental" materials stresses that they are mere lumps, things resolved to their elements. The "ancient image" is most likely the statue of Athena in the Acropolis, the "famous ivories" the chryselephantine statues by Phidias, the golden bees probably delicate small works contrasting with the works of Phidias. The golden grasshoppers were to Thucydides signs of luxury and aristocracy:

> The Athenians were the first to lay aside their weapons, and to adopt an easier and more luxurious mode of life; indeed, it is only lately that their rich old men left off the luxury of wearing undergarments of linen, and fastening a knot of their hair with a tie of golden grasshoppers. . . .

The golden grasshoppers, and the other images of this section, are signs of both peace and aristocracy, of an entire secure and luxurious way of life predicated on the efforts of the human will and reason to minimize flux and evil.

The failure of this particular civilizing effort is notorious: "Many ingenious lovely things are gone. . . ." The analogy between Periclean Athens and western Europe in the period extending from the Franco-Prussian to the First World War is perhaps not so evident:

> We too had many pretty toys when young:
> A law indifferent to blame or praise,
> To bribe or threat; habits that made old wrong
> Melt down, as it were wax in the sun's rays;
> Public opinion ripening for so long
> We thought it would outlive all future days.
> O what fine thought we had because we thought
> That the worst rogues and rascals had died out.

The "pretty toys" of Europe are one with the "lovely things" of Greece, the difference being that our toys are more abstract, are matters of law, habit, opinion, thought; "fine thought" being comparable to the "sheer miracle" of the first stanza in that it is refined and fragile. The "sun" that is to melt old wrong is the antithesis of the moon that casts things about in the first stanza, and the stanza suggests what the outcome of reliance on the full light of reason is to be; these ripening habits and opinions will also rot.

In these opening stanzas, then, the major tensions and processes of the poem are presented with both concreteness and cogency. The tone of sardonic mockery that underlies the stanzas is one of Yeats' most commonly used devices to keep him from the sentimental pontificating that such a subject might, in a lesser man and poet, promote. The tone, as G. S. Fraser suggests in a discussion of "I am of Ireland," represents "that note of sardonic mockery which for Yeats, as for most Irishmen, was something positively valuable in itself, a necessary preservative against the softness that turns the romantic attitude into the sentimental one." The tone is indeed the chief instrument permitting Yeats to speak in one voice of the love and despair with which he contemplates the state of man. The elegiac note that permeates much of modern literature from Proust to Edith Sitwell is here at once presented and measured.

The third stanza continues the analysis of false expectations entertained by trusters of the will and reason. The use of mockery and the persistent playing on "show" and reality ("ancient tricks") continues to elaborate the point of view of the humanitarian who thought that gunpowder was really for fireworks rather than for bloodshed. With the fourth stanza the tone shifts as the poem moves from intent to reality, from the drowsy chargers of the palace guard to the nightmare of murder by drunken soldiers:

> . . . A drunken soldiery
> Can leave the mother, murdered at her door,
> To crawl in her own blood, and go scot-free;
> The night can sweat with terror as before
> We pierced our thoughts into philosophy . . .

The philosophy is fabricated, artificial, and—because of its one-sided emphasis on the importance of reason—incapable of facing and controlling evil.

The "philosophy" is *not* the philosophy of Yeats' *A Vision;* when Yeats told Olivia Shakespear that the poem was not philosophical, he meant that it had nothing to do with his "philosophy" that was then emerging through the special gifts of Georgia Yeats. In fact the poem is extremely free in its use of various philosophies. The "philosophy" of the first section that was pieced together is the humanitarian philosophy derived from Mill, Spencer, Bury and others, its chief motivating idea being the idea of progress. This poem is one of the strongest and most effective critiques—it is really a negation—of the idea of progress.

Against the failure of humanitarian intent, Yeats examines the possibility of maintaining a stoic indifference. The only recourse of non-sentimental integrity is to see, to know, to be aware of and therefore protected from mutability. No work (no fabrication, no toy, no thing) can stand, "No honour leave its mighty monument." The man who knows this "Has but one comfort left: all triumph would / But break upon his ghostly solitude." But this attitude is being measured, and the tone, which has shifted from qualified lament to sardonic mockery to indignation to stoicism, now shifts once more to a flat, loving, desperate compassion:

> But is there any comfort to be found?
> Man is in love and loves what vanishes,
> What more is there to say? . . .

He then returns to the objects of the opening stanza and points out that no one had dared admit that any "incendiary or bigot" would destroy the Athenian olive or the golden grasshoppers. The first section of the poem is circular in its movement, and within that circularity it presents the flux and terror as well as the nobility of experience. It sets, in short, the basic vision of life within which the remainder of the poem will take place. It also develops the limitations of the options that seem available (lament, stoicism, indignation, mockery) and enters a further possibility, the dominant attitude of the poem, which at once accounts for and transcends the evident variety of possibilities.

After this overture, Yeats develops fully, in the following five sections of the poem, the various materials presented in the first section. In section two, Loie Fuller's Chinese dancers serve as symbol of both the circularity and the flux of part one, but they also symbolize the formality of historical pattern and the interpenetration of levels of being that, for Yeats, is the cause of historical change. A "dragon of air" seems to fall among the dancers and takes them out of their conscious limited bodies, and this concrete situation is the appropriate sign of the general human situation:

> All men are dancers and their tread
> Goes to the barbarous clangour of a gong.

The "Platonic Year" "whirls out new right and wrong," and in its place "whirls in the old," with no regard for the interests of humanity. Both the moon and the gong are representative of this larger circle. Although this section is primarily concerned with circularity in its imagery, its structure is emergent rather than circular: it begins with a simple reminiscent anecdote, proceeds to an explication of the anecdote, and concludes with a statement of the meaning of the experience. It extends and develops by resymbolizing, setting in a new context, one dominant image of the first part (the dragon), so that it may be contemplated in yet another set of circumstances.

The same general pattern is followed in the third section, except that an attitude rather than an image is carried over from the first section and freshly symbolized. Stoicism, formerly recommended as an escape from both fear and sentimentality, is once again examined and found wanting, and once again the essential discrepancy between will and reality is stressed. In this section the solitary soul is identified with the swan, seeking an ultimate self-realization before death. But man is no swan; he is lost in the labyrinth he has made "in art or politics." He is lost in accidental matters that keep his soul from its true integrity, and with this possibility in mind, Yeats appears, with an outrageous and winning deliberateness, to try on an attitude for size:

> The swan has leaped into the desolate heaven:
> That image can bring wildness, bring a rage
> To end all things, to end
> What my laborious life imagined, even
> The half-imagined, the half-written page;

> O but we dreamed to mend
> Whatever mischief seemed
> To afflict mankind, but now
> That winds of winter blow
> Learn that we were crack-pated when we dreamed.

The poem returns once again to the point it had reached at the end of section one. Man *is* in love and loves what vanishes; he may be crack-pated in his dreaming, but he lives in a world subject to the foul storm, the winds of winter, and even the stoic suicide will not release him from that fate.

The brief fourth section takes up the weasel symbol from the first section:

> We, who seven years ago
> Talked of honour and of truth,
> Shriek with pleasure if we show
> The weasel's twist, the weasel's tooth.

At the same time that it stresses the tone of mockery that was strong in sections one and three, this quatrain turns the mockery against the mocker: there is something fruitless in the posture, something not only unpleasant but self-indulgent. This is recognized in the fifth section when mockery is advocated in a series of three stanzas urging mockery of the great, mockery of the wise, and mockery of the good. But the fourth stanza explicitly undercuts this point of view:

> Mock mockers after that
> That would not lift a hand maybe
> To help good, wise or great
> To bar that foul storm out, for we
> Traffic in mockery.

In the first five sections of the poem, then, Yeats has tested and rejected various attitudes possible in viewing the current state of the world, and he has rejected them in favor of an attitude that sees the current world under the aspect of the eternal human condition. Humanitarianism without a sense of evil will not stand up; mockery of human effort is not valid; stoicism is no refuge; sentimentality is perhaps worst of all. The only possible deduction from the experience treated in the poem is that only an attitude of persistent courage combined with a full apprehension of evil will serve men, given the universe that they are given.

With the attitude set firmly, the final section of the poem then uses the figure of Lady Kyteler to dramatize the nature of historical process.

In Lady Kyteler it is possible to see a civilization suffering the influx of evil, accepting superhuman power of vicious origin, turning to ancient wrongs. Lady Kyteler's fate analogizes the fate of the modern world:

> Violence upon the roads: violence of horses;
> Some few have handsome riders, are garlanded
> On delicate sensitive ear or tossing mane,
> But wearied running round and round in their courses
> All break and vanish, and evil gathers head:
> Herodias' daughters have returned again,
> A sudden blast of dusty wind and after
> Thunder of feet, tumult of images,
> Their purpose in the labyrinth of the wind;
> And should some crazy hand dare touch a daughter
> All turn with amorous cries, or angry cries,
> According to the wind, for all are blind.
> But now wind drops, dust settles; thereupon
> There lurches past, his great eyes without thought
> Under the shadow of stupid straw-pale locks,
> That insolent fiend Robert Artisson
> To whom the love-lorn Lady Kyteler brought
> Bronzed peacock feathers, red combs of her cocks.

When the flux of history briefly ceases, when the dust is cleared away, when all illusions and artifices are dropped, the emergent image of meaning is the image of Robert Artisson and Lady Kyteler.

Yeats offers as explanation of the section a single note which clarifies somewhat Robert Artisson and the horsemen but leaves both Herodias' daughters and Lady Kyteler unexplained:

> The country people see at times certain apparitions whom they name now "fallen angels," now "ancient inhabitants of the country," and describe as riding at whiles "with flowers upon the heads of the horses." I have assumed . . . that these horsemen, now that the times worsen, give way to worse. My last symbol, Robert Artisson, was an evil spirit much run after in Kilkenny at the start of the fourteenth century.

The violence of the horses is at worst an amoral violence; some of the riders are conceded handsomeness, and their horses have "delicate sensitive" ears and fine manes. These forces of innocence break and vanish as the forces of evil gain strength. At a single stroke they are replaced by Herodias' daughters, who are in turn superseded by Robert Artisson and Alice Kyteler.

Dame Alice Kyteler is a figure well known to students of witchcraft and demonology; she appears in almost all compendious histories of European witchcraft and is one of the very few witches brought to trial in Ireland. Dame Alice flourished in the diocese of Ossory (Kilkenny

County) in the early fourteenth century. Apparently she had been practicing witchcraft and general outrage for a good many years; however, her heresies might have passed without historical trace if it had not been for the zealous Richard Ledrede's accession to the Bishopric of Ossory. The bishop's first Synod (1317) legislated emphatically against deviants from the faith, and in 1324 he brought charges of heretical sorcery against several persons, headed by Alice Kyteler.

Lady Kyteler immediately fled to Dublin. After some delays caused by the influence of Lady Kyteler and her relatives, Bishop Ledrede managed to bring the case to trial. A historian sympathetic with the bishop applauds the result:

> Lady Alice Kyteller [*sic*], her son William Outlaw, and their confederates, . . . all beyond doubt a bad lot, . . . were found guilty . . . Lady Alice . . . fled to England, where she spent her remaining years. William Outlaw acknowledged hs fault and abjured his heresy in St. Mary's Church; but, relapsing, was sentenced, as part of his punishment "to cover with lead within the next four years the entire Cathedral church . . ." Of the others, Sarah, daughter of Petronilla, saved herself by flight; Petronilla was burned at the stake. . . ; the fate of the rest is unknown.

The accusations against Lady Kyteler were numerous, but most of them simmered down to the charge that she had rejected the Church and had enjoyed unholy intercourse with a certain demon, Robin, son of Art (filius Artis): "The said dame had a certain demon, an incubus, named . . . Robin son of Art, who had carnal knowledge of her, and from whom she admitted that she had received all her wealth." The name Robert Artisson has the authority of Holinshed:

> In these daies lived in the diocesse of Ossorie the Lady Alice Kettle, whom the bishop asscited to purge herself of the fame of inchantment and witchcraft imposed upon hir . . . She was charged to have nightlie conference with a spirit called Robert Artisson, to whome she sacrificed in the high waie nine red cocks and nine peacocks eies. Also that she swept the streets of Kilkennie between compleine and twilight, raking all the filth towards the doores of hir sonne William Outlawe, murmuring secretlie with her selfe these words:
>
> > "To the house of William my sonne,
> > Hie all the wealth of Kilkennie Towne."

It is easy to see how this story would appeal to Yeats: the grotesque comedy of the last couplet; the casual tragedy of Petronilla; the peculiar mixture of religious and practical motives in the covering of the cathedral; the exotic sacrifice; the blend of sexual and religious motivations. More important, however, is what he selected from the entire history and how he integrated it into his vision of humanity. The chief interest of the tale for Yeats resided in its violent depravity and in its capacity for symbolizing in intimate concrete terms the interaction of levels of being, the unification of natural and supernatural, so that Lady Kyteler in all her relative pettiness could symbolize the same great interaction of natural and supernatural that he found in the myth of Leda and the Swan or Mary and the Dove. The pride of the peacocks and the barnyard domesticity of the cocks could contrast with the god-like beauty of the swan in earlier sections of the poem; the figure of Robert Artisson could be integrated with the drunken soldiery of the earlier sections; and the lovelorn Lady Kyteler could stand for all the terrible and desperate surrender to evil that had gone through all of life, had caused the fall of civilizations, and was indeed as central a fact of the universe as was the attempt, through artifacts of art or politics, to overcome the whirling antitheses of the inhuman universal pattern. Unlike the Virgin or Leda, with their long record of associations in religion and romance and history, Lady Kyteler could stand singly and unequivocally for a surrender without grace or beauty to a force simply and unambiguously evil.

What this concluding image does is first to explain and extend the meaning of the whole poem, to answer the questions posed by the opening assertion ("Many ingenious lovely things are gone . . ."), and second to set the poem in relation to Yeats' better-known poems on historical change ("The Second Coming," "Leda and the Swan"). It leads, moreover, in its complex inclusiveness, to more general speculation on the ideas and attitudes, the special folding together of technique and concept, person and world, that could motivate such a construct as "Nineteen Hundred and Nineteen."

For the structure and concerns of the poem are peculiarly those of our world; we should not be put off by the bizarre appearance of the surface, this curious mélange of items drawn from a knowledge at once wide and extremely personal. In the poem, the personal has been so transmuted as to become the common property of the race, and the eccentric has been so ordered and imagined as to become central and prophetic. If we move back from the poem briefly and turn our attention to the spiritual problems that it has faced and, within its limits, overcome, its centrality to the modern mind and world will become more clear.

The poem does not simply declare that things are bad, nor does it simply declare that things have always been bad, that man is born to trouble, that original sin exists, though it in no way contradicts those notions. The poem rather examines the difficulties that a modern man faces when evil emerges in his world, and much of the structure grows directly from the fact that its reference is immediate and contemporary.

The chief difficulty for a reader of the poem originates in the poem's arrogant demand that we know ourselves.

In "Nineteen Hundred and Nineteen" Yeats speaks as a poet with prophetic intentions, and for the prophet one major problem is metaphysics. The metaphysical challenge handed to Yeats and his contemporaries was, generally speaking, that the universe was probably chaotic; life was perhaps meaningless; so far as there was any meaning, it was artificial and imposed, not inherent in any postulated exterior reality. As William James phrased the problem,

> There is no really inherent order, but it is we who project order into the world by selecting objects and tracing relations so as to gratify our intellectual interests. We carve out order by leaving the disorderly parts out; and the world is conceived thus after the analogy of a forest or a block of marble from which parks or statues may be produced by eliminating irrelevant trees or chips of stone.

In such a world, order or meaning is illusory, and on the precarious surface that men have created, they live in constant danger of eruptions from forces not comprehended and controlled. The psychology of the twentieth century, especially that of Freud, is predicated on such a view of the human condition, and much of the literature (that of Conrad, for example) argues that we live in darkness and walk in the feeble illusion of light that can only be perpetuated by a conspiracy of silence. Some things, as one of Conrad's characters says, will not bear looking into.

So Henry Adams found, and one of the most revealing utterances of the age is his description of his journey through Switzerland after his sister's terrible death in Italy. In that trip he saw Mount Blanc "as it really was," as a chaos of purposeless forces. What he saw was, in T. E. Hulme's phrase, "the world as cinders," the senseless flux and congregation of atoms, organized briefly but disintegrating rapidly, forming this or that pattern that was apparently real and significant, but never holding to that pattern of significance with any permanence. Pattern and meaning were in the eye of the beholder, and though the discovery of pattern and meaning was the highest function of man, Adams could see no essential difference between one pattern and another. Certainly Adams was ironically posing when he prayed to the Dynamo as men of the Middle Ages prayed to the Virgin, but the anguish thus masked and treated had a metaphysical base: it meant that to Adams there was no point in distinguishing between the Will of God, the Order of Nature, and Man-made Order; all order was man-made, the Virgin and the Dynamo were one. When he saw Mount Blanc as his metaphysics assured him it "really" was, the "stage-scenery" of his senses collapsed.

The problem faced by Adams, by Conrad, and by Yeats, was further intensified by the fact that in a chaotic universe—or a multiverse—the possible variety in Orders was endless, or if limited at all, then limited by the range of intellectual, imaginative, and emotional combinations possible to the human entity. In such a world the concept of absolute truth could have no efficacy, for the correlation between statement and fact was embarrassingly subject to change as the apparent design of chaos changed. What could exist, in the place of statement correlated with data and consistent within itself, was a multiplicity of self-consistent hypotheses that "organized" force in the sense of directing it toward goals arbitrarily selected or, at best, sanctioned by human motives. The variety of options available to the cultivated mind of the twentieth century has had as its chief result a terrible paralysis of the will.

One would search far in modern philosophy to find any attitude or doctrine that is interested in the discipline of the moral will. Pragmatism, pluralism, radical empiricism, and logical positivism have combined to encourage a distrust of metaphysical interests and to affirm the proposition that the universe is quite literally what human beings make of it. Our politics of naked force and practiced expediency thrives on the belief that there is no extrahuman standard or design to which political systems or acts can be referred, and even the weary effort of the conservative elements of western Europe cannot mask a cynical acceptance of power as the only possible rule in a purposeless universe. In the churches, academies, and chancelleries of the world, the entire intellectual tone justifies Rilke's anguished cry, "The world has fallen into the hands of men."

It is this world to which "Nineteen Hundred and Nineteen" addresses itself. The poem's stress on the essential emptiness of the merely human, the world "carved out" by men, the statue or garden that the humanitarian wishfully declares the total truth, gives the lie direct to a world that continues to deceive itself in the face of all the evidence, and—by so deceiving itself—lays itself open to the incursion of evil. In the poem everything, the humanitarian aspiration and the delicate handiwork of the goldsmith, stands in pathetic isolation against the whirling force of history, which is on no one's side. The universe of the poem is—like the universe of James or Adams or Conrad—not comprehensible from the merely human point of view, seems to be run on principles not intelligible by the measurements of men. Its postulated form is not that of statue or park but of whirling dust, from which can emerge nakedly and brutally the image of a force inimical to the persistence of human artifacts.

The universe of the poem may have a purpose, but it is not a human purpose. The human purposes presented in the poem, like the human purposes that Adams saw, are multiple, and one of the main attempts of the poem is to present and evaluate several of the main attitudes possible in facing the universe. Humanitarianism, cynicism, stoicism, Platonism, and variants of each of the four are tested, only to be rejected in favor of an attitude that includes them all, accounts for more than does any of them, and preserves for men a full measure of dignity while not minimizing in any way the evil to which men are subject if not heir. The attitude is, in the simplest terms, the attitude of the contemplative, and it has the advantage first of admitting more and second of affirming more.

The contemplative attitude, as displayed in this poem, admits more because of its willingness to wait, to permit the emergence and watch the shifts and permutations of its own workings and of the workings of the world. Whether, as in some sections of the poem, it is recording external events or, as in other sections, it is examining internal and personal events, the contemplative attitude refuses to do violence to the truly existent facts. It is passionately involved in the various events—in the aspirations and fall of Athens, in the fumbling good will of Europe before the great wars, in the mockery of good, wise, and great, in the terrible perversity of Lady Kyteler—and being so involved cannot deny or distort. In this refusal to deny or distort resides the ultimate affirmation of the contemplative and the full acceptance of responsibility.

In this acceptance and affirmation one finds the true greatness of Yeats. Poet he certainly was, brilliantly articulate and technically skilled, but he was a certain kind of poet, different from most of his contemporaries because of his devotion to a mode of thought that has its roots in a tradition greater than the merely poetic. He was first and above all a contemplative prophet with a dramatic sense of his personal responsibility for what he saw and what he did, and with a symbolic sense of the generic importance of his experience. From his definition of himself and of his role comes much of the glory of his poetry, and from momentary relaxations and follies comes much of its failure. More often than not, and even in his less ambitious efforts, his hold remained firm, and the poetry took on the resonance and power that we have seen in "Nineteen Hundred and Nineteen."

Reprinted from B. H. Lehman et al., *The Image of the Work* (Berkeley: University of California Press, 1955).

Yeats and Contemporary Irish Poetry

8

W. B. Yeats

To begin the twentieth century with Yeats is to affirm its continuity with the preceding age and to consent to its special flavor. By 1900, when he was thirty-five years old, he had developed a style that he then took to be his very self; at the close of his life thirty-nine years later, he was still restlessly seeking a style adequate to his continuously developing self and the historical flux of a world entering the agony of the Second World War. Like other protean masters of modern art, Stravinsky or Picasso, he underwent a succession of styles, outgrowing and casting aside a fully developed manner only to return to it again to follow out its unrealized possibilities. Following his work from its beginnings, his belief that William Morris was the happiest of poets and that Dante Gabriel Rossetti was a proper model, the cloudy tenderness and twilight dimness, the early formulation of a theory of symbolism based on his studies in Blake and in the occult, his aesthetic nationalism that resulted in the Abbey Theatre and *Kathleen ni Houlihan*—it is possible to see general strands of continuity in attitude and sector of experience chosen for poetic treatment (for attitudes as much as experience were elected rather than accepted). He exhibits also a deep conservatism in art and politics that checks the tendency toward improvising and gives his romantic interest in self-exploration a fixity and a rigor that it would otherwise have lacked. "Too soft" was a verdict that Pound made on most work in the Symbolist Tradition, and though he did not complain of the softness of Yeats' later work, its systematic symbology made it unpalatable to him. In fact, for Yeats' immediate successors, notably Eliot and Pound, his later poetry had no inventive relevance, though Pound's early poetry owes an evident debt to the style Yeats had established by 1900 and then refined and altered to such a point that the division between early and late Yeats has become a major critical puzzle.

Yeats presents the anomaly of a poet with two distinct accomplishments that can be associated with two historical periods often thought of as opposite. He is anomalous in other ways that make serious readers question his claim to be the greatest modern poet; he might better be described as a great poet writing in the modern period. Many of the intellectual and social concerns that obsessed intellectuals contemporary with him he found irrelevant; he had no use for the interests that were central to Shaw or Russell; he was indifferent to depth psychology and modern physics, and the issues raised by the Russian Revolution were secondary, in his attention, to those raised by the founding of the Irish Free State. While theologians agonized over the decay of religious faith and institutions, he was content to accept the tradition of heterodox mysticism as it came to him through the writings of Blake, Blavatsky, and Mathers and such organizations as the Theosophical Society and the Order of the Golden Dawn. The major developments in modern visual and literary art that have changed the general sense of artistic form and reference were antipathetic to him; he preferred the norms of the pre-Raphaelites. He seems, when so generally described, an intellectual provincial, committed to a minor aesthetic movement, a limited nationalism, and an eccentric religiosity.

Yeats himself was aware of the difficulties that his interests presented not only to his readers but to himself. In 1919 he wrote of the problem that, in his youth, his primary concern presented to him. "Hammer your thoughts into unity"—this sentence persisted in his head: "For days I could think of nothing else, and for years I tested all I did by that sentence. I had three interests: interest in a form of literature, in a form of philosophy, and a belief in nationality. None of these seemed to have anything to do with the other. . . ." The development of a coherent world view from these unpromising materials may be accounted a tribute to Yeats' genius, and in the later poetry he did so with an amazing vigor. Even in his youth he did manage to shape a style, a mode of thought and perception as well as a distinctive manner of writing and a special subject matter that allowed him to be, of all the poets who came to maturity in the 1890s, the only one who shaped a valid body of work:

> I was unlike other of my generation in one thing only. I am very religious, and deprived by Huxley and Tyndall, whom I detested, of the simple-minded religion of my childhood, I had made a new religion, almost an infallible church of poetic tradition, of a fardel of stories, of personages, and of emotions, inseparable from their first expression, passed on from generation to generation by poets and painters with some help from philosophers and theologians. I wished for a world where I could discover this tradition perpetually, and not in pictures and poems only, but in tiles round the chimney-piece and in the hangings that kept out the draft. I had even created a dogma: "Because those imaginary people are created out of the deepest instinct of man, to be his measure and norm, whatever I can imagine those mouths speaking may be the nearest I can go to truth."

This statement suggests how he did in practice attain unity, whatever the theoretical problems that remained unsolved. His primary motives, and his main technical designs, as poet were dramatic and traditional. The tradition he created was, as he once phrased it, the tradition of himself, the special set of Irish mythology and history, cabalism, and alchemy that he formed into a rich compelling structure; and beyond those external bookish forces, the accidents of his life that he transformed into essences, the dramatic figures he recognized in experience and presented in art.

One of the dangers for critics of Yeats is to take with such seriousness the difficulty of shaping vital forms from these materials that they ignore the art, the forms that grew from the shapes of experience into the permanent matter of the imagination. Few poets have taken their poetic substance from material so varied and odd as that with which Yeats worked; but complex as those materials are, inherently interesting as they are, they are of a different order of complexity from that of the finished works, the poems first but also the plays, the essays, the stories, the autobiographies. The materials, his life-long relation with Maud Gonne, the commanding figure of his father, Ireland in torment, the documents of neo-Platonism and Hermeticism, the complications of the Abbey Theatre, of the Hugh Lane controversy—these are in themselves interesting, so that it is possible for critics to think of Yeats' poems as footnotes to his spiritual, erotic, and political autobiography, but the poetry remains, dramatic always, but the lyric poetry primarily, as the very reason for interest in the biography. And would the political history of Ireland hold the attention it now does if Yeats had not written? This seems a large claim, but as Yeats once remarked, the great poet creates his audience, so that it is legitimate to add that he also creates an audience for his subject matter, his concerns, his origins.

He began in Dublin, in 1865, son of the distinguished irascible painter, John Butler Yeats and his quiet withdrawn wife Mary Pollexfen Yeats. The only compliment, Yeats would later say, that ever turned his head was his father's statement that the Yeats family had ideas and no passions, "but by marriage with a Pollexfen we have given a tongue to the sea cliffs." The contrast between his mother, who exchanged tales with serving maids before the fire, and his father, who was so theoretical in his view of life that he gave his son a lecture on the principles of perspective rather than rushing him to an optometrist when the boy revealed that he could see out of only one eye—this contrast with all its complications remained central to Yeats' sensibility throughout his life. His characteristic vision of life was dual; whenever one concept entered his mind, another followed it in quick contrast, and his belief that "Between extremities / Man runs his course" took its origins in the extremes of his childhood environment, the West of Ireland contrasted with the intellectual centers of Dublin and London, the emotional and cerebral life in direct opposition. This habit, as his autobiographical writings indicate, was life-long.

Yeats was raised as a bohemian with aristocratic predilections. He attended no university but at first attempted to follow his father's course as a painter. He wrote from childhood, and it is important that his earliest surviving writings tend with natural gravity toward dramatic form. His first book, *The Wanderings of Oisin*, in its original format, contained numerous dramatic poems, many of them suppressed in succeeding editions of his work, and even the long narrative title poem is in a form of rhapsodic dialogue. His second book of poems has as its title poem the play *The Countess Cathleen*, written expressly for Maud Gonne, who had entered his life at the time of the publication of *Oisin* in 1889.

The story of Yeats and Maud Gonne has been told in detail often enough to allow merely the briefest reference to its outline. His feelings for her were so serious that one has to say that few men have ever suffered for a woman as Yeats did for Maud Gonne. She was the trouble of his life; she was beautiful, cold, cruel, fickle, demanding, and it is hard to believe that she realized the extent of her unfairness and mischievousness. To say that Yeats loved her is too much and not enough. He adored her, devoted his personal and poetic energies to her service, allowed her to disrupt and muddy every clear valid relation he had with other women; and she was his escape from any other deep involvement. She took from him everything except his freedom, and that was what he most required. Whatever miseries his frustrations caused him, and they were great, they were probably less than he would have suffered in marriage to her, and more rewarding. This statuesque woman with the marble heart released a passion in him that allowed him to create in his poetry a figure that will have a practically endless life.

Yeats was the greatest love poet of the twentieth century, and his poetry up to 1917 was dominated by the dramatic beloved that he shaped from his experience with Maud Gonne. The woman of the poems (or rather the chief woman, for there are other, more obliging women in the verse) is a figure with heroic stature and dedication to an ideal distinct from yet related to the poet's aspirations. She is aloof and austere, unyielding and powerful, beautiful and cold. Her beauty is unattainable, and her passion goes into abstract politics. She has none of the qualities, other than beauty and passion, that sensible men

seek and admire in women: she is not generous, elegant, or affectionate. Nor does she have the abstract ideal features of the conventional
poet's *inamorata*. She is busy; she has children; she ages; she participates in violent politics; she has bad taste in men; she is pathetically
childlike; and she is extraordinarily brave to the point of foolhardiness.
The women of other lyric poets are pale abstractions when seen against
this vivid, forceful figure.

The cruel beloved who walks like a goddess, spreads strife among
men, and ignores her lover's suffering—she is a recognizable form in
the literary imagination, and in the poetry Yeats wrote in the 1890s, he
brought to bear on his work over a century's meditation on the figure
of the demanding cold woman who appears so persistently in the literature and art of romantic Europe. She required devotion and was un-
moved by it, and her impassive demands make her finally unattractive,
so that one drama in Yeats' love poetry emerges from a lifelong process
of adoration that ultimately outwore its object and allowed him to see
this goddess as a limited being. Once he had lived through this process
he could move past the illusion to a physical reality, in the love poetry
written after 1917, on which a new system of values in love could be
explored.

That end was remote, and from 1889 to 1917, a primary motive of
his lyrics was to contemplate and in effect create this figure: take the
love poetry out of those volumes from *The Rose* up to the 1917 edition
of *The Wild Swans at Coole,* and surprisingly little remains. If sex and the
dead, as he would later remark, are the chief concerns of his work, the
erotic impulse takes first place in the lyrics of his early and middle
periods, and his entire early stylistic development as well as his
changes in basic disposition toward experience are intimately evident
in the love poetry. In *The Rose,* for instance, he formalizes his passion
by historical analogy and hyperbole:

> Who dreamed that beauty passes like a dream?
> For those red lips, with all their mournful pride,
> Mournful that no new wonder may betide,
> Troy passed away in one high funeral gleam,
> And Usna's children died.

It is at once superb and fumbling, as is the entire poem. Within a few
years he would not purchase rhymes with such archaisms as "betide,"
and the tone of appositive explanation in the third line is awkward; but
no other poet of his generation developed the mastery evident in the
first and the two final lines. In his poem his impulse toward the heroic
received a form adequate to his ambitions. His grand ambitions are the
reach and limits of these early love poems, and they are alien to cur-

rent readers largely because of their hyperbole. This generation tends to restrict hyperbole to satirical purposes; Yeats' style came from more generous habits. There is in these poems an overflow of impassioned tenderness that is always close to despair—despair at the remoteness of the beloved and equal despair at the limits of language, which can neither seduce nor adequately present the adored figure. Angels, saints, the Rosicrucian rose and lily, eternal beauty, the Virgin Mary— nothing is adequate to his passion. The beloved merges into an ideal realm where her features are lost.

She was to embody a generalized mood; the concern is with psychological states rather than any fixed being. The basic temper of the very early poems, the amorphousness of the woman, the separation of love from temporal existence, the search for the disembodied condition of white birds (souls) rather than men and women, the poet's sense that he is "haunted by numberless islands"—the lyrics of *The Rose*, although more sophisticated in texture, extend the habits of vague longing that had dominated the poetry to 1889, when Maud Gonne entered his life. Maud Gonne gave fresh and particular emphasis to a predisposed mood; she tapped a reservoir of rich feeling and gave it an object.

The basic mood persisted in the poems written between 1892 and 1899 and collected in *The Wind Among the Reeds*. He was still tempted by Swinburnean rhythms, by the faded effects of tapestry, by the blandishments of the epithets mournful, sad, dim, and pale, and by a falsely imposed simplicity that was betrayed by the involuted syntax and complicated symbology. Part of the richness of *The Wind Among the Reeds* comes from the appearance of another tone in Yeats' love-poetry. In the book there are obviously two women, and although he attempted by editorial arrangement to minimize the potential drama of the divided image, one of the women is obliging, and the other continues the aloof demanding habits of the heroic beloved of *The Rose*.

At this point, while perfecting and bringing to a relative dead end the early style, the poetry moves toward the complexity and fullness that distinguish the body of his work. The constant figure of the demanding lover remains central, but a lighter, more human woman appears. This figure is also stylized, so that she seems to come from an unfinished room in *The House of Life*. These lines from Rossetti have the tepid air of *The Wind Among the Reeds*:

> Then loose me, love, and hold
> Thy sultry hair up from my face. . . .

But the amiable woman of Yeats' 1899 volume represents the most favorable aspect of the white goddess of the pre-Raphaelite dream. Her pallor and her long heavy hair are her chief characteristics:

> Beloved, let your eyes half close, and your heart beat
> Over my heart, and your hair fall over my breast,
> Drowning love's lonely hour in deep twilight of rest . . .
>
> ("He Bids his Beloved be at Peace")

> . . . that pale breast and lingering hand
> Come from a more dream-heavy land,
> A more dream-heavy hour than this;
> And when you sigh from kiss to kiss
> I hear white Beauty sighing, too . . .
>
> ("He Remembers Forgotten Beauty")

The impulse of the poem is to find through sexual relations some reality beyond the senses, so that man and woman in love embody and evoke a force that transcends their nature. In Yeats' early poetry this belief is not placed in a perspective that includes ranges of being such as history, politics, and the dead; later, he would establish such a perspective.

The complication of experience and poetic method that marks *The Wind Among the Reeds* sets the stage for the more extensive development in the verse of Yeats' middle period, from *In the Seven Woods* (1903) to the first edition (1917) of *The Wild Swans at Coole*. The period from 1903 to 1917 is at once a defined body of work with a style and set of subjects that distinguishes it from the early and later work and a connective tissue between the early and late accomplishments. This becomes most strikingly evident when one contemplates "Adam's Curse," a poem that begins with the characteristic dramatic utterance of the middle period, continues with the charm and tact that distinguishes the love poems of Yeats' work to 1917, and ends with a return to the cosmic suggestiveness of the earlier work:

> We sat together at one summer's end,
> That beautiful mild woman, your close friend,
> And you and I, and talked of poetry.
> I said: "A line will take us hours maybe;
> Yet if it does not seem a moment's thought,
> Our stitching and unstitching has been naught.
> Better go down upon your marrow-bones
> And scrub a kitchen pavement, or break stones
> Like an old pauper, in all kinds of weather;
> For to articulate sweet sounds together
> Is to work harder than all these, and yet
> Be thought an idler by the noisy set
> Of bankers; schoolmasters, and clergymen
> The martyrs call the world."

                                    And thereupon
           That beautiful mild woman for whose sake
           There's many a one shall find out all heartache
           On finding that her voice is sweet and low
           Replied: "To be born woman is to know—
           Although they do not talk of it at school—
           That we must labour to be beautiful."

           I said: "It's certain there is no fine thing
           Since Adam's fall but needs much labouring.
           There have been lovers who thought love should be
           So much compounded of high courtesy
           That they would sigh and quote with learned books
           Precedents out of beautiful old books;
           Yet now it seems an idle trade enough."

           We sat grown quiet at the name of love;
           We saw the last embers of daylight die,
           And in the trembling blue-green of the sky
           A moon, worn as if it had been a shell
           Washed by time's waters as they rose and fell
           About the stars and broke in days and years.

           I had a thought for no one's but your ears:
           That you were beautiful, and that I strove
           To love you in the old high way of love;
           That it had all seemed happy, and yet we'd grown
           As weary-hearted as that hollow moon.

This poem already demonstrates the characteristic structure of such admired later poems as "Among School Children," moving from cir-
cumstantial reality through conflict to the rhapsodic apprehension of
symbolic reality. The language ranges from colloquial to high rhetorical, and the tone from literal flat description to sardonic satire to enrap-
tured passion. This remarkable range, even in so quiet and unpreten-
tious a poem, was not within Yeats' powers until he had learned
through his experience in writing for the theatre how to modulate language to give the impression of a voice with a body behind it. He
learned, too, to set his widely suggestive symbols within a more extensive context, so that the contact between time and eternity, so often the
implied subject matter of his early verse, could be overtly and effectively presented. This habit of composition came to engross his concern
and dominate his style in lyric as in dramatic writing.

    From 1899 to 1917, Yeats developed an idiom that allowed him
greater range in his love poems and also the power to treat occasional
and satiric public subjects. The love poems reached out to include moments of brief physical passion abstracted from the legendary beloved
of the earlier poems, and to treat those affectionate relationships with

women that Yeats found so crucial to his personal and intellectual well-being. A new boldness and a new denseness of reference came into his work. He continued his elegiac poems for Maud Gonne, and his poems of farewell to her ("Broken Dreams," "Fallen Majesty," "Her Praise," "The People," "His Phoenix," and "A Deep-Sworn Vow," among others) appear in his work as implied dramatic sequences, thus foreshadowing a device that he would follow later in "A Man Young and Old" and "A Woman Young and Old." As the love poems continue to develop, they exhibit a curious alternation of bitterness and wisdom, of isolation and familial connection, of regret and gratitude, that composes a very complex sense of the erotic and affectionate life. The poetic enterprise of Yeats from 1903 to 1917 was unique. The grandeur and comprehensiveness of the later poetry tend to blind readers into considering this middle period as transitional and, in effect, unsatisfactory. The occasional poems on the Hugh Lane controversy and on the Easter rising impose themselves on critics' attention because they require ancillary material for full reading. Yet there is in the simple lyrics of personal affection and passion an original poetic undertaking, showing a capacity for inclusiveness and candor in treating relations between men and women, a maturity, that is exceptional. The impressiveness of these poems comes from their emotional fullness, their inclusion of friendship, solicitude, intellectual comradeship, gentleness of manner and generosity of heart as elements appropriate to the bonds that unite men and women; and the impressiveness of these basic sweet human qualities is increased by their being presented in a scheme of life that does not deny lust, resentment, self-pity, and malicious disgust.

If we had only the poems written by Yeats up to the 1917 edition of *The Wild Swans at Coole,* we should think of him as essentially a poet of personal passion and affection. It is only from the retrospective position of the later work that "The Magi" seems a more significant poem in his middle period than "Presences" or "Friends." Taste shifts and changes, and as the revived interest in *art nouveau* makes Yeats' early work more accessible to this age, so the interest aroused by the personalist work of Sylvia Plath or Robert Lowell may make Yeats' middle period more attractive than it has been in the recent past. For like that of other major artists, Yeats' work has such variety that it is difficult to imagine a taste that would deny legitimacy to a great bulk of his poetry.

Yeats' life and work are so interconnected, and both so complex, that it is at once tempting and impossible to determine what precise effects rose from what precise causes. Maud Gonne, for instance, was as much the excuse as the cause for the elegiac tone of the early poems, and the tone of the middle period could be explained by a multitude of events: Yeats' direct involvement through "Theatre business, management of men" in public life, his close association with Ezra Pound, the technical demands of the theatre on his verse, the example of Synge, the embitterment that followed upon Maud Gonne's marriage, even simple impatience with the tone and texture of his earlier work, or a late but elaborate maturity. And the change that came to his work in 1917, the expansion of its subject matter, the sense of controlling mastery of reality, the recklessness of external judgment, the capacity for creating fresh personae—this too is subject to multiple explanation. His marriage to Georgie Hyde-Lees in 1917 brought a new stability and order to his life, as well as the learning and insight of that witty, sensitive woman; shortly after the marriage he referred to her as "a perfect wife." His diminished responsibilities at the Abbey Theatre after 1911 released his lyric energies and allowed him to make prolonged studies in philosophy, history, and occult phenomena. The events in revolutionary Ireland stirred him deeply and compelled him to examine his historical environment afresh. From 1912 on he was busy writing his autobiography, so that he was forced to look on the design of his life and find what destiny it embodied and proposed.

What these several activities have in common is concentration, bringing to a center the numerous concerns that his youth had generated and opened to study. He was still, even as he would be on his death-bed, striving to hammer his thoughts into unity, and the personal and literary events of the period 1911 to 1917 granted him, and even demanded that he grasp, the opportunity to define a center and to radiate from it the energy thus compacted. The process was further accelerated by the collection of his work issued by Macmillan between 1922 and 1925, in which he could see—and often correct—the work that he had done to date. He lived in a process of defining and beginning, shaping the contours of his being to that moment and projecting beyond it yet another series of possibilities.

T. S. Eliot once remarked that a man wanting to write poetry beyond the age of twenty-six must develop a sense of history. The age is arbitrary, but the general idea is not. What Eliot had in mind was the necessity for the poet to move beyond the limits of his personal experience into the wider possibilities suggested by the experience of the race. Yeats had the good fortune in his Abbey years to be forced imaginatively into the position of a spokesman for other voices, and the legends of heroic Ireland had granted him an extension beyond his personal life. He had also learned an idiom, flexible, various, inclusive, that granted him a fine poetic instrument. And after his period of prolonged study, he could turn his technical abilities toward a wider sub-ject, so that he could eventually say, "I am a sixty years old man; it is 1925," and know what both statements meant.

From this period of study and concentration came a document, *A Vision*, that has become for many readers a road-block against the study of Yeats' later poetry. One result is the *canard*, and it is that, that Yeats began as a simple direct emotional poet and became in his later years an eccentric, over-intellectual, difficult, obscure modern poet. His early and middle poetry, in both syntax and symbol, was often more obscure than the great bulk of the later work—the notes to the original edition of *The Wind Among the Reeds* were extensive and puzzling, and many of the poems in that volume are unintelligible without recourse to obscure books and curious personal associations. Although some of the later poems have this characteristic, the great bulk of them have a primary literal meaning that is perfectly clear, and often difficulties in one poem are soluble by reference to some other poem where the sym-bol in question is used in a clearer context. The best explanatory com-ment on a poem by Yeats is frequently another poem by Yeats, or his collected poems. There is a grand architecture to his work that gives it a scope parallel to that of an epic or an immensely inclusive novel, with the advantage of lyric intensity.

A Vision is a complex work of historical psychology. It is not a comprehensive theory of history; its substance is all drawn from the history of Western Europe with brief asides on Oriental culture and practically no reference to other elaborate cultures that have arisen throughout the geographical world. Its assumption is that all cultures, and all men, are fixed in the same general pattern, that this pattern can be divided into distinct historical epochs which in turn are associated with certain psychological types. Rather than the customary metaphor of the seasons, Yeats uses the 28 phases of the moon to represent the several historical phases, granting him more counters to manipulate and a corresponding greater complexity in historical and psychological judgment. Complications increase when it becomes evident that men are frequently, even usually, born out of phase; Shelley is assigned to Phase 17, Byron to Phase 19, while the Romantic Period comes early in Phase 21. Two phases, that of the full moon (15) and the dark of the moon (1) transcend the human condition—human life is not possible at full or dark of the moon. The human consciousness cannot exist without antinomies.

The problems raised by *A Vision* are too vast for the limits of this essay; it is possible only to suggest the function of this elaborate con-struct in Yeats' poetry. *A Vision* is perhaps best thought of as a con-struct in its own right, an extended philosophical work with certain poems closely related to it and even dependent on it for their meaning. Yeats himself created some mischief by expressing public scepticism about the objective importance of his system. When, first through automatic writing, then through trance-like speech, his wife began communicating the elements of the system, Yeats reports that he was so excited that he offered to give up his entire life to articulating the knowledge; but the communicating spirits replied that they had come to bring him metaphors for his poetry. This statement, which should be taken as a form of self-protective irony on Yeats' part, has had dismal results, chiefly a tendency on the part of critics to seek in *A Vision* an explanation of symbols that are, in the poetry, clear enough in meaning and function. This has resulted in having reasonably lucid poems obscured by the rich specialized vocabulary of *A Vision*. It might be more profitable to think of *A Vision* as being primarily concerned with the thought that Yeats wanted to *keep out* of his poetry, thought necessary to Yeats in making the poetry, a scaffolding but not necessarily part of the final structure. In the "Introduction" written in 1928 and later, Yeats talks of Blake's fondness for the diagrams in Law's *Boehme*, "where one lifts a flap of paper to discover both the human entrails and the starry heavens. William Blake thought those diagrams worthy of Michael Angelo, but remains himself almost unintelligible because he never drew the like. We can (those hard symbolic bones under the skin) substitute for a treatise on logic the *Divine Comedy*, or some little song about a rose, or be content to live our thought."

The diagrammatic shapes of his system were "stylistic arrangements of experience," that helped him "to hold in a single thought reality and justice." But with that symbolic frame established, he could then live his thought and give it dramatic voice and body.

A Vision was thus liberating. It opened a large subject matter and granted him historical measures for the violent public life that burst out before him in the Ireland of Michael Collins and Kevin O'Higgins. It gave him imaginative ingress to the world of Periclean Greece, Augustan Rome, the Byzantium of Justinian, the Quattrocento. The historical pattern emerging from his studies, the revelations from his wife's automatic writing and speech, and his own imaginative projections from these sources—this allowed him to place and estimate events and persons. And it allowed him to continue his dramatic lyrics with the sense that there was no need for any general context in the poems themselves. The results were a few cryptic lyrics, several poems in a new historical manner, and an extension and subtilizing of his earlier motives. The bulk of the poetry was not, however, so radically affected as one might at first believe; the basic change was in Yeats' morale, his confidence in facing the poetic problem. Many factors contributed to the concentration of power that would characterize the later poetry, and *A Vision* was one.

Of the poems that rose directly from the system of history, several have become so well-known that their very phrasing has passed over into the common idiom of English. Public men attempting to describe the urban crisis in the United States find themselves quoting "The Second Coming":

> Things fall apart; the centre cannot hold;
> Mere anarchy is loosed upon the world,
> The blood-dimmed tide is loosed . . .

And though one's sense of the best and worst may shift, the cogency of these lines is widely admired: "The best lack all conviction, while the worst/Are full of passionate intensity." This poem on "the growing murderousness of the world" not only grew from his studies but in a sense extended them, gave them a new base. It was completed while *A Vision* was still in very rough outline form. The primary outline divides history into periods of almost equal length. The basic unit is the millennium, and historical civilizations cover roughly two thousand year periods, divided into single millenia, which are in turn divided into five hundred year periods. "The Second Coming" plays upon this basic idea and combines it with popular chiliasm only to reverse the expectations of the Christian and substitute for the expected savior a rough beast, sphinx-like in its monstrosity. "Leda and the Swan" shows the start of the second millennium of classical civilization, love and war, Helen and Clytemnestra, emerging from the intercourse of Zeus with Leda. Each new age begins with the impress of the superhuman on the human, and with the death of one civilization another enters the historical drama. They interpenetrate, each living and dying within the other. Opposition and conflict are the law of historical as of individual being. Momentary stasis is possible for a civilization (Byzantium), and for individuals the marriage bed is a symbol of the resolved antinomies—unfortunately, Yeats wryly remarks, man falls asleep. But unresolved conflict is the law of historical and personal being.

The intersection of cultures in Yeats' poetry may best be understood in his "Two Songs from a Play." The first song is a choral introduction to his prose play, *The Resurrection*, in which three of Christ's followers, a Hebrew, a Syrian, and a Greek, guard the eleven apostles who await the resurrection of Christ. Outside a Dionysian revelry takes place, but it is an ugly parody of the mysteries, with homosexuals acting female roles. The scene is described by the Greek, and arguments between him and the Hebrew touch upon the possibility—not accept-

able to the Greek—that a god can take bodily human form. Before the
action of the play, the chorus sings:

> I saw a staring virgin stand
> Where holy Dionysus died,
> And tear the heart out of his side,
> And lay the heart upon her hand
> And bear that beating heart away;
> And then did all the Muses sing
> Of Magnus Annus at the spring,
> As though God's death were but a play.
>
> Another Troy must rise and set,
> Another lineage feed the crow,
> Another Argo's painted prow
> Drive to a flashier bauble yet.
> The Roman Empire stood appalled:
>
> It dropped the reigns of peace and war
> When that fierce virgin and her Star
> Out of the fabulous darkness called.

The virgin of the first line is Pallas Athena who rescued the heart of
Dionysus after he had been murdered by the Titans, and from that
heart the god was born again. The Magnus Annus is the large historical cycle that a civilization lives through, and the closing line of the
first stanza sadly foreshadows the activity of the play itself, in which
the end of classical civilization is presented as a perverse play by the
street revellers. At the close of the second stanza, the virgin Athena is
replaced by the Virgin Mary, and the fabulous darkness of Christianity
spreads over the world.

At the close of the play, the Greek is so shattered by discovering
that the resurrected Christ does have a beating heart, that he too is re-
born, that this, like the death of Dionysus, is myth become flesh, he
cries out:

> O Athens, Alexandria, Rome, something has come to destroy you. The heart of a
> phantom is beating. Man has begun to die. Your words are clear at last, O Hera-
> clitus. God and man die each other's life, live each other's death.

The gods are immortal men; men are mortal gods: they are, historically, alike perishable. The play concludes with the second song:

> In pity for man's darkening thought
> He walked that room and issued thence
> In Galilean turbulence;
> The Babylonian starlight brought
> A fabulous, formless darkness in;
> Odour of blood when Christ was slain

Made all Platonic tolerance vain
And vain all Doric discipline.

Everything that man esteems
Endures a moment or a day.
Love's pleasure drives his love away,
The painter's brush consumes his dreams;
The herald's cry, the soldier's tread
Exhaust his glory and his might:
Whatever flames upon the night
Man's own resinous heart has fed.

Reading the poems is helped by reading the play; and a general knowledge of Yeats' historical system helps reading both play and songs. But
there is nothing in the songs that demands much more specialized
knowledge than could be provided by recourse to a sound reference
book on mythology and some general sense of history. The tragic poignancy of the closing stanza demands the kind of generous objective
feeling for the human fate that great art imposes on its audience—no
more than that, and no less.

"Two Songs from a Play" appear in *The Tower* (1928) along with
"Sailing to Byzantium," "Nineteen Hundred and Nineteen," "Leda and
the Swan," "Among School Children," "All Souls' Night," and the remarkable sequence of lyrics "A Man Young and Old." This volume, appearing only a few years after Yeats had received the Nobel Prize, revealed to the critical and reading public that the Yeats of the Celtic
Twilight and Abbey Theatre, the Yeats who in effect had received the
Nobel Prize, had been transmuted into a new, harder, more inclusive,
more objective, and more masterful poet. Sentiment had become passion, opinion conviction. The book also had a profound dramatic
center, growing from Yeats' capacity for moving through a variety of
voices while retaining a tone of passionate conviction and commitment
to the values of art, courage, love, friendship, and wisdom. Later,
Yeats was to say that he was surprised at the bitterness of the book,
but it is hardly bitter in any unrelieved sense. It is often harsh and vindictive in its tone, even sardonic, but this is relieved by outbursts of
tenderness, pity, and awe. At times the poet seems to occupy an *optique* that is outside the human, but never inhumane.

The book is generally reckless in the best sense of the term: indifferent to eternal judgment. The poet treats his experience directly and
fully, but with the freedom that grows from a capacity to look on his
own being as a datum. The manuscripts of the poems shows that they
grew often from a very personal and pathetic situation or feeling to an
austere and passionate one, as if the aim of the poetry were to release
the inherent pattern of experience rather than follow its overt contours.

Even in the details of prosody there is a sense of free indifference to merely conventional notions of form. "Sailing to Byzantium," for instance, uses off-rhyme with great frequency: young-song, dress-magnificence, wall-soul-animal; and other poems are equally free. Freedom without relaxation, with continued concentration and tension, is the norm of the verse, in dramatic structure, in symbolic use, in linear measure.

Here all the conflicts of Yeats' thought are brought to focus: art and nature; youth and old age; man and woman; past and present; body and spirit; love and death; instinct and intelligence; passion and intellect; heart and soul; natural and supernatural; time and eternity. These primary contentions that had obsessed his being and his art and had been presented implicitly and obliquely in preceding work were here directly faced. The book has an air of definitiveness, accomplished finality. In part this comes from the book's subject, which could be phrased in a single sentence: I am a dying man in a dying civilization. The book shares in the sense of cultural crisis that distinguishes other poems of the same period, notably "Gerontion," *The Waste Land*, "The Hollow Men." Within this milieu of a disintegrating culture, however, *The Tower* presents the poet as the courageous contemplative man whose victory resides in his capacity for seeing such a world without blinkers and discovering within it those human values that make the reality of such terrible years not only endurable but in a real sense conquerable. None of the standard anodynes are called into play, and in "Nineteen Hundred and Nineteen" Stoicism, Platonism, and cynicism are successively denied as possible responses to a world where there is no comfort to be found.

The Tower placed Yeats once again in his position as innovator but it showed that he was a poet capable of handling the problems that are thought of as particularly modern. His idiom was at once traditional and colloquial, capable of moving from the realistic opening of "Among School Children," with the nuns teaching in an actual schoolroom to the ultimate symbolic revelation of the tree as a sign of possible unity of being. He was capable of extrapolating from the Black and Tan terrors and the Irish Civil War those designs of violence that increasingly mark the twentieth century. In technical skill and in historical understanding he had attained "right mastery of natural things."

There is in *The Tower* also a valedictory or testamentary tone, notably in the title poem: "It is time that I wrote my will. . . ." The poet seems willing to settle for subjective isolation as the only solution to his problems, both personal and historical. The book closes with just such an assertion:

Such thought—such thought have I that hold it tight
Till meditation master all its parts,
Nothing can stay my glance
Until that glance run in the world's despite
To where the damned have howled away their hearts,
And where the blessed dance;
Such thought, that in it bound
I need no other thing,
Wound in mind's wandering
As mummies in the mummy-cloth are wound.

Yeats' own pride and dissatisfaction with *The Tower* may have grown from his belief that there was a deathfulness in its very perfection. *The Winding Stair* (1933) would move beyond the accomplishment of *The Tower* toward exploration of physical passion and assertion of commitment to the temporal world.

More than one-third of the poems that Yeats wanted to appear in the definitive edition of his lyrics were printed in the three last books of his career: *The Winding Stair* (1933), *A Full Moon in March* (1935), *Last Poems* (1939). The last fifteen years of his life, though developing from his massive prior work, composed a creative outburst of energy without parallel in English letters. He was in those last years freed of some of the monetary troubles that had plagued him throughout his life, and he was no longer compelled to do editing and reviewing in order to maintain his household. His long association with the Abbey Theatre that had consumed much of his powers had come to an end, and though he continued writing plays he was not absorbed with details of management and personnel and policy. All his force could then be devoted to the lyric.

These last years are his most brilliant. The versatility of the verse is as astonishing as its variety. He moves from poems expressing his own personal attachments to persons and places to poems in which his own being is seen as a representative social and historical being. He turns then to poems where the historical and the eternal meet, moving through a series of levels of being to an ultimate assertion of values. He imagines himself as a country slut who enacts "the black mass of Eden," celebrating her own physicality. He assumes one mask and then another, becoming a dramatist in an extended series of lyrics that shows what he takes to be the redeeming feminine qualities. He writes simple brief songs and in a moment of folly undertakes the writing of violent marching songs for the Irish blue shirts. He praises aesthetic ignorance and explores the intellectual problems of the Irish Protestant Ascendancy of the eighteenth century. His imagination moves restlessly over all the subjects and figures that he has treated, and he both perfects his technical abilities and returns to forms that he had explored earlier and abandoned, so that some of his most compelling poems are ballads.

So too with the major symbols of his poetry; the sun and moon, the bird, especially the swan, the tree, the four elements, are examined freshly, and some of them are eventually dropped from the poetry, so that the swan virtually disappears in the last two books, and the sun and moon lose their symbolic force in the final book. The figures who in his life have become legendary symbols, Maud Gonne, John Synge, his father, John O'Leary, Lady Gregory, are evoked in his memory and looked on for their ultimate meaning. It is a crowded stage, and the tone is steadily dramatic, mainly in the manner of tragic joy that he thought of as the highest and most appropriate emotion for the human condition.

The verse remains traditional and experimental. The forms are those of *The Tower*, meditative poems in decasyllabic lines, with the *ottava rima* a favored stanza, songs in a stress prosody often making variations on the fourteener so that a line of four main stresses is followed by one of three. The voice thus rendered is capable of enormous range.

And as one looks over the entire body of Yeats' verse, the striking feature is the variety and variability of the poetry, in its forms, its symbols, and its attitudes. For Yeats never remained content with any success; he moved on, questioning his achievement, searching for the more appropriate mode, the fuller articulation of what he took to be his role as poet in the universal drama. These last years are summary, not in the sense that they make up an abstractable and identifiable body of ideas and methods but because they embody this rage toward self-transcendence:

> Grant me an old man's frenzy,
> Myself must I remake
> Till I am Timon and Lear
> Or that William Blake
> Who beat upon the wall
> Till Truth obeyed his call;
>
> A mind Michael Angelo knew
> That can pierce the clouds,
> Or inspired by frenzy
> Shake the dead in their shrouds;
> Forgotten else by mankind,
> An old man's eagle mind.

Nothing is ever settled. The poems in *The Tower* had an air of finality that the succeeding volumes did not have, so that even the final lines of the *Collected Poems* which would become the epitaph on his grave stone leave the spectator in a condition of anguished balance between life and death:

> Cast a cold eye
> On life, on death.
> Horseman, pass by!

"Between extremities / Man runs his course." These lines open what Yeats thought of as his most typical poem, "Vacillation." The conflict within the poem is basically between the Swordsman and the Saint, and the poet takes an intermediate position. Conflict does not end with these primary figures but involves the tension between remorse and joy, and *The Winding Stair* as a whole is intent on casting out remorse so that tragic joy may prevail. One major symbol, that of the divided tree, at once defines the arena of the poem and illustrates how, in his maturity, Yeats worked his symbols for all they were worth:

> A tree there is that from its topmost bough
> Is half all glittering flame and half all green
> Abounding foliage moistened with the dew;
> And half is half and yet is all the scene;
> And half and half consume what they renew,
> And he that Attis' image hangs between
> That staring fury and the blind lush leaf
> May know not what he knows, but knows not grief.

The sources for this symbol are several, but the motive for their use is single, controlled by the poem's whole. The tree is one of the most often remarked of Yeats' symbols, and he used it frequently and throughout his career. Its importance is evident in the drafts of "Among School Children," where the briefly appearing hawthorn tree is asked whether it is all or the creator of all. The tree is a god-like force, and whether hawthorn, chestnut, or hazel, it has supernatural weight. Like birds, trees participated in a dual nature, rooted in earth, feeding on air, organic and fluent, between heaven and earth, self-complete. From his early studies in Blake and in the cabala, he learned of the dual trees of life and knowledge, and in the *Mabinogion* he learned of Peredur's divided tree and cited it in his essay (1897) on "The Celtic Element in Literature." He contemplated the tree of Attis in *The Golden Bough*, *Hasting's Encyclopedia of Religion and Ethics*, and Julian's hymn to the Great Mother of the Gods. The tree of Peredur was composed of two great opposites, moisture and fire, and although in the *Mabinogion* it merely took its place as one more odd item in the landscape, Yeats, by integrating it in his total understanding of the generic symbol, endowed it with rich connotations. The tree that eventually appeared in the poem was original in the sense that it was a new complex of elements, the pine tree of the priests of Gallus, the trees of life and knowledge, Peredur's tree, and the organic form of the Romantic imagination. Several cultures were thus folded together into the special form required by Yeats' imagination. But the tree has been so taken from its origins that it is no longer theirs. What the poem offers, under the concentration forced upon it by the limits of stanzaic form, is a tree that is ancient, dual, widely distributed in the human imagination, and made up of both mere stupid persistent life and the all revealing flame of deathless knowledge. The stanza has a wide and deliberately suppressed context that Yeats hopes will in part be widely suggestive; but its function in the poem limits those associations.

This stanza is characteristic of the way in which Yeats, in his late years, used his most intently contemplated images. Even when they are not presented with such elaborateness, they gain from their appearance in other poems. This symbolic structure is related to the drama of the verse as embodied in the dramatic forms of the poet himself and those personae he creates. The result is an interlocking structure of dramatic symbolic lyrics. Each poem has its form and its rich texture, and is in turn enriched by its relation to all the other poems. Nor should the term symbolic indicate that the main texture of the bulk of the poems is so dense and packed as that of the tree of "Vacillation." Often the profundity of the verse comes from the very simplicity of statement, as in "Her Anxiety":

> Earth in beauty dressed
> Awaits returning spring.
> All true love must die,
> Alter at the best
> Into some lesser thing.
> *Prove that I lie.*
>
> Such body lovers have,
> Such exacting breath,
> That they touch or sigh.
> Every touch they give,
> Love is nearer death.
> *Prove that I lie.*

If the poem were anonymous and isolated from any body of work, its beauty would be clear; related as it is to the other lyrics (twenty-five in all) of love and death in "Words for Music Perhaps," it takes on wider associations and meanings while retaining its integral power.

And so it is with the body of Yeats' lyric poetry. The poems have their individual vitality, and they have a further vitality when related to the whole of his work and the curve of his career and life. Yeats is not a poet who yields himself entirely through his poems; he remains a man, and a man of a time and place. Much of the power of his work grows from the integrity of his sense of himself as poet and man, and at least part of its reference is to the unity of being that he sought and perhaps achieved only in the marmoreal stillness of the study as the poems revealed themselves to him. He is a poet primarily but also a man of letters. He founded one of the most continuously successful of national theatres, the Abbey, and if only his dramatic writing and criticism had survived, he would have to be reckoned with as a figure in theatrical history. His prose, expository, narrative, and autobiographical, is distinguished in style and both revealing and moving in subject. He lived a life at the center of the Irish state as it became one of the first nations to reclaim its identity as the colonial structure broke up.

But it is as a lyric poet that he will be remembered. His participation in the movements of modern art, as suggested earlier, makes him seem an eccentric. He wanted always, what too much of modern art denied, a vision of heroic possibility. At the end of his life he wrote an introduction to his collected essays in which he made clear his opposition to much modern poetic theory:

> I have never said clearly that I condemn all that is not tradition, that there is a subject-matter which has descended like that "deposit" certain philosophers speak of. At the end of his essay upon "Style" Pater says that a book written according to the principles he has laid down will be well written, but whether it is a great book or not depends upon subject-matter. This subject-matter is something I have received from the generations, part of that compact with my fellow men made in my name before I was born. I cannot break from it without breaking from some part of my own nature, and sometimes it has come to me in super-normal experience; I have met with ancient myths in my dreams, brightly lit; and I think it allied to the wisdom or instinct that guides a migratory bird.

And he goes on to assert the importance of "A table of values, heroic joy always . . . and a public theme. . . ." That table of values was not to be abstract but realized in the full artistic work. What that meant is suggested by his last letter:

> It seems to me that I have found what I wanted. When I try to put it all into a phrase I say, "Man can embody truth but he cannot know it." I must employ it in the completion of my life. The abstract is not life and everywhere draws out its contradictions. You can refute Hegel but not the Saint or the Song of Sixpence.

The work was the realization of the life. The poet would, in carrying out his role, fulfill his destiny and create a new public. He may have succeeded beyond any hope. He is now one of the most widely read poets in English, and his work seems established with the same security as that of Donne or Wordsworth. There have been few poets in any language so varied, intense, and integral as Yeats.

He was, in many ways, a man of his era, in spite of his notorious rejection of much of modern thought and art. He studied and made extensive use of the Cambridge anthropologists, as Joyce and Eliot would after him, and he shared the widely diffused preoccupation with theory of history. He accepted and even advocated the essential isolation of the artist from the dominant norms of the society, and he assumed an irreconcilable conflict between the claims of art and those of mechanistic science. He deplored the idea of progress and sought fresh sources of religious feeling in Eastern thought. Of the major artists of the twentieth century, he made the most searching inspection of theory of symbolism, and as early as 1895 he had settled on a syntax and diction that were to set directions for the main writing of the first half of the century, banishing archaism and inversion, striving toward a natural measure that would not violate traditional forms.

Yet he remains an outsider, as if he were the prototypical poet who found himself suddenly in the twentieth century and had to shape poems under forbidding conditions. The greatest modern poet would seem less an historical anomaly if he were thought of as a great poet writing in the modern period. He himself thought that his function as critic and poet was to reassert the great criteria that poetry has always lived under. Describing the poet's function, to be more type than man, more passion than type, a dramatic form in the human imagination, Yeats concluded that " . . . we adore him because nature has grown intelligible, and by so doing a part of our creative power." As Yeats has.

Reprinted from *The Sphere History of Literature in the English Language,* Vol. 7, *The Twentieth Century,* ed. Bernard Bergonzi (London: Sphere, 1971).

9

Serious Work:
The Poetry and Prose of Seamus Heaney

Seamus Heaney's work has a wonderful clear integrity, from his book reviews through his longer essays, from his initial poem on "Digging" to his long sequence of works exploring the north of the human soul. Heaney has style, developed over years of study and writing, working on and thinking of poetry. Like his near-contemporary John Montague, he comes from the lost six counties of North Ireland, so that he carries a considerable cultural burden, threatened by the demand for opinions on the condition of that battered and torn portion of the world and by his direct sad involvement in the life of its populace. He has fought free of easy declarations, knowing as he does the bitter complexity of the human condition throughout the world and its special forms in the country of his childhood. What he has done, quietly and thoroughly, is to explore the heritage caught in the bogs of Ireland, the reminders of a violent legacy, evident in the relics folded into and preserved in the soft ground, which he takes to be the ground of the soul.

Poems 1965–1975 contains his first four books, and the *Preoccupations* present pertinent prose that can be used to elucidate his motives, especially the essay "Feeling into Words," the extended essays on Hopkins and on Yeats, and the revealing essay on Wordsworth and Yeats. Heaney apologizes in his preface because some of the essays have the tone of lectures; he need not apologize for these fluent, intimate discourses. His verse has style because it has a voice, and the same could be said for the essays and reviews. They are interesting, as well, because Heaney writes distinguished poetry; the essay on Yeats, for instance, is the single most interesting essay on the limits and importance of his poetry that I know.

These two books, then, give a fairly full account of one of the best intellects now writing verse. They should be read and contemplated seriously. The opening poem "Digging" is programmatic, and I imagine that it will always be read as an overt delineation of his poetic field. Digging is the traditional activity of Irish farmers, his father, his grandfather:

> The cold smell of potato mould, the squelch and slap
> Of soggy peat, the curt cuts of an edge
> Through living roots awaken in my head.
> But I've no spade to follow men like them.
>
> Between my finger and my thumb
> The squat pen rests.
> I'll dig with it.

The poetry has the aspiration to become part of a productive culture, with physical weight and substantial results. Following the poetry from this point, one can see in the books a movement out from the immediate involvement in the natural landscape until, with no visible effort, the poetry moves from the poem of man in nature to man as a partly alien natural form, violent, conscience-stricken, plagued with the guilt of his own unearthliness. Nature, history, and pre-history become a single unit, the human joy and sadness finding its ambience. Hence when poems treat current events or historical events with current relevance, the poems seem natural ("For the Commander of the 'Eliza'," "Requiem for the Croppies," the poem prefatory to *Wintering Out*, "The Other Side").

Toward the close of *Wintering Out*, the third volume of Heaney's work, appears "The Tollund Man," a justly celebrated poem in two parts, and Heaney discusses the poem's origin in his readings in P. G. Glob's *The Bog People* (see "Feeling into Words" in *Preoccupations*). But to make what Heaney did of the sacrificial victim to the goddess of fertility, he had to have his long prologue of obsession with the ground of history. The Tollund Man is, in Heaney's phrase, a turfcutter, part of the line of ancestry evident in "Digging," and a justification of Heaney's sense of the continuity of the human condition. Human sacrifices are part not only of pre-history but of current events in the north of Ireland and events in the Irish past. For this reason, if Heaney were to see the Tollund Man in Aarhus (as he later did), then

> Out there in Jutland
> In the old man-killing parishes
> I will feel lost,
> Unhappy and at home.

The last book in the present collection *North* (1975) is the best. Poets like to hear that their most recent work is their best, but I will have some qualifications about the book not included in this collection:

Field Work (1979). *North* continues within the framework already discussed, and in these poems Heaney manifests a ready control over his subject and idiom. The poems are not clogged with alliteration and internal rhyme as they sometimes were in, for example, "Servant Boy" (c. 1969--71):

> Your trail
> broken from haggard to stable,
> a straggle of fodder
> stiffened on snow. . . .

Trail-stable, haggard (hay-yard)-straggle, stable-straggle-stiffened, broken-snow—at such times Heaney seems more interested in what he can do with words rather than what can be done through them; then the poems clog, call too much attention to their means, the archaic word close to Heaney's sense of landscape as the Ur-soul and often so functioning but here too dominant in its tonal effects. This mild aberration does not damage the poem, but with *North* one is affected by the unity of subject and implication. It all coheres in a fierce quiet splendor: there is no need to raise one's voice when the domestic, filial, local, pre-historic, historic, and present fuse into a controlled and deeply stirring whole. All the poems work at so high a level that it is hard to single out any one as dominant. In this book no poem is excused for defects because it contributes to an entire impact, but I should like to single out a few titles that remain as residues in the reader's sensibility: "Funeral Rites," "Bog Queen," "Punishment," "Act of Union," "Whatever You Say Say Nothing." The last of these poems is overtly on current events, but much of its impact comes from its relation to poems like "Punishment" that treat the pre-historic, so that the current can become permanent:

> I can feel the tug
> of the halter at the nape
> of her neck, the wind
> on her naked front.
>
> It blows her nipples
> to amber beads,
> it shakes the frail rigging
> of her ribs.
>
> I can see her drowned
> body in the bog,
> the weighing stone,
> the floating rods and boughs.
>
> Under which at first
> she was a barked sapling

that is dug up
oak-bone, brain-firkin:

her shaved head
like a stubble of black corn,
her blindfold a soiled bandage,
her noose a ring

to store
the memories of love.
Little adulteress,
before they punished you

you were flaxen-haired,
undernourished, and your
tar-black face was beautiful.
My poor scapegoat,

I almost love you
but would have cast, I know,
the stones of silence.
I am the artful voyeur

of your brain's exposed
and darkened combs,
your muscles' webbing
and all your numbered bone.

I who have stood dumb
when your betraying sisters,
cauled in tar,
wept by the railings,

who would connive
in civilized outrage
yet understand the exact
and tribal, intimate revenge.

The ending seems almost too topical, but the north of Ireland and the history of Ireland generally are exemplary, embodying in centuries of hatred and courage and outrage an extremely wide range of human possibility. After Bangladesh, the Biafran War, Argentina, and El Salvador, the north of Ireland seems in this century an emblem of man's external fate and internal destiny, for which there is no ready simple solution. Heaney certainly offers none, and the stockade of his direct experience merges with the primitive murdered adulteress:

This morning from a dewy motorway
I saw the new camp for the internees:
A bomb had left a crater of fresh clay
In the roadside, and over in the trees

Machine-gun posts defined a real stockade.
There was that white mist you get on a low ground

And it was déjà-vu, some film made
Of Stalag 17, a bad dream with no sound.
Is there a life before death? That's chalked up
In Ballymurphy. Competence with pain,
Coherent miseries, a bite and sup,
We hug our little destiny again.

Of all the fine poems in the book, this one seems to me among the most moving and troubling. What Heaney manages in this book is an amalgamation of history and the soul that is normally the province of the novel or drama. All poets who matter are engaged in that enterprise. He asks, "Is there a life before death?" and implicitly answers, yes, in the sympathetic imagination that, to paraphrase his admired Wordsworth, is the breath and finer spirit of all experience.

"What then?" sang Plato's ghost, "What then?" The refrain from another of Heaney's admirations, Yeats, applies to the book not included in this compilation, *Field Work* (1979). The book has been much admired, and it should be, for its accomplishment and air of finish. There are no hesitations, no poems that trail off, or seem in any way inadequate; the mastery continues. There are several elegiac poems, some written on occasions, several that are touching. But the book has an interim tone: having conducted life and phrase to this point, what then? I do not say this to depreciate Heaney's work and achievement but in a spirit of interest. Heaney once thought of writing drama accompanied by contemporary music, perhaps Irish music adapted to the thrust and drive of rock music. Why not? It seems to me that Heaney has developed a powerful instrument that is perhaps too powerful to become the servant of occasions, even when the result is so finely accurate and touching a poem as his "Elegy" for Robert Lowell. His considerable talent seems, for the moment, caught between trains, and my interest is, "What direction will it take?" Heaney is, as the two books under primary review clearly indicate, a serious human being, not solemn, capable of wit and humor, but serious. He is much too serious to allow himself to be caught in the station designated "Our Most Even and Consistent Talent Now Writing Poetry in English." He is, but I cannot imagine his being satisfied with that.

I conclude this review with uneasiness about the previous paragraph. Critics of contemporary writers should not interfere with them, and I should like to reiterate that my rather quizzical conclusion comes from an interest that grows from what we all seek, admiration and some envy of this wonderfully articulated work. Nothing should detract from the rich integrity of Heaney's poetry; it should be widely read with attention and, inevitably, reward.

Reprinted from *Southern Review*, Spring 1982.

10

Poetry Is Alive and Well in Ireland

Anthony Bradley has edited an anthology of *Contemporary Irish Poetry* with care and good sense. His introduction, necessarily general, still has cogent things to say about the Irish poets who emerged after the renaissance from 1890 through 1911. His first poet was born in 1893, his last in 1951. The book is inclusive, the selections first-rate, the biographical and textual notes brief and useful. It is really excellent and should be consulted especially by those who have only a sketchy awareness of Irish poetry of the twentieth century exclusive of Yeats, a few poems by Synge, Joyce's lyrics, and an occasional poem by James Stevens or AE. Without Yeats, the poetry of modern Ireland does not have a figure with the resonance of Pound, Stevens, Williams, or Eliot. Austin Clarke is an estimable writer, as is Patrick Kavanagh. Valentin Iremonger, Denis Devlin, Donagh Macdonagh, Padraic Fallon, and W. R. Rodgers wrote memorable poems.

Contemporary Irish poetry really has its center, however, in the work of a group of writers born in the 1920s, those now the age of Ginsberg, Creeley, and Snyder in this country. None of the poets born shortly before the close of the First World War produced bodies of work comparable to those of Robert Lowell or Robert Duncan in America. But two writers born in the late 1920s, Thomas Kinsella (1928) and John Montague (1929) have composed a considerable and admirable body of work, and it is the good fortune of the literary world that Wake Forest University Press has produced two volumes of work by Kinsella that form an interim Collected Poems (*Poems, 1956–73; Peppercanister Poems, 1972–78*) and one inclusive volume of *Selected Poems* by Montague. Their work, along with that of Anthony Cronin, Pearse Hutchinson, and Richard Murphy, is central to the canon of contemporary Irish poetry. They write substantial poems and books, they are professionally able craftsmen, and they have the special magic of artistry beyond craftsmanship. They have learned from the tradition of Ireland, Europe, and America; they have local roots and international reach.

Of their successors, only Seamus Heaney and Derek Mahon have produced an œuvre that is substantial in quantity and fine in quality. Mahon is generously represented, as he should be, in Bradley's anthology, but the projected full collection of his work to date (he has published four books and a pamphlet) is not available. Like Heaney and Montague, he comes from the lost six counties of the North, and his work has the vigor and force of theirs. Heaney's work is more known in this country, and the publication of *Poems, 1965–75*, along with his fluent and informative essays (*Preoccupations*) and his most recent book, *Field Work*, certify his continued productivity and the genuine achievement that he has already made at the age of forty-three. Heaney's work already deserves praise and attention. He is the most even and consistent talent now writing poetry in English, and especially in the book called *North* (1975, included in the compendious *Poems, 1965–75*) he manages an amalgamation of pre-history, legend, and the contemporary that is extremely moving.

In what remains of this review, I should like to treat Kinsella and Montague, giving more weight to Montague because he is the less known to American audiences. The two poets are very distinguished writers, and compared with Americans contemporary with them— Merwin, Kinnell, Bly, Snyder—they stand up very well, as they do in comparison with such English contemporaries as Gunn and Hughes. They are poets coming from a rich native culture in a land whose troubles epitomize the troubles of the entire world at present, and they are international as well, in knowledge and poetic understanding. Kinsella, for instance, is one of the best translators of Irish (notably of *The Táin*), and he is also a master of the meditative mode in traditional English meters, though his rhythms are those of spoken Irish. At first, his work was more metrical than rhythmical, too close to Auden, who served as a model. The early poems suffer from excessive abstraction:

> I nonetheless inflict, endure
> Tedium, intracordal hurt,
> The sting of memory's quick, the drear
> Uprooting, burying prising apart
> Of loves a strident adolescent
> Spent in doubt and vanity.
>
> ("Baggot Street Deserta")

When they work, however, they work because of this glamour of his imagination. A poem beginning "As I roved out impatiently / Good Friday with my bride . . ." recalls all too quickly "As I walked out one evening / Walking down Bristol Street. . . ," and especially when other poems in the early volumes are so Audenesque. But "In the Ringwood" is the first of Kinsella's poems where his sensibility uses meter rather than merely follows it, so that we get the special Kinsella rhythm. He does not always maintain his voice; "Baggot Street Deserta" might as well be "Regent Street Deserta."

Establishing and maintaining a style has been Kinsella's main problem. He solved it temporarily in *Wormwood* (1966) and *Nightwalker* (1967). In the publishing history of the poems, the two books were included in a single volume in 1968, which has been for me the best of his work, and after reading the poems written since, I find that judgment confirmed. The initial poem in *Nightwalker*, "Our Mother," has puzzled and moved me for years. What exactly is happening, I cannot say, but an old lady is dying, and in the next bed of the hospital, a child is crying from the pain of an operation. The child's mother is present, and the poem is spoken by her father. If I read the poem correctly, all three women are crying:

> All three women, two in my care,
> The third beyond all care, in tears.
> Living, dying, I meet their stare
> Everywhere, and cannot move.

So the poem ends, but the description of the child's mother is so compelling that I will quote the pertinent two stanzas:

> Her mother watches, struck dumb.
> Tears of recognition run
> For the stranger, daughter, self, on whom
> In fascination her eyes feed,
>
> As mine on her—a revenant,
> A rain-worn, delicate
> Stone shape that has looked long
> Into that other face direct.

One allusion in the poem suggests that the "other face" is that of the Gorgon, related to the child's suffering, and the revenant that has survived the recognition of death. This poem is rather typical of Kinsella, for it is moving, strikes a deep root of human experience, and has a terrible coldness. There are light moments in his work, but they are not characteristic. Bleakness seems the ultimate outcome; the epigraph to "Nightwalker" is "The greater part must be content to be as though they had not been," and the first line reads "I only know things seem and are not good." The poem ends:

> The earth, at the full,
> Hangs in blue splendour in the sky.
>   I believe I have heard

> Of this place.
> In the mind darkness tosses:
> The light deceives. A vivid ghost sea
> Quivers and dazzles for miles.
>
> Let us take the waters.
> Stoop down, run the fingers along the brink.
> It has a human taste, but sterile; odourless.
> Massed human wills . . .
>
> A dust plain flickering . . .
> I think this is the Sea of Disappointment.

Not all the poems have so dark a tone, but the bleakness is always ready to assert its permanence. They are sobering poems.

After the poems written through 1968, Kinsella continued writing, always with power and energy. The *Poems, 1956–1973* compose a striking unity. In 1970, Kinsella changed the design of his life, teaching at least half the year at Temple University, writing steadily and printing the poems under the imprint of the Peppercanister Press: hence the title of the second collection, *Peppercanister Poems, 1972–1978*. The level remains high, and Kinsella has learned from the conventions of current American verse. He is one of the few poets of British origins who seems to control free verse readily, and as he grows, he will continue to be one of the most distinguished men of letters. The trouble his work presents is the threat that he will become a poet of occasions: the death of Kennedy, the murders in the lost six counties. In his more recent work he seems less capable of creating the occasion for poetry. A further trouble with Kinsella's work is that it excites admiration but not envy, so that poets reading his work may see that it is very good without wishing (the highest praise) that they had been granted the poems that are Kinsella's. Art need not be likable, however, and Kinsella reaches levels of power that are not within the reach of many able talents.

In speaking of Kinsella's work, I used the term "glamour of the imagination," thinking of magic and charms of the sort that is part of the native Irish, the Gaelic, tradition. In a special way, Kinsella and Montague embody that tradition more fully than the poets of the Irish Renaissance. Yeats gets some of its qualities, but usually in such plays as *The Only Jealousy of Emer*. The lyric and narrative poems treating Irish legendary matter seem much too artificial. Like Kinsella, Montague is as deeply steeped in Gaelic culture as he is in the literary traditions of France, America, and England. He edited the *Faber Book of Irish Verse*, covering poetry from its beginnings in Gaelic to very recent work (a wonderful book and a fine companion for Bradley's *Anthology*).

Montague is more immediately attractive than Kinsella, and he often writes poems that would excite the envy and admiration of any poet, from "All Legendary Obstacles" through "Edge." His poetry works with most charm when affection moves toward passion. As a love poet he is comparable to Lawrence and Graves, with Graves serving as his master. Graves functions well for him, especially since his immersion in French and American poetry leads him to modulate the standard forms that Graves mastered. Montague's ear is not entirely reliable, but he does not fall into the conventional line that sometimes plagues Kinsella. When he moves beyond the personal and erotic poem, Montague shows an extremely varied control of prosodic vocabulary. The section chosen from *The Rough Field* (1972) indicates his power of bringing together deeply personal family love with his indignation at oppression and bringing all together under the common wild dog rose. These poems cover pages 101 to 127 and form a good entry into the poetry.

Scholars will have as merry a time with Montague's texts as they do with those of Graves. The poems just cited are far less than half those printed in *The Rough Field*. The book under review is highly selective, and often I wonder why some poems were included and not others, and I regret that a poet who so carefully composed his books is not presented fully. Perhaps, like Wallace Stevens, Montague thought a Collected Poems a preamble to death.

This book, then, should be read as an introduction to an extremely fine poet, and a sensible reader will seek out the individual volumes from which it is selected, especially *The Rough Field* and *The Cloak*, so carefully set by Liam Miller's Dolmen Press. This selection, including some hundred and twenty-five poems, is not just the tip of the iceberg, but it omits a great deal of splendid work, as well as some of lesser impact.

There is no way in so limited a review to suggest the entire range of Montague's work. How to suggest the qualities of a poet who writes savage political poems, poems of familial affection and loss, poems with a lustful passion as attractive as it is startling, poems evoking natural landscapes with rich overtones of charged emotion, tender eloquent elegies for the gifted who die too young, and all these with an increasing command of the traditions and innovations of centuries of human experience? It cannot be done, so I will simply quote two entire poems, both typical of Montague's love poetry. The two poems appear on facing pages of the *Selected Poems* (pp. 164–5), and although they are enriched by their original appearance as part of the poetic sequence that forms the book *The Great Cloak* they have independent merit.

DON JUAN'S FAREWELL

Ladies I have lain
  with in darkened rooms
sweet shudder of flesh
  behind shadowy blinds
long bars of light
  across tipped breasts
warm mounds of
  breathing sweetness
young flesh redolent
  of crumpled roses
the tender anxiety
  of the middle-aged
a hovering candle
  hiding blue veins.
eloquent exhaustion
  watching light fade
as your drowsy partner
  drifts towards the
warm shores of sleep
  and you slowly awake
to confront again
  the alluring lie
of searching through
  another's pliant body
for something missing
  in your separate self
while profound night
  like a black swan
goes pluming past.

The poem treats legendary matter and brings it into an ambience at once personal and symbolic. It is a poem both simple and rich. At the end one does not even mind the term "profound night," which in another context might seem an affectation. Here it is saved by the black swan that goes pluming past.

On the facing page appears a poem that begins as anecdote and ends with the personal becoming legendary and symbolic. Very few poets can write with any full understanding of the working of the minds of others, especially women. Montague manages:

SHE WALKS ALONE

In the white city of Evora, absence accosted me.
You were reading in bed, while I walked all night alone.
Were you worried about me, or drifting towards sleep?

I saw the temple of Diana, bone white in the moonlight.
I made a private prayer to her, for strength to continue:
Not since convent days have I prayed so earnestly.

A dog came out of the shadows, brushed against my leg.
He followed me everywhere, pushing his nose into my hand.
Soon the cats appeared, little scraggly bundles of need.

There were more monuments, vivid as hallucinations.
Suddenly, a young man stepped out of the shadows:
I was not terrified, as I might have been at home.

Besides, he was smiling & gentle as you used to be.
"A kiss" he pleads "a kiss" in soft Portuguese.
I quickened my step, but he padded behind me.

He looked so young, my heart went out to him.
I stopped in the shadows under the Cathedral.
We kissed, and the tears poured down my face.

Taking Montague only as a love poet (he is much more than that), we should bear in mind that these two fine poems are representative of the quality of his work and that they are a very small percentage of the total poems rising from the erotic experience. Moreover, the selection he has made omits several poems of extraordinary brilliance. Montague is already a very important poet, and he continues to grow steadily.

It is heartening to read Bradley's *Contemporary Irish Poetry: An Anthology* and then to extend one's reading into the fine large collections of work by Heaney, Kinsella, and Montague. Montague and Kinsella have just turned fifty; Heaney is forty-three; Yeats' first book in his truly grand manner did not appear until he was fifty-six. With good luck, Irish poetry may well have three poets of genuinely major stature during the next decade.

In this review I may seem to have slighted Heaney's work, but I have written extensive praise of it in the previous chapter and his poetry is generally better known in America than that of Kinsella and Montague. With more space, I could talk extensively of other poets, notably Derek Mahon. But any reader can easily choose from Bradley's anthology the poets who attract further attention.

Reprinted from *Georgia Review*, Fall 1982.

Literary Movements

11

The Beat Writers: Phenomenon or Generation

When the beat writers emerged in 1956 they struck so responsive a chord that they became the most widely discussed phenomenon of the late 1950s. If they represented a "generation," they replaced a remarkably short-lived and little-lamented "silent generation" which had dominated the first five years of the 1950s. Even in the accelerated pace of twentieth-century living, two generations per decade rather crowds things. Whether they represented an entire generation or a spasm of revulsion, the beat writers attained symbolic status, as did the until-then little-remarked Bohemian communities of New York's Greenwich Village and San Francisco's North Beach. When the San Francisco columnist Herb Caen dubbed the members of current Bohemia "beatniks," the derisive appellation stuck. Beatnik life became a subject of general interest, and that special nexus of jazz, Buddhism, homosexuality, drugs, and squalor was graphed and discussed in a wide range of media that reached a large audience.

It was easy to deride the nonconformist existentialist costumes, the sheer unpleasantness of texture in the dreary fakeries of beatnik art, and no one could defend the aimless self-destructiveness and occasional pointless criminality of conduct. But two basic problems were not so easily dismissed. The first was the genuine vigor and force of Allen Ginsberg and Jack Kerouac, the extraordinary wit and hilarity of Lawrence Ferlinghetti and Gregory Corso, the obvious intelligence, learning, and decency of Gary Snyder and Philip Whalen, the hard integrity of Michael McClure—in short, the simple literary expertise of several gifted writers who participated in many of the excitements and obsessions of current Bohemia. The second problem, essentially social, was how to estimate the importance of this extra-official mode of life. Was it spindrift or the point of an iceberg, this sudden revelation of resentment and bad feeling? Was it American Bohemia newly garbed, new beatnik being old bum writ bold? One commentator closed his very unfriendly article with somber tone: "A hundred million squares must ask themselves: 'What have we done to deserve this?'" A hundred million seems a modest estimate, but whatever the census, the refrain of puzzled commentators was a steady and repeated "What's wrong?" To many people the chief force of the beat movement was the suggestion that all was not well with our unrivalled happiness.

If not puzzled, commentators were pleased to see that the tradition of revolt was not dead, and many a patronizing phrase approved of youth having its fling. A surprising number of people seemed to assume that rebellion per se, whatever its means or ultimate goal, is a good thing. After ten years of literary dandies carefully machining their Fulbright poems in a social atmosphere of cold war and general stuffiness, the beats were welcomed. What troubled the most tolerantly disposed critics, however, was the refusal of beat and beatnik to play their proper social role. Their elders had a hazy rosy memory of their own daring youth in which they had been true radicals, that is, left New Dealers relatively active in political affairs. To their sense of things, the true rebel might take his origins in blank resentment of the world, but he went on to formulate his motives in terms of some ideal mode of social organization. But the beat movement simply denied the role of social critic and took an indifferent and passive posture before the problems of the world. Fallout, population, medical care, legal justice, civil rights—the beats were concerned actively with these problems when they impinged on the printing of books with certain taboo words, or on the problems of dope addicts cut off from their source of supply, or on the rights of poets to say slanderous things about policemen. Otherwise their approach was sardonic, apocalyptic, or impudent.

With very few exceptions, the beat and beatnik compose a social refusal rather than a revolt: as Allen Ginsberg announced to his audience in Chile, he is a rebel, not a revolutionist. They take no particular pleasure in tearing down a social fabric that they see as already ruined, and their attitude toward society is suspicious and evasive rather than destructive. When their attitude becomes destructive, the result is pointless antisocial acts; they then cease to be beat and become unemployed delinquents. Many beatniks are college students who, after two or more years of college, are not certain that they intend to go on into the business and professional worlds that swallow up the graduates of American colleges and universities. So they take a year off and loaf and invite their souls on Grant Avenue or Bleecker Street or the Left Bank. Some find the atmosphere so congenial that they linger through several years, and a few of them become permanent Bohemians. In such an atmosphere the tone is naturally antiacademic and antiofficial.

In this sense the beatnik world is a continuation of the Bohemian world already familiar to observers of American life. The beats are differentiated from past Bohemians by their religiosity (Zen Buddhism, Christ-as-beatnik with sandals and beard), experimental interest in hallucinogenic drugs and occasional dabbling in addictive drugs, proximity to criminality (largely through association with drugs), and fascination with moral depravity for its own sake. The traditional antidomesticity of the Bohemian world is still prevalent, as well as the concomitant relaxation of sexual mores in this predominantly male society.

The differences between the intellectual and religious concerns of current Bohemia and those of the 1920s or 1930s are modes of differentiating the attitudes of those eras from our own. It seems to me fairly plain that American Bohemia in reacting against suburbia tends to produce a reverse image of the society that makes the hydrogen bomb, throws its money around an idiot frenzy, and refuses to vote for school bonds; the same moral flaccidity, the same social irresponsibility, the same intellectual fraudulence operate throughout the two worlds that are, finally, not opposed. Freud in the 1920s meant sexual liberation, whereas psychoanalysis in Bohemia and suburbia in the 1950s was primarily a mode of keeping going. The borderline between beatnik and psychiatric patient shifts constantly, claiming one and releasing another, and a surprising number of people in current Bohemia are under psychiatric care. This in turn reflects the rising commitment rate of American mental hospitals and the steady increase in the numbers of people seeking psychiatric aid so that they can continue their business and professional life. The indifference toward politics exhibited by Bohemia is matched by the neglect and cynicism of suburbia. The beatnik contempt for simple comfort and cleanliness is the counterpart of mindless possessiveness, status-seeking, and other elaborate forms of greed.

It would be easy to multiply points of comparison: the grey flannel suit and the existentialist costume, the smiling religious purveyor of togetherness and the egotism of Christ-as-beatnik, ranch house and pad, cocktails and marijuana. But it was not merely the direct parody that attracted so much attention; rather, the illusion of community promoted by the hip jargon, the agreed values, the common rites, and relaxed tone—this was the chief source of attraction and interest. What was sought by commentator and reader alike was a way of life that would answer their feeling of pointlessness and guilt in looking at their own unrewarding accumulation of commodities. The beatniks not only evaded a society that, even its friendliest critics are quick to admit, has lost all community of motive; they went further and created an impenetrable community that turned the well-adjusted member of suburbia into a frustrated outsider. They shaped a way of life at once public and arcane. No wonder that the spectacle of Grant Avenue has produced so many dances of uncomprehending rage.

And yet is it not pathetic that the alternatives of American society should be posed in terms of Beatville and Squareville? If the beat and beatnik are the only answer to the wasteful cupidity of suburbia, then the country is in a very nasty spot. In truth, there is a vast fund of good sense and social responsibility in this country, and the only problem is to allow its voice to be heard more clearly and loudly. And if a rebellion is necessary, it will be fostered by people who have a sense of commitment to the insulted and injured of the world, who feel and act on an ideal of human conduct that sponsors change in individual experience, and who do not waste their substance on pointless conformity and aimless complaint. Some of those people live in suburbia, some in Bohemia, and many of them just anywhere; they respond to and shape their environment, and from such responsible shaping come the seeds of community and, finally, civilization.

In talking about the social phenomenon of the beat and beatnik, I deliberately distinguished between the two terms. The term "beat" I take to be descriptive, and its primary reference is to a group of writers, especially, who participate in certain common attitudes and pursue common literary aims. They may use the beatnik milieu as their subject and their ideas and attitudes may be widely shared by current Bohemia. The beatnik, on the other hand, is either not an artist or an incompetent and nonproductive one. The beatnik provides the atmosphere and audience of Grant Avenue and analogous areas, and he is frequently an engaging person. He may write an occasional "poem," but he has no literary ambitions.

The beat writer, on the other hand, is serious and ambitious. He is usually well-educated and always a student of his craft. Sometimes, as is the case with Gary Snyder, he is a very learned man, and his knowledge of literature and its history is dense and extensive. Allen Ginsberg's public posture on literary matters is that of an innocent who writes from impulse, but he knows better. And one of my objections to Lawrence Ferlinghetti is that he is much too literary in tone and reference. He writes for the man in the street, but he chooses a street full of Nation subscribers and junior-college graduates, that is, Grant Avenue. In fact, the only untutored writer of the lot is Gregory Corso, and in his work this is neither a merit nor a handicap. His stock in trade is impertinence, and he learned that out of his own impish nature.

The reception of the beat writers, the extraordinary interest taken in the novels of Kerouac, Ginsberg's little pamphlet of poems, Ferlinghetti's Coney Island of the Mind (which has sold over 40,000 copies), the

San Francisco issue of *Evergreen Review* (entering its seventh printing), and the publicity accorded the beat way of life by national magazines—all this has passed into not only social history but also literary history. When Meridian Books put out its anthology of *New Poets of England and America* in 1957, it included none of the beat writers and none of the writers of the San Francisco school and the Black Mountain group. Any anthology of recent poetry now appearing would practically have to include Ginsberg and Snyder, to say nothing of the nonbeat writers who have by accident been associated with them: William Everson (Brother Antoninus), Robert Creeley, Robert Duncan, Denise Levertov, Charles Olson, Kenneth Rexroth, and Jack Spicer, to name only those I take to be most distinguished.

The beat writers are not, in short, the only writers in America who live outside the universities and are not interested primarily in perpetuating the iambic line. This fact needs underlining, for one unhappy result of the publicity attendant on the rise of the beat was, simply, the tarring of all writers with experimental motives with the single brush *beat* or the further implications that the only valid experimental writers *were* beat. The terms "San Francisco Renaissance" (awakening would be more fitting) and "San Francisco writers," for instance, were cheerily applied to any writer who knew Allen Ginsberg or was published by Lawrence Ferlinghetti. As a matter of fact, only one of the writers on the City Lights list was even born in California. The writer in question is Robert Duncan, who is one of the best poets now writing in English and as nonbeat as a person can get.

The association of the beat writers with San Francisco is not entirely fortuitous. From about 1944 on, the area has been distinguished by considerable artistic activity, and during that period it was one of the strongholds of experimental poetry. There was a great deal of other literary activity, and I do not intend to depreciate the products of Stanford's writing program or of the Activist group associated with Lawrence Hart or the numerous writers who simply lived in the San Francisco Bay area because life was pleasant there or because they had jobs in the various colleges. But what especially distinguished writing in the Bay area was a group of people—mainly poets—who were interested in creating and establishing a community of literary interest. They were like coral insects building a reef that might ultimately create the calm and pleasure of a lagoon. They were interested in forming a culture rather than in shaping unimpeachable structures out of the detritus of a museum civilization. The poetry they wrote and liked was deeply religious in tone, personalist in dramaturgy, imagist in iconographic habit, and experimentalist in prosody. With this poetics was associated a loose cluster of concerns and attitudes—anarcho-pacifism in politics,

relatively conservative (especially Roman Catholic) religious preoccupations, a generally receptive attitude toward Eastern art and thought
that grew naturally out of the Pacific Basin orientation of the great port
of San Francisco, intensive interest in the traditions of European ex-
perimentalism, and perhaps above all a very deep elegiac sense of the
destruction of both the natural world and the possibilities of the American dream (its waste in the great wars and the frozen polity of the
postwar period) dramatized in the brutal exploitation of California as
its population swelled. Whatever was wrong with the poetry written
out of these basic concerns, it was not a poetry that refused to meet
squarely the challenges of great subjects.

This was accompanied by a widespread feeling of poetic community that took its center in activities organized by Robert Duncan,
George Leite, and Kenneth Rexroth. George Leite's *Circle* magazine appeared first in 1944, and from then until 1950 he published ten issues
of work local and international in origin. Its closest analogue in that
period was the British magazine *Now*, which included many of the
same contributors, and though Leite's editorial taste was far from infallible, the level of achievement was often very high. Some of his contributors—Henry Miller, Kenneth Rexroth, Josephine Miles, George P.
Elliott, Robert Duncan, Brother Antoninus—have come to be well-
known figures in current American letters, and a surprising number of
his other contributors have been consistently productive. The attitudes
that *Circle* espoused, both political and aesthetic, were hardly what
could be called generally acceptable, and the magazine embodied the
blithe indifference to the official culture that marked the early or post-
war stages of the San Francisco Renaissance.

During the period of *Circle's* publication, Berkeley and San Francisco woke from their literary sleep of years. The chief figure in this
awakening was Kenneth Rexroth. He was a poet nationally known at
the time, printed by Macmillan and New Directions, and one of James
Laughlin's advisors at the latter publishing house. He was interesting,
well informed, friendly to the young. He gave the impression of truly
patriarchal longevity. I said to him once that I had lost all my illusions
about the Soviet Union at the time of the Finnish war. He said, "That
just shows how young you are. I lost *my* illusions with the Kronstadt
Rebellion." It was only much later that I came to realize that at the time
of the rebellion he was fifteen years old, for he gave the impression
that he had turned his back on Lenin with sorrow and withdrawn his
counsel from the baby Soviet republics, leaving them to stumble on
into disaster. He had a trick of imaginative projection that allowed him
to suggest he was a contemporary of Lenin, Whitman, Tu Fu, Thoreau,
Catullus, Baudelaire, John Stuart Mill—they were all so real to him.

The amount of labor and confusion that he saved younger people was immense; one could be painfully working his way out of Dublin Catholicism, and he would talk of Buber or Lao-Tzu. Or with difficulty one could be moving toward understanding of his locale, and he would make some casual statement about Pacific Basin culture, adducing Morris Graves as exemplar. It would be easy to multiply instances. His recent collection of essays—*Bird in the Bush*—gives some idea of the range of his interests and talk.

Beyond his work as poet and critic, Rexroth organized discussion groups at his home, chiefly on political subjects though he conducted some literary seminars. He was certainly one of the best close readers of texts that I have ever encountered, and his technical knowledge of verse was wide, detailed, exact. I stress this because he has insisted recently on the indifference of such analysis to the study and writing of verse ("I write poetry to seduce women and overthrow the capitalist system"), and the record should be clarified. Chiefly, however, the discussions were political and religious with literary figures (Lawrence, Blake, Yeats) seen in the perspective of Schweitzer, Buber, Berdyaev, Kropotkin, Emma Goldman, Toynbee, Gill, Boehme, Thoreau, Gandhi —the list could be extended indefinitely. When poetry was discussed directly, it tended to be French poetry since Apollinaire or the most recent British poetry; he was at that time engaged in his extensive translations from Léon-Paul Fargue, Cros, Carcot, Milosz, Desnos, Reverdy and in editing his anthology of British poetry since Auden. In addition to various poets and ordinary people, the discussions were attended by many of the conscientious objectors who after the war migrated in large numbers to the Bay area and had much to do with establishing the range of intellectual interest. For example, many of the founders of the famous listener-sponsored radio station KPFA-B (with branches now in Los Angeles and New York) were among the participants, and now that the station has become more staid and respectable, it is practically forgotten that the title of its governing board— Pacifica Foundation—was not a geographical but an intellectual designation.

In Berkeley too, partly because of the sudden upsurge of enrollment at the University of California after the war, there was a great deal of extra-academic literary activity. *Circle* was published there, and Bern Porter brought out some individual books of poetry. Robert Duncan, however, was most instrumental in organizing discussions and readings of poetry, and he was the first person in the Bay area who gave large-scale public poetry readings. These readings drew on the large and relatively mature postwar student body at the university for audience. As one sour witness put it, every clique must have its claque. Very true, but the extraordinary thing about the poets was their very great variety, their degree of disagreement. Through the poetry readings in Berkeley and San Francisco and—when it began operation in 1949—over KPFA, a fairly large audience was created that accepted and took interest in poetry readings.

From about 1950 to 1953, there was a period of dispersal when this embryonic literary community developed no further, and it was with the opening of the Poetry Center at San Francisco State College that poetry in the Bay area entered its most recent phase, in which the beat writers were involved. Through the Poetry Center, Mrs. Ruth Witt-Diamant brought to the area most of the important poets of the Anglo-American world, and it was largely because of the generosity of W. H. Auden that she was able to start this always precarious enterprise. Through her hard, thankless labor, a fixed center was established for poetry readings where widely recognized poets could be heard and young poets only emerging could get an immediate audience. As the writers associated earlier with the area began drifting back from their travels, things began to quicken again, and a newly emergent group of younger writers revived the earlier excitements. There were continuities between the by-now older poets and the younger, so that Michael McClure was in some ways a disciple of Robert Duncan, and Gary Snyder and Phil Whalen took much of their poetic method from Kenneth Rexroth. Duncan, through his association with Black Mountain College and his participation (by contributing) in *Origin*, helped to bring to the attention of the writers of the area the work of Charles Olson, Robert Creeley, and Denise Levertov; and Rexroth, who remained tirelessly interested in and receptive to experimental writing of all kinds, also kept people informed of the new and as yet generally unknown.

In other words, when Lawrence Ferlinghetti came to San Francisco in 1953 and Allen Ginsberg in 1954, they were not entering a cultural void, even restricting the sense of culture to experimental writing. It seems to me fruitless to argue whether writing in the San Francisco area has been notably original, just as it is fruitless to ask whether the San Francisco painters are really separable from the main currents of recent painting. In both instances it seems more useful to consider the quality of work produced and the extent to which the producers of the art learned from each other. In both painting and poetry, it seems to me perfectly clear that there *are* San Francisco schools, that is, significant groups of artists who have learned from each other profitably and have produced work capable of competing on equal terms with work produced in other cultural centers. In painting—David Park, Elmer Bischoff, Ernie Briggs, Sam Francis, Richard Diebenkorn, Clyfford Still;

in poetry—Brother Antoninus, Robert Duncan, Michael McClure, Kenneth Rexroth, Jack Spicer, Gary Snyder, Phil Whalen. Naturally all these artists have affinities with painters or writers from other parts of the world, and it is for this reason that their names are often associated with those of artists with whom they have nothing in particular to do.

When the beat writers came to the San Francisco area, then, they found a sounding board, so that Allen Ginsberg wrote *Howl* and related poems only after moving out to the West Coast and read it first to Bay area audiences. The audience and structure of public address were there, and the literary atmosphere was receptive. Snyder, Whalen, and McClure, who were in effect a second wave of the Bay area awakening, joined forces with him, and when first Kerouac and later Corso made the trip, they also found an amiable reception. The presence of Lawrence Ferlinghetti as publisher also provided an outlet for at least Ginsberg and Corso, and so another phase in the literary life of the San Francisco area began.

In giving the historical background to the association of the beat writers with San Francisco, I am not trying to depreciate the personal role played by Allen Ginsberg in revivifying the poetic life of the Bay area. Too little stressed in all the public talk about Ginsberg are his personal sweetness and gentleness of disposition. He was a person more cohesive than disruptive in impact, and it was largely through his personal qualities, his extraordinary abilities as reader of his own verse, and his genuinely selfless dedication that the sense of literary community was again established. And he wrote well. In spite of all the miscellaneous demurs against *Howl*, it still stands as a moving and important poem, and I suspect that it will hold up for a long time. And Lawrence Ferlinghetti, with his quiet easiness of manner, his very great skill as public reader, and his persistent courage, was a force of equal importance and pertinacity. It takes nothing from either of them to say they were supported by an environment that, in turn, they changed. Their great contribution was in the expression of new motives and their creation—or recognition—of a new audience. The singular force of the beat writers is manifest in the fact that they did not merely reflect the audience of American Bohemia; they substantially altered that audience, and in so doing they liberated and clarified motives until then only imperfectly realized. The intensity of reaction to their work indicates that the motives embodied in Kerouac's *On the Road* and *The Subterraneans* strike some sensitive hidden nerve that is more important than, before the appearance of those works, many had cared to admit.

I have taken such historical pains because there are two confusions that I think should be unraveled. First, the best experimental poetry in the United States is not necessarily beat, anymore than the beatnik pattern of conduct is the only valid response to the life of the organization man. Second, the beat writers, with the exception of McClure, Snyder, and Whalen, are all easterners whose relations with northern California are either fugitive or nonexistent. A person moving from the Left Bank to Greenwich Village to North Beach is not leaving home but is remaining in a basically constant society. The scene changes but the emotional milieu is fixed, existentialist costumes, jazz, and all. When Kerouac writes of the West Coast, he does so with a tourist's eye; it is all copy, raw material to be exploited, not substantial. No one objects to this seriously, but it is a little annoying to Californians to hear William Burroughs described as a San Francisco writer when he has not, so far as I know, ever set foot in the state. It is all the more annoying when the result is a distortion of historical fact that muddies waters.

More important than such minor pique, however, is the question of the association of all experimental writing with the beat movement. What happened in 1956 when the national news media became aware of the beat writers was a taking off of the lid. Laments had been issued because of the dullness and sameness of American poetry, and as the cold war thawed, there seemed room for a little more freewheeling treatment of experience. At the same time, there ws no reason for taking such a matter too far, and the beats were suited for a surprisingly moderate role. They presented a spectacle of a romantically dark community that repelled and attracted, that satisfied and thrilled without inviting. It was possible to feel at once sympathetic, envious, and superior to the way of life they embodied. So too with the writing; if this was all that existed outside the finicky preciousness of the dandy and the plodding wholesomeness of the women's magazines, who could seek or be interested in a change of intellectual diet? In effect, it was possible to talk their work to death by considering only their odd habits, and since their contempt for the intellect preserved them from any rational critical self-defense, they could become figures of derisive fun. The fact that Gregory Corso publicly boasted that he has never combed his hair has led to the belief that he could not then have taken much care with his poetry. The quality of the work could then remain unexamined.

Of the writers represented in this casebook, several seem to me important figures, not merely as social phenomena but as literary artificers of some accomplishment. The best comments on *Howl* are probably those made by Kenneth Rexroth and Mark Schorer during the obscenity trial, and they suggest its remarkable qualities quite clearly. I have always felt that Ginsberg is the genuine article, and if he keeps on writing he will probably become a very important poet. Both he and Ferlinghetti are extremely gifted readers—entertainers—and they have been extraordinarily effective in bringing poetry to a widened audience.

A certain amount of ironic comment has been made on the importance of oral delivery and the writer's physical dramatic presence to the full impact of the poetry of Ginsberg and Ferlinghetti. Their poetry, and that of McClure and Whalen (and Snyder, to a lesser extent), attempts notation of the actual movement of mind and voice in full vernacular. It seems difficult to take this poetry off the page largely because the mode of poetic notation that fits the movement of American speech is still in the realm of the nonconventionalized. Accustomed to syllabic, stress and foot verse, the normal audience for poetry is not prepared to take into consideration intensity (loudness), pitch, and duration, and the concept of breath pause is far from being ritualized. The usual prosodic assumption is that the precise notation so readily accepted for music is not possible for poetry, that poetry will have to bumble along with concepts that more or less fit the products of another tone and tempo of speech. This seems to me predicated on a happy combination of ignorance and laziness, ignorance of the past and laziness in the face of actual problems of current experience. The primary problem of poetry is notation, through the appearance of poem on page to indicate the reality of articulation. A poem is a score.

Looked on in this way, much of the notation of this poetry ceases to seem odd or frivolous. The capital letters, the broken lines, the long long long lines, the shift from vernacular idiom to lofty rhetoric, these are attempts to shift from conventional idiom to actual, to increase the vocality of the verse. The experiments with jazz accompaniment are more dramatic instances of the stress on precision of notation.

Related to the concept of vocality that underlies much of this poetry and brings it over into the world of performance and entertainment is the concept of intimacy that affects both prose and poetry. The beat poet is best considered as a voice, the beat prose writer as an active revery. Into this revery come past and present, but the revery is chiefly preoccupied with keeping up with the process unfolding outside and inside the narrator. Hence the long sentences, endlessly attempting to include the endless, the carelessness—even negligence—with the ordinary rules of grammatical function, so that noun, adjective, and verb interchange roles; after all, if the process is endlessly unpredictable and unfixed, grammatical categories are not relevant. It is a syntax of aimlessly continuing pleasure in which all elements are "like." Release, liberation from fixed categories, hilarity—it is an ongoing prose that cannot be concerned with its origins. There are no origins and no end, and the solid page of type without discriminations is the image of life solidly continuous without discriminations in value, and yet incomplete because it is literally one damned thing after another with no salvation or cease. There are no last things in this prose whereas the very division of experience into lines compels the discrimination of element from element. Even a poetic catalogue, which is by definition one thing after another, moves in blocks which have weight, and even if each unit weighs the same, the total weight increases with each succeeding integer. Not so in prose, the only limits coming from the size of the page. The ideal book by a writer of beat prose would be written on a single string of paper, printed on a roll, and moving endlessly from right to left, like a typewriter ribbon.

Is there anything especially new about this sense of endlessness in prose or of vocal notation in poetry? *Finnegans Wake* and Molly Bloom's soliloquy at the close of *Ulysses* could also be printed on a ribbon without violating James Joyce's intention, and the classical experimental poetry of the twentieth century had as one chief aim the kind of precise notation that I have suggested as a major motive in beat poetry. There is nothing new under the sun, even the American sun, granted, but this would not disturb the beat writers. They are perfectly happy to place themselves in a tradition of experimental writing, and they are alert to the existence of writers they can claim as ancestors. They assume that this experimental tradition should be consolidated and extended, and they do not consider it as part of the conventional work of English writers. The experimental era could be looked on as an attempt to vivify the conventions of English verse and prose, that is, as extension of the normal performances of, say, Dickens and Tennyson, corrective to it, part of the loyal opposition. In this sense, it can be assimilated into the institution of literature as generally—that is, academically—understood, just as Blake can be memorialized in Westminster Abbey.

In another sense, the experimental writers destroyed convention in order to create a completely new way of looking at experience and cannot be assimilated into the existing institution. In this view, the aim of literary creation is not to enrich the tradition but to expose its poverty and irrelevance so that it can be swept aside in favor of a literature more responsive to the realities of experience. The question raised by this aim has wide implications, for education, for politics, for human understanding. I have heard William Carlos Williams say that the poet who invented a new measure, a new line, would change the world radically. The scientists at Alamagordo certainly did change the world, as did the biochemists who produced antibiotics, and the technicians working on increased automation. Whether a literature proportionate to technological change is in the process of being shaped is certainly a question worth asking. But by the same token, one might also ask whether this literature is not merely an expression of the hopelessness and consequent frivolity that affects a world shaken to its foundations as its population, power, and problems multiply.

These are fundamental questions that may be too large for the context of beat writing. In the history of American life and letters, the phenomenon of the beat may have been a spasm rather than a "generation," and the final importance of the movement will be seen only when a larger *œuvre* is available from its several writers. The test of literature is the knowledge it realizes, using knowledge in the fullest and least exclusive sense, and literature realizes knowledge by the labor of that intelligent love we think of as art. It may be an unfair comparison, but to read Theodore Dreiser after reading Jack Kerouac—Dreiser knew so much and had so intelligent a love of life and art that he could compose an image of an entire society. He established a norm for American writers, and it is against the measure of human force represented by Cowperwood, Witla, Carrie, Jennie Gerhardt, Lester Kane, and Clyde Griffith that any claim to embodying an image for a generation has to be placed.

The image shaped by the beat writers is partial, but without it any sense of life in these post–atom bomb years is incomplete. The solution is not, as is often absurdly suggested, to add Bohemia to suburbia and divide by two, thus achieving a golden mean or a shabby compromise. The solution is to be, where you are, what you are, with such persistence and courage as can be called to life. The best of the beat writers exemplify precisely that state of secular grace. In this world of shifting conflicts the integrity of the person might not be enough, but without it, all else is lost.

Reprinted from *A Casebook on the Beat*, ed. Thomas Parkinson (New York: Thomas Y. Crowell, 1961) by permission of Harper and Row.

12

After the Beat Generation

It is little over ten years since the beat generation appeared as a force in American life, and now the hippies appear, sometimes called beatniks, but different. A lot has happened since 1956, including the beat writers, and these forces alter the extra-official options that seem accessible to those young people who are not satisfied with the environment that asks them to adjust if they are to have monetary and social rewards, at least such rewards as that environment grants. Many characteristics of the beat generation or decade remain part of the hippie milieu: the virtue of voluntary poverty, refusal to accept the institutional world of jobs and domesticity and school, exploration of hallucinogenic drugs, interest in Oriental or Amerindian religion and ritual. Other forces have intervened: the Freudian revisionism of Marcuse, Rieff, Brown; the exploration of media as coercive forces by MacLuhan and others; the brief period after 1960 of legal systematic exploration of LSD-25, psilocybin (and drugs molecularly similar) by Leary, Alpert, and psychiatrists both here and in England; the articulation of a new poetics by Olson, Creeley, Duncan, Levertov—and its ascendancy in the academy; the development of popular music through Dylan, the Beatles, and the numerous folkrock groups growing endemically out of the San Francisco area, with light shows and posters bringing new sensation and elegance; and the continued expansion of their motives and powers by the several beat writers, Burroughs, Ginsberg, Snyder, Whalen, McClure, Ferlinghetti, so that especially Snyder and Ginsberg became legendary figures.

Ginsberg now has such star quality that he is a celebrity, like Norman Mailer or Stokely Carmichael. Snyder has not had so much public exposure, probably because he has spent most of the past decade in Japan, where he writes and studies. He is a legend for several reasons: he is not merely interested in Buddhism but studies Japanese and Chinese so thoroughly that he is fluent in conversational Japanese and translates easily from both languages. His knowledge of Zen Buddhism is not that of a dilettante but, insofar as this is possible for an Occidental, of an adept. He is at present completing a study of the history of Zen rituals for the Bollingen Foundation, based on records that have not been available to an Occidental nor systematically studied by anyone.

Snyder is skilled in the use of his hands. If he were put down in the most remote wilderness with only a pocket knife, he would come cheerfully out of it within two weeks, full of fresh experience, and with no loss of weight. There is a physical, intellectual, and moral sturdiness to him that is part of each movement he makes and each sentence he phrases. He is gracious, soft-spoken, incisive, and deeply intelligent. He is also an extraordinarily skillful poet, and his work develops steadily toward more thorough and profound insight. If there has been a San Francisco renaissance, Snyder is its renaissance man: scholar, woodsman, guru, artist, creatively maladjusted, accessible, open, and full of fun.

It is perhaps his "accessibility to experience" that makes Snyder so engaging to the young. He not only talks with but listens to them and allows himself to be guided. He is over thirty—born 1930—but ageless. He is willing to work for weeks with young people who want to coordinate a reading of his poetry with a light show. He accepts their values and motives as legitimate and refuses to stick them with his special desires. He could serve as a model for those parents and older people who at once throw up their hands in alarmed despair and dance in rage when they contemplate the young.

Snyder can take his position partly because so much of what he admires and has learned from—Amerindian lore, the wilderness, hallucinogens, Buddhism—is at the core of experience for the hippies. He can accept them because he is responsible for their environment, having in part created it through his work and life. I single out Snyder because, of all the beat writers, he has maintained the most vital connection with the new art and milieu. Other writers, like Gregory Corso or Jack Kerouac, have removed themselves from the density of current Bohemia, and Michael McClure has had his own special work to do, though he has lived in the Haight-Ashbury for years and has defended and served as spokesman for the hippies. And Allen Ginsberg has become a bridge between the new and the staid, so that Diana Trilling can very touchingly describe his courteous presence and polite explanation at one of Tim Leary's shows.

There is, then, a real continuity between the new and precedent Bohemia that can be symbolized by the figure of Snyder. The differences are very great, however, and accounting for them is not easy.

Media

By now McLuhanism has become a fad that McLuhan himself can mock with some glee. This is unfortunate because *The Gutenberg Galaxy* and *The Mechanical Bride* have permanent value. If one has the sense of *déjà vu* on reading *Understanding Media* and the feeling that long practical jokes are not funny on looking at *The Medium is the Massage*, this is because the earlier books had phrased the main points so thoroughly and well that repetition gains nothing, nor does parody. Attending the Fillmore or the Avalon Ballroom in San Francisco should reveal how fully the medium has become the content—the explosive electronic guitars, the beat so intense that it becomes a vibration, the light shows, and not least of all the playful costumes and the playful use of luminous paint on floors, walls, and people. Playfulness—though the beats were individually humorous and a great deal of their work witty to the point of hilarity, their milieu was somber to the point of being glum. Comparing the dark world of cool jazz, crowds gathered at small tables in murky surroundings, bobbing their heads, with the light world of the Fillmore or Avalon, where everyone is dancing with everyone else—the change is enormous and comes in part from the very media in which one exists. It is a group experience, both for the artists and for the dancers, and the isolation that so depressed observers of jazz some ten years back is now gone, as is the passivity. The sense of excitement and release so generated, even of abandon, is in vivid contrast with the control, the rigor, of both music and audience at an earlier point.

The same could be said of the typography of various publications, from *Coyote's Journal* to *The Oracle*. A current joke says that *The Oracle* comes out every four weeks because that's how long it takes a hippie to read a newspaper. Well, *this* newspaper takes me four weeks to read because it is typographically coercive and refuses to let my mind move in the normal glib rectilinear pattern. Each page or line thus takes on its own identity, and it is easy to get lost in the process. The use of photolithography by the Coyote Press also allows Phil Whalen to present his notebooks as they occurred. And the relative cheapness of these processes is matched by the cheapness of mimeographing, especially when coöperatively sponsored.

If typography itself can give the impact of immediacy, the use of electronic devices also changes the very method of composition. Allen Ginsberg's *Wichita Vortex* was composed on a tape recorder while he travelled through the Middle West in a microbus; Lawrence Ferlinghetti's *Starting from San Francisco* has a record inserted in its cover; and poems like Michael McClure's beast poems should be recorded on tape so that their articulation is clear. The day may not be far off when all poetry will be "published" on tape, and readers of poetry will be as few as readers of musical scores, though listeners may well increase.

McLuhan, then, is a prophet honored in his own time, for in much of the art, whether posters, music, light shows, or printing, the medium is the message. While pseudo-artists make "environments" so grubby that they sicken, the Fillmore and Avalon ballrooms make environments of light, vibrations, dance, fun, and freedom. And all without the artificial paradises of marijuana or liquor.

Why San Francisco?

Gertrude Stein complained of Oakland that "There's no there there," and my complaint about New York is that there's too much there there. Visitors (read tourists) to the Haight-Ashbury often ask, "Is this all?" meaning are these four plus city blocks where *there* is and can it be enough? San Francisco is a small city—forty-nine square miles, around 750,000 population. But it is even smaller. It is easy to walk from Union Square to Fisherman's Wharf and Ghirardelli Square. Then it's possible, again easily, to walk to North Beach, then back through Chinatown to Union Square. Very few people manage this itinerary because they can't believe it. If children get tired, put them and yourselves on quaint cable cars or busses. It's a walkable city, like Paris or Venice or Barcelona. I sound like the Chamber of Commerce, agreed, but I'm trying to express something else, that the only viable cities are those that can be covered significantly on foot. Ovid's Rome was like that, and Socrates' Athens, and Yeats' Dublin.

The three norms of American experience are the city, the small town, and the wilderness. The small town has been so savagely treated in Garland, Robinson, Anderson, Faulkner, and Lewis that it has never recovered the nostalgic fondness that an earlier generation invested it with. The city as an image has lost the glamor that Crane, Dreiser, and Fitzgerald experienced: "O my City, o my white!" Fitzgerald exclaimed, and of New York. The sense of freshness and purity there suggested cannot be sustained by any American city now and the wilderness that Thoreau roamed and Whitman extolled has become a dream sustainable only through the vigorous work of such organizations as the Sierra Club. In Dante's Paradiso there are no artifacts, whereas the Inferno is full of them, and William Cowper declared that "God made the country and man made the town." It is useless to decry this as primitivism, romanticism gone wild. For too long human beings have had this contrast deep in their minds, so that if one were to paraphrase Shelley, it might seem simply accurate: "Hell is a large and populous city rather like Detroit." The city is man's highest creative dream; the wilderness rebukes his incompetence.

San Francisco both as city and as center for exploration of wilderness has deteriorated badly over the past thirty years, but of the larger American cities it is one that maintains internal cohesion and opens out on the sea and the mountains. People think of Kenneth Rexroth as a city, or more specifically San Francisco, poet but very few of his poems are specifically urban in subject; the bulk of his work is set by the ocean, in the mountains. San Francisco is west—wilderness; it is also east, a Pacific basin city; and like Seattle and Vancouver, it is beautifully situated. The only advantage it has over the northwestern cities in locale is a more benign climate and longer settlement, and this might be why there has been some exodus to Vancouver especially (not only because of the draft). San Francisco is, for Americans, the city at the end of the world.

The step beyond that is to eastern thought; to the wilderness; to a mode of being that is not of the world.

Community

They are set apart. Young people from the suburbs remember their houses, each set apart from the other, and the automobiles that encapsulate the father on his way to work, the mother on the way to the supermarket, the children on the way to school. Walking, especially at night, especially alone, is a suspect enterprise. What is there to see but more separation in walking? The suburb itself is set apart, designed to allow the troubles of the world to appear in miniature commercially interrupted intimacy on the television screen, and there only. *I have my cave with Bartok on the hi-fi and Van Gogh prints on the wall, so let the environment I drive safely through on the freeway deteriorate daily—private wealth, public squalor, but I have my private wealth. Or do I? Isn't it menaced constantly by the threat of Negro immigration, violence on the streets—driving through west Oakland, a molotov cocktail landed on the hood of my car, fortunately not burning, and I have to drive through there every day to work. Taxes go up every year, and my debts with them, so I can never get that sports car, and all for good-for-nothings who sit on their asses and draw welfare. I never thought there were tax-brackets like this. My children don't respect me; my wife takes two more martinis before dinner than she used to, but then I take three more, and she's at the gin bottle during the day, but boy those sale lunches, I can't really work much after two o'clock in the afternoon.*

This imaginary monologue is not so imaginary as one would like it to be; the sense of apartness and solitude is very deep in American society and there are few agreed rites that bring people together. The magical word in current American discourse is *community* just as the black-magical word is *alienation;* and closely related to the sense of community, ritual, and identity is the concept of drugs, often seen as antithetical to the alcohol that current young people associate with suburban society. But alcohol is not the only poison used by adults, poison or stabilizer as one wills, and the various tranquilizers, barbiturates, and stimulants that so often form part of the home pharmacy have been adapted to the uses of Bohemian culture. Sometimes the results are disastrous, so that the only non-opiate drug that I have consistently heard downgraded by sober seekers is methamphetamine, a drug that is usable in injected form only as a kind of convulsive, draining and in no sense productive, so that methamphetamine seems of all the several new drugs or uses of drugs the one that merits the fear and anxiety that society has for the past decades associated with the opiates, and especially with heroin. I am well outside my limited area of expertise when I approach the subject of drugs, but for any interested student of current Bohemia—and that is, essentially, what hippiedom is—the subject of drugs, hallucinogenic and addictive and stimulant and pacifying, is central. Books on the subject appear at an alarming rate, so that I get the panicky impression that experts on LSD and marijuana write faster than I can read (or want to). Two recent books I can recommend without the fear that they will bore or misinform: *The Marijuana Papers* from Bobbs-Merrill; *LSD, Man and Society* from Wesleyan University Press. The first of these has the most reasoned and sensible discussion of LSD and marijuana that Dr. Tim Leary has yet made; the second has an essay by Frank Barron on "Motivational Patterns of LSD Usage" that exemplifies all the virtues of scientific method and of belles lettres that expository prose can embody.

All of us know or have opinions about Tim Leary, and I suspect that most of those opinions are quite wrong. He has been called the high priest of LSD and has at times acted like the lapsed papist that he is with the conviction that he has found the true eucharist, the body and blood of the lord god himself, that can be served up as part of a highly ornate ceremony or ritual in which a community of the alienated can find its motives most properly shaped; his adverse critics grumble that any parish church can put on a better show several times each Sunday morning. The Tim Leary show is universally considered a bomb hardly atomic.

Defective as the show may be, LSD users as a group do in fact have a rich feeling of community, of occupying not only the same historical point in time but a single spiritual plane in the cosmos. They share a sense of having broken through to a level of experience hitherto reserved only to a small group of mystics after a lifetime of devotion. They share an incommunicable experience, one that defies by transcending the tropes of languages—there is no other to which the experience is equivalent, and only faint clues and indirections can come close to it. Not that any one tries very hard to bring the experience over into language—even the Beatles, the Rolling Stones, Big Brother and the Holding Company and other rock (or cube) groups have to rely on their large vibrations to make part of the experience common in public terms. When they do, they run the risk of irate censorship.

The main drugs used in hippie ceremonies, LSD and marijuana, are not for solitary use. There are many solitary drinkers and heroin addicts are by definition solitary, using a drug that reduces all appetites to the vanishing point and even makes its user constipated. But marijuana is social, and those teachers who are not willing to forego after-dinner cognac in favor of a shared roach won't much enjoy a characteristic graduate student dinner party. There is, however, a considerable body of marijuana literature and even a literature of heroin. LSD is social mainly in the sense that without a comfortable and friendly ambience, and without the help and restraint of friends, it can lead to conduct that is self-destructive and socially deleterious. The LSD circle is a society of mutual aid and protection; and in bitter moments some commentators have looked on it as a group of paranoids united by a common enemy. What are the appeals of the drug, as Frank Barron asks: "Why on earth would a drug that profoundly affects consciousness and the efficiency of mental functioning in ways that are difficult to predict and that are potentially dangerous to the person who uses it become popular, especially among the young, the well educated, and those who are well chanced in life?"

Barron gives several answers: some persons interested in aesthetic appreciation or expression; some seeking religious experience; some needing a cure for alcoholism; some under psychiatric guidance; some seriously disturbed persons potentially psychotic or suicidal; some social delinquents; finally, and for our purposes, persons in late adolescence or early adulthood whose psychological development has encountered the "identity crisis" (a term that one devoutly wishes had not occurred to Erik Erikson). Alcoholics, neurotics of various grades, psychotics, delinquents—whatever the hippies are, they do not fall easily into any of these groups, unless they are classed with all of us who are neurotic in this age of panic. For they are adolescents and young adults, and they are seeking a personal identity, and often aesthetic apprehension and religious insight. There can be little argument that the religious and aesthetic instruction—and the moral instruction—offered by the American religious and educational institutions are far from adequate or attractive, and as liberal education in any sense of the term continues to be flattened by graduate and high schools, both endowed with pre-professional motives, the need of the young will continue. They may turn to what seem bizarre alternatives, but they see very little viable in what is generally offered to them. Their response is a reaction against the world that modern science and technology and state collectivism are shaping.

The new community based on common participation in drug-centered rituals has a wide apocalyptic streak in it and the panel discussion of Tim Leary, Allan Watts, Allen Ginsberg, and Gary Snyder is constantly being interrupted by voices from the audience and by Snyder, asking what new valid institutions can come out of the new orientation toward some form of religious society. Leary's insistent *Turn on, tune in, drop out* is more and more being answered by "Drop out into what?" Community is generally recognized, even by very reactionary Republicans, as better than collectivity; and non-functioning— non-human—individuality seems not a desirable end in itself. To drop out into solitude means very little; to react to existing institutions is, in effect, to confirm them. When Snyder wrote his diatribe against the Pentagon, there was considerable flurry in the offices of *The Oracle* and the Bonaparte Press, both of which were unwilling to accept the hatred expressed in the poem and the vindictive tone. Lawrence Ferlinghetti's comment on the poem was that Snyder's generation was showing, that the tone of old radical indignation was inappropriate to the current young. Yet it should be plain that poetic and prophetic truth are not to be conditioned by the motives of any limited group, however love-prone it may be.

Here is the point where the nature of the hippie movement or community becomes most clear—it is a group of people without what Erikson, accepting the basic motives of Western civilization, took to be identities, that is, they lack largely any sense of significant work and any corresponding vindication of their being. Using a word that has proper religious connotations, *vocation* is the object of their quest, as it is that of any serious person, and *vocation* rises from a sense of debt and dedication. If love is meaningful, it is close to hate and linked with it, has a capacity for passionate exclusion and exaltation at once; the loved object is separate from and transcendent to all others, and is an other, an object that does not depend on one's feelings or perceptions. This is what *vocation* requires; and the lack of such sense is what makes many sympathetic people, like myself, look skeptically on the slogans urging one to make love not war, which would look plain silly if translated into its basic meaning (fuck, don't fight). Love and a vocation are preferable to domesticity and a job; meaningful work becomes scarcer and harder to find—these are basic premises not only for the serious young but also for their serious elders who don't want their entire dream of human possibility to go down the drain.

Dropping out, then, seems to suggest some meaningful area that one can drop *in* to, and the current phase of the hippie movement is making earnest and probably doomed efforts to find or construct such an area. Community may be what they want, but they are becoming sure that the city is not the place to find it. Hence small groups withdraw from urban areas with the forlorn hope of finding land that will support them. "Will support them"—for one of the naïvetés of the current young is a belief that land does support; after all, using Kroeber's work on California Indians as a norm, the Indians lived off the land. But that land has been grazed and over-grazed, bought up for summer homes and sub-developments and for factories in the field uninhabited except by migrant workers and equally migrant machines—it's simply not available in any workable quantity, especially with current price and tax structures.

So that those earnest seekers without skills prized in the world will end as have so many American utopians, nowhere, and with some bitterness in the bargain. Some of them will remain committed to their ideals and develop an art or craft that will assure their continued support when they need seed grain or the rental of a tractor or to meet a tax bill that has doubled because their farm land has been reclassified as residential. Poets can, if they like, retire to a small isolated semi-wilderness area where they can grow their own vegetables, making raids (poetry readings) on the institutional world without impairing the integrity of their function; and carpenters are always in demand, especially those with genuine craftsmanly talent. Without capital, in the form of money or of transactable ability, negotiable in an external world, the rural communities toward which the hippies are now gravitating will simply not function. Already, some of the more sagacious and competent former residents of the Haight-Ashbury who have established what they hope will be subsistence farms are finding themselves inundated by their former colleagues taking the comfortable but unreal positions of lilies of the field, and these subsistence farmers turn away in disgusted grumbling, saying, "They toil not, neither do they spin. The hell with them."

Whether this urge toward the subsistence farm is realistic or not, it responds to deep needs in the young. Substitute *survival* for *subsistence,* and perhaps the nature of the needs will be clearer. These young people have been born since 1945, and common sense should tell us that you cannot frighten an entire generation to numbness with the atomic bomb and soothe them with television. Further, the aim is to allow total humanity to survive, not in the mere physical sense but in the sense that all the possible dimensions will survive. Many otherwise sensible people look on the idea of the macrobiotic diet as a fad, rather like Buddhism, without asking themselves whether Kleenex bread and polluted diluted morality might not be the real fads that are not proper to the physical and psychic nature of man. I have never been able to understand the argument that you cannot change human nature unless it means that its manifestations differ; but certainly the fact that you can get several million people to hunch weekly before the Ed Sullivan show suggests that you can change several million human natures. This, I suppose, is a fad; but I don't understand why the desire for tasty food is looked on as a brief aberration in human history.

The urge toward the expansion and exploration of consciousness evident in the use of LSD is not to my mind a fad at all but one of the most important developments of the twentieth century and a development that answers to needs basic in men at all times. For those who like the organic progressive metaphors of evolution, this will seem an extension of awareness leading perhaps to some revelation of God; to those of reactionary disposition, the expansion of consciousness may lead instead to a recovery of states of being that the monotonizing and mechanizing of life have kept away from vision, returning to human awareness a lost God. And to those of simple humanistic faith, it might be an energizing force compelling men to realization of their possibilities that have been merely hinted at darkly in past aesthetic and religious articulations. Whatever metaphor we prize, it should be clear that the use of psychedelic drugs is too important to be left to the military.

The legacy of the beat writers can be seen in several forms: a relaxation of American poetics that has affected the entire range of our poetry; an urge toward community symbolized by new living habits, family structures, and rituals, as well as the increased use of drugs as a common center for shared experience; voluntary refusal of the blandishments of American commercial culture; sometimes faddish but more frequently deep personal exploration of Eastern philosophy following up but not necessarily interlocked with use of hallucinogens. These phenomena have been qualified and extended by developments in such media as lithography, folk-rock music (notably the use of electronic guitars and tape recordings), and the very fresh use of light as medium in the light shows. The American Indian as example of man living in a harmonious ecology with animals and plants and mountains and valleys has taken on heroic status. An anti-urban movement toward a pastoral-wilderness existence has become powerful enough to make one believe in a possible shift of population back to rural areas where smaller groups can create the sense of community that is so lacking in our ruined cities.

Clearly these phenomena are symptomatic of deep motives in American society that the beat writers exemplify as much as cause. But figures like Burroughs, McClure, Ferlinghetti, Snyder, and Ginsberg have become culture heroes to the young—this is their modern literature as much as Faulkner, Eliot, Fitzgerald, and Hemingway were mine. They compose only part of the contemporary literary pantheon but a significant part. Especially Ginsberg and Snyder seem to embody religious and spiritual and social motives that correspond with those of our young, who experience a profound spiritual void that American life cannot satisfy. If psychedelic drugs are too important to be left to the military, life and death are too important to be left to the military structure and the industrial mess that currently dominate this tormented country.

Reprinted from *Colorado Quarterly*, Summer 1968.

13

Current Assumptions about Poetry

I was tempted, in writing this, to turn my attention to the poetry of my distinguished colleagues, Robert Pinsky and Seamus Heaney—to Pinsky's quiet mastery of the meditative conversational mode and to Heaney's profound wrenchings of language which explore the north of the human soul. But that would have been too easy a pleasure. Instead I decided to be at once more general and more personal, relying on memory and intuition and, partly to avoid slandering persons, making only casual reference to particular poets and texts. What I have to say is not at all favorable toward current assumptions about poetry—those implied in the relation between poet and reader, those tacit conventions that always underlie contemporary arts until they are formalized overtly, assimilated into the traditions or set aside as curious fads and fashions of merely historical interest.

The most inclusive and releasing statement of poetic assumption appears in the first section of Whitman's *Song of Myself:*

> I celebrate myself, and sing myself
> And what I assume you shall assume,
> For every atom belonging to me as good belongs to you.
>
> Creeds and schools in abeyance,
> Retiring back a while sufficed at what they are, but never forgotten,
> I harbor for good or bad, I permit to speak at every hazard,
> Nature without check with original energy.

The key lines are "And what I assume you shall assume" and "Nature without check with original energy," "original" meaning both primal and originating. Whitman intends to release the animating natural energy that exists, often in bondage, in the simple separate person. At the same time his faith in the ultimate unity of the human spirit convinced him that in so doing he would be uttering "the word Democratic, the word En-Masse."

I mention Whitman because so much of modern and especially contemporary American poetry seems concerned with completing Whitman's unfinished book. Some of the current assumptions are shared with Whitman. First, no poem has a prescribed form but is instead a unique shape due to the uniqueness of each person and the uniqueness of each experience. Predictable repetition of sound or rhythm is mechanical; the unpredictable is organic, and a poem is a series (not a set) of surprises. This requires a continuous emptying of the mind, a laying to rest of the cerebral faculties at the end of each line in order to permit the entrance of the novel and unexpected. At its worst, this assumption about measure grants the originality of merely placing words in an unprecedented order, an achievement that, oddly, would be better conceded to the world of electronic computers where the failures of complete originality would be systematically avoided. Measure, rather than meter, as a guide to rhythmic composition in words (poetry) seems reasonable, and it is true of Wordsworth and Yeats that they did not compose in the sequence of the metronome any more than did Chaucer and Milton, or Stevens and Williams. The rationality of poetry—its measure—is emotional and imaginative as well as cerebral; it always has been. When unpredictability becomes a desired norm, the result is a paradoxical monotony. The capacity for accepting the apparently irrelevant, what Norman O. Brown calls the creative tolerance for chaos, is not an end in itself, as it too frequently is assumed to be in contemporary practice. That tolerance and that capacity for admitting what is superficially inadmissible are means of establishing genuine, rather than apparent, resemblances. Great and even good art does not impose unity on chaos; it discovers the unity that is not visible and brings it into the definite realm of rational beauty, using rational in the full sense of the ratios of mind, heart, indeed the entire body, and intelligence. Artists need not be intelligent; art always is.

Hence in the primary element of measure, the linear unit, the assumption of uniqueness and consequent unpredictability is redundant and can become vicious if taken as an end in itself. The assumption is antithetical to the art of poetry and to art itself. Poetry is the dance of language, necessarily involving formal design and the kinesthetic repetitions of rhyme. The rhyme need not be end rhyme, but rhyme, whether controlled by stanza form or simply following the leads of vowel tone, is a major source of revelation of resemblances otherwise not accessible.

Related to the assumption of an infinity of linear forms is the concept of the concrete as being desirable as an end in itself. Language is by its very nature vocal in its tonal structures and abstract in its reference. It can, in Pound's terms, present an emotional and intellectual complex but not an object. The very term "concrete" refers more to an emphasis or motive than any possible use of language. The proper term might be definite or specific. But the stress on the definite and specific presents hazards, for what is specific to one person is often personal and obscure to another. The desirability of the definite and specific creates further problems when it is related to the concept that all material and all experience are inherently poetic; thus, there is no hierarchy of values that determines decorum in matter or diction. Decorum means simply what fits at any given moment, and if linear structures are unpredictable, there can be no prior assessment of pertinence to any larger structure. Anything is then welcome and valid because it exists as language, whether in the common lexicon or taken from documents, letters, diaries, textbooks, or mathematical formulae. The result can too often be a hodge-podge of the irrelevant.

Quotations from documents are valid in such a poetic because they are by definition specific, that is, they carry their own context. But this neglects the chief mission of the poetic enterprise, the creation of new contexts. It may be argued that any statement provides a new context for each word in the statement, but the poetic statement proposes an ordered richness of measured language that is dense enough to have specific gravity not otherwise to be experienced. The language need not be specific or definite. The tacit assumptions behind much contemporary practice would exile from the canon such poetic lines as "Death is the mother of beauty" or "Man is in love and loves what vanishes." They are not definite or specific. They are, rather, cogent and dense with implication.

The mystique of the concrete and specific has led to some wonderful and exciting poems, but it closes off too much of poetic possibility. It grows from a recognition that traditional symbolism has lost its weight, that abstract language is too often a substitute for, rather than an enrichment of, experience. Orders have to be constructed from the raw material of experience. This argument is familiar enough. The question it raises is whether poetry is not involved in a great continuous work of transmutation rather than reflection of the given. If that is the shaping spirit's obligation, then it should be remembered that the experience of justice is perhaps the greatest sensual experience attainable, that justice may be an abstraction, but that the red wheelbarrow is no less abstract and much less important.

The assumptions noted about measure and iconography are closely related to the dramaturgy of much current poetry. We have happily passed through the confessional period so that the guilt and incompetence of harried people call less vigorously for attention.

Poetry, especially lyric poetry, asks for the poet a privileged position, involving a permitted egocentricity; and thus it used to be thought that what happens to the poet was intrinsically interesting. At its worst, this means that sincerity is an artistic virtue, which would have surprised Tintoretto, Shakespeare, Whitman, and Yeats.

In certain respects, the dramatic assumption is the base of the system that I have been constructing. It should be clear that Whitman, for example, in all his work from the first *Leaves of Grass* onward was sharply aware of the fundamental paradox in his concept of the poet's nature and function. He was a "self," a simple separate person, but when he uttered the "word," it was the expression of that person and the expression of the general identity of the race, more particularly of the American people. The poet harbored the rigidities of past creeds and the secondary knowledge of schools in temporary suspension so that he could give voice to the community of being and thus release primal energy that would grant genuine originality. The poet was the center for the conservation, retrieval, and creation of human possibility.

Poetic identity is not easily gained. Any human identity is not given but an earned construct. What is often taken as "individuality" is rather a complex type, unique not in its elements, widely shared with other members of the culture, but in their composition. So much goes into the forming of an identity that simple modesty requires the recognition that we are, all of us, products of family, religion, political and other ideologies (for most of us, what Robert Bellah calls the American civil religion), work, love, comradeship, money, recognition, the gratitude or ingratitude of children, the awareness of death, the perception of nature, the association with artifacts—all of these are our teachers and shapers. There is within us all a shaping spirit as well, ordering and evaluating and attending to the realities of our offered and imposing world. That spirit, as Whitman reminds us, is both our undeniable community, our commonality, our commonwealth, and the source of our originating power and responsibility. Combining our identity as complex types with our identity as "original" spirits makes us, in Yeats' term, more type than man, more passion than type.

Originality for genuinely creative persons, in all the arts and sciences, is an inevitable by-product rather than a primary aim. The same could and should be said more often about individual poems, about the poetic line, about the iconography of poetry. The poetry that we so often consider unique, from Chaucer through Robert Duncan, is unique in its mastery of the entire possibilities of human identity rather than in its placement of words in an unprecedented order, an inescapable result of the articulation of identity. Identities are not granted to us at birth but in one sense held in suspense as the events that we are compelled to accommodate present themselves to us and in another sense hidden until actualized by our capacity to permit, organize, and particularize what to the unknowing appear to be the accidents of experience. There are no accidents to the artist. That is the true base for his claim to a privileged position.

I keep returning to the danger of the unpredictability of the line, to the notion of the concrete as a virtue or even a possibility in image and metaphor, and to the norm of individuality. The notion that one perception leads "instanter" to another that has a necessary connection with the first perception seems to me pernicious, a gross misunderstanding of Whitehead and of Dewey because it neglects their sense of the significant experience (the artifact of science or art) as an event rising from a process with only potential significance. The process to Whitehead is prepoetic, more generally preartistic and prescientific. For Dewey, art is to be seen as experience, but he discerns in the specifically artistic experience the presence of a shaping spirit. What distinguishes an event for Whitehead and a work of art for Dewey is the fact that they forever alter the process. Only in that sense are they part of it. I am speaking here primarily of the poetics of Charles Olson, not out of any dislike of Olson but because of my great respect for him, a respect so widely shared that misunderstandings of his not always clear presentation of the poetic process have become conventionalized into a rather dull set of possibilities. The strength of his poetics has been fortified by the analogy with action painting, that the process of shaping the work of art is the work of art. This is a piece of mystification that leaves me speechless.

Such a mistaken sense of the unity of process and event underlies a great deal of contemporary verse, and, without maligning any individual, I point instead to the exemplar of the Black Sparrow Press, the best avant-garde press in the country. Many books on its generally distinguished list and many poems within the best books illustrate perfectly the convention of the new academy of the original. For if one follows the convention of "following the process," the result is measure without rhythm, concreteness without specificity, definiteness, gravity or density, and personality without identity.

This poetics is especially dangerous to the young. There is something puzzling to me about the pertinence of these doctrines to people who do not control a large vocabulary of forms. I keep it no secret that I think that our greatest living poet is Robert Duncan, nor is it any secret that he loves Olson as person and memory. Much of his own poetics, complex as it is, includes many ideas associated with projectivism and ideals associated with Black Mountain. But Duncan knows Whitehead and Dewey very well indeed and presents a much more sophisticated poetics. He masters multiple poetic forms in multiple languages, and he is self-assertively a derivative poet who looks on originality as a burden as well as an achievement. He is a good example of a poet with an identity of complex origins attained only after the labor of art and of a poet with access to that underlying common reality that is the human community. But he is not a conventional poet; he is a traditional poet in the fullest and deepest sense of the term.

There is much more to say about the assumptions of contemporary poetry. One could speak of the drive toward an Ur-language that one finds in Heaney and in Geoffrey Hill and David Jones; of surrealism and Orientalism; of poetry of anthropological origins and references; of the poetry that seems like some dreadful hangover from the brief dandyism of the fifties, that produces unforgettable lines of profound overtone, like "The guests are at the tangerines and Vichy / Before the meal." These lines are, alas, typical of a kind of poetry that is obviously academic in the original and pejorative sense of the term. I guess they are profound. I guess they are about original sin: you can't trust anybody. But they, and much of parallel poetry, are trivial and silly.

There is one final aspect to American poetry, one last assumption, that I cannot forebear to mention. That is the assumption that productivity is creativity. In my current position it is often my fate to read the collected work of relatively young people, people in their thirties. In one instance I did some mathematics and found that one young person had published three hundred poems before reaching the terminal year of Christ and Catullus, that is, thirty-three. The poems were sausage turned out by a machined process, and not at all edible sausage. It occurred to me that Yeats wrote four hundred poems in over fifty years at hard labor and Frost three hundred and fifty over a longer period, that Eliot wrote very few poems and Donne a relative handful. But they felt a responsibility to their best selves, their true audience, their true identity. Yeats said once at the Rhymers' Club that "I do not know whether any of us will be great or famous, but I know one thing: there are too many of us." One could say the same of modern American poems.

I do not want to end on a negative note. The poetry of any period is inevitably full of guff and humbug. Most art is very bad. Criticism is not merely evaluative; it is also moral and diagnostic. What I have been doing here is diagnostic criticism: here be dragons, phony ones for the most part, that should be questioned. The poetry of the past thirty years is extraordinary in its variety and often dazzling in its accomplishment. We should be proud of it, cherish it, foster it. But we should take it seriously as the potential conscience and consciousness of the race and more particularly of our nation, as a reservoir of human possibilities within all of us that might otherwise be lost or, worse, neglected. Taking our poetry seriously, however, means giving it the kind of scrutiny that we give to the poetry in the canon, from Chaucer through Stevens. To do less would be to insult our poets and ourselves.

Reprinted from *Critical Inquiry,* Summer 1981.

14

Yeats and the Limits of Modernity

Yeats was a modern poet but not a modernist. If he had died in 1900, he would probably be remembered as the Celtic Pre-Raphaelite poet who through his studies in heterodox mysticism, especially as represented in Blake, had developed the most extensive and elaborate theories of literary Symbolism that the British Isles produced. So Arthur Symons realized in his 1899 dedication to Yeats of *The Symbolist Movement in Literature*. Pound accepted that definition of Yeats and in reviewing *Responsibilities* in 1914 distinguished Yeats' Symbolist associations from the newly emerging poetry that he identified with Imagism.[1] Yeats was not merely unable to accept the emerging art of modernity, however; he was constitutionally and by vocation opposed to it. Of all the great modern poets, he was the least beguiled by the art whether literary or visual that has come to be regarded as classical modernism. And his reaction was not caused only by his nineteenth-century associations.

In spite of the affections of his early years and their undeniable impact on his verse through *The Wind Among the Reeds*, Yeats from the beginning of the century was a twentieth-century poet treating the problems of the modern world in an idiom that by the close of his deepest association with the Abbey Theatre he had established firmly. When Thomas MacDonagh sent him a body of poetry, he commented on it as the author of *The Wind Among the Reeds* could not have done. The following letter is dated 1 April 1910:

> I find that I did not give you back all your manuscript. I have just found the enclosed. I have been very much interested to read them, they are eloquent, full of real feeling. The principal criticism I must make upon them is that you allow yourself to use some words, and combinations of words, which interfere with the keenness of the emotion for they are rather worn out conventions, the difficulty of rhyming has kept certain words living in poetry which we do not use in speech. I think we should get rid of these words the moment we are certain that we do not keep them for their positive value but because they get us out of a difficulty. I

notice in the first poem or rather in the first sonnet the word "rife" in the sestet. I can remember as an event of importance my first renunciation of that word. You use it because it enables you to rhyme to a very charming line—two lines further down. Then again one should never use inversion to get one out of a difficulty but only if at all when it gives one some new emphasis or some new cadence. I often ask myself when I have written a poem, could I have said this or that more simply in prose, and if I could I alter the poem. I am off to England tomorrow . . .

Yours ever,

W. B. Yeats[2]

What Yeats wrote to MacDonagh would fit easily into Ezra Pound's "Some Don'ts by an Imagist" of 1913, intended as a rejection slip for *Poetry Magazine*, and it is hard to imagine William Carlos Williams in his later years finding anything objectionable in the notions of diction and syntax here expressed. Yeats, however, wrote practically no free verse, thinking of it as "devil's metres" (Pound, p. 378) while making some concessions to the work of D. H. Lawrence. For Yeats after the turn of the century, the metrical norm was syllabic and accentual, the rhythmic norm established by the impression of a living voice. In meter and rhythm as in syntax and diction he had been schooled by writing and producing plays for what was then the great experimental and innovative theatre of the Western world. His use of symbol and image were further qualified by his sense of the need for communicating with an audience drawn more, as he saw the matter, from the masses than from the classes. The practical dramatist and producer became, though he might have resented the term, the practical poet.

Under this set of techniques rested another reality that embodied an impassioned generality that validated art and was rendered accessible by technique, an extrasocial and permanent reality variously described as passion or personality and contrasted always with character and with individuality. This reality established a norm that, as the world of art changed in its movement toward classical modernity, became a rebuke to what Yeats saw as the abstract and mechanical. In part his devotion to this norm made the emerging art of Vorticism, Cubism, and Futurism an abomination to him. Manet had annoyed him; as for Wyndham Lewis and his associates, no matter what Ezra Pound might say in person or write in *The New Age* as "Bernard Dias," their abstraction—similar, in his mind, to the flat materialism of Manet—denied the kind of beauty that he loved to the point where he thought there was but the one kind.

Yeats' relation to modernism and its manifestations has often been connected with Ezra Pound and rightly so, although the Pound who came to London with copies of *A Lume Spento* as calling cards and the chief motive of being with Yeats, the only living poet from whom he could learn, was himself far from modernity and had not even approached the technical proficiency and innovation that Yeats expressed in his letter to MacDonagh. Pound in 1910 was still Yeats' disciple and even took as an epigraph to one of his poems the opening line of one of Yeats' lyrics "Reconciliation": "Some may have blamed you" (VP 257). Pound's poem has none of the resiliency of syntax or clarity of diction that Yeats had already mastered.[3]

In the crucial period from 1910 to 1913, Yeats had two great difficulties in his professional life, his immersion in "theatre business, management of men" (VP 260) and his deteriorating eyesight. He could read for only two hours a day, having to dictate the body of his letters and have the numerous plays from the Abbey Theatre that spilled into Woburn Buildings read aloud. He also suffered from a night blindness that fell upon him with twilight. His Monday evenings at home provided him with some company, but the remaining nights of the week brought devils and loneliness to the man that Pound saw as the greatest living poet. Charles Ricketts managed to get him to the Russian Ballet, and he found it "most exquisite, most profound. The only beautiful thing I have seen on the stage of recent years."[4] So he wrote to Lady Gregory, but he did not return.

He managed an occasional trip to France, mainly to visit Maud Gonne in Normandy and to attempt with some success to disengage himself from theatre business. But his principal energies were consumed by arguments about ownership of the Abbey and attempts to buy out the interest of Miss Horniman and to placate the restless actors and actresses who had made a name with the Abbey and were now beguiled by attractive offers from commercial theatres and companies. The patent of the Abbey required that the theatre perform plays by Irishmen or at least plays on Irish subjects and restricted them from using other plays in English written before 1800, so that reading and choosing from among the various scripts presented to the management by Irish playwrights added to his burden. He and Lady Gregory, as his numerous letters to her show, really managed the theatre even after Lennox Robinson took over the production of the plays. Policies had to be shaped, attacks from Dublin, Liverpool, Chicago, and Philadelphia had to be answered, and there were always Yeats' own plays to be revised and prepared for publication and staging.

When Yeats thought of modern poetry he thought of Lionel Johnson and Ernest Dowson, his beloved dead friends of the Rhymers' Club, and planned a lecture on modern poetry that would begin with them and would conclude with a long section on his admired comrade Sturge Moore. Plainly he could not include William Watson, Rudyard Kipling, or, in spite of their friendship, John Masefield. I think that in considering Yeats and modernity we should be more surprised by the freshness of his work written between 1900 and 1914 than dismayed by his lack of admiration for his own contemporaries or their successors. The visual arts were also not accessible to him, partly because of the defects in his sight but largely because of a constitutional dislike of art that was, as he understood the Impressionists, passive before the world, or, as he saw the Cubists and Vorticists, committed to a mechanical abstraction as mode of perception. Whether literary or visual, art should manifest a conscious desirous shaping of visual and dramatic forms. He saw modern visual art as rhetorical, that is, as the opposite of the poetic. The arts from 1900 to 1914 underwent radical innovation; Yeats had other motivations, and in what others regarded as growth and the release of possibilities he saw only limitation and confinement of the spirit.

Yeats found himself driven to reflection by the advent of the new visual art and poetry publicized by Marinetti in his London presentation of futurism, an event that helped lead Lewis and Pound to publicity under the aegis of Vorticism as presented in *Blast* and Pound to Imagism as articulated in *Poetry Magazine* and given representative form in his *Catholic Anthology* (where Yeats' "The Scholars" first appeared). Yeats reacted to the notions of the modern in the essay "Art and Ideas," in *The New Weekly* of June 20 and 27 of 1914 (E&I 346–55).

The essay places its audience in the Tate Gallery with paintings by Millais and Rossetti that present the heroic images of Ophelia and of the two Marys. Yeats is taken back to his childhood and forgets "the art criticism of friends," as he observes "wonderful, sad, happy people, moving through the scenery of my dreams" (E&I 346). He finds there what he sought in childhood, images associated with the poems and religious ideas that most moved him. He is seeking what he had always wanted and what often evaded him, a touch of the sacred. Rossetti had found it when he turned to religious themes, reacting against "the pedantic composure of Wordsworth, the rhetoric of Swinburne, the passionless sentiment of Tennyson" (E&I 351–52). Poet and saint alike could have no use for such desecrations of the spirit. The trouble with this attitude was that it could neither refute nor use ideas, thus limiting the scope of art and life, demeaning emotion itself.

As often happens with Yeats, there is confusion in the essay because Yeats wanted very much to accommodate realities that were superficially incompatible. What he wanted was "an organic thing . . . the flow of flesh under the impulse of passionate thought" (E&I 354), and much as he might admire Rossetti and his associates, their lack of thought was limiting for them. Hence he could feel in the ideas on which he had based his early life a lack of power. Beautiful, sad people moved through his dreams, and he found them compelling and admirable, beyond the negative criticism of his friends who, in their own aesthetic, were also fighting free of the Pre-Raphaelitism that Yeats evoked as critique of the contemporary drive against imitation. Yeats was a man devoted to power and to beauty at once, as his work at the Abbey evinced, and he held a lifelong interest in organization and a lifelong curiosity in the origins of historical change. Pride of the intellect and sedentary meditation were qualities he could decry, but power came from the intellect in action: "Why should a man cease to be a scholar, a believer, a ritualist before he begin to paint or rhyme or to compose music, or why if he have a strong head should he put away any means of power?" (E&I 353). The question seems oddly out of joint with the general tone of the essay, but Yeats is speaking of himself, a strong head, a ritualist, a believer, and in certain respects a scholar.

Yeats was a man of power in his acts of founding both the Irish Literary Society in London and the National Literary Society in Dublin as well as the Irish National Theatre. He joined the Irish Republican Brotherhood, and at the end of his life he had every right to ask whether *Kathleen ni Houlihan* had sent out "certain men the English shot" (VP 383). He enjoyed not only the prestige of his senatorship but the attention it granted his speeches on censorship and on divorce. He used his membership on the Academic Committee of the Royal Literary Society to aid Joyce during the World War. He was shrewd and cunning in his use of power, and many of his lyrics, notably those on the Hugh Lane pictures, were acts of spiritual power. A touch of the sacred; a place in the world. The evocation of passionate thought; the creation of an audience.

These coexisting motives suggest the range of Yeats' interests both poetically and publicly. He was always affected by his early ideas of the symbol stressing essence and vertical suggestion, increasingly qualified by an urge toward the definite and public. His sense of mimesis was therefore more complex as he developed past the early reflections on Blake and Shelley toward the grand complex poems treating the problems of the world ("Nineteen Hundred and Nineteen," "Meditations in a Time of Civil War") with specific references to actions of the Black and Tans and the gunmen who attempted the overturn of the new Free State and with grand historical and mythological references that created a framework that let him see his private and public experience in a larger frame. In his middle period, from 1900 through 1917, however, he remained uncertain of what exactly his poetry referred to, so that when his father wrote to him in 1916 about imitation, he presented a complicated reply: "In the last letter but one, you spoke of all art as imitation, meaning, I conclude, imitation of something in the outer world. To me it seems that it often uses the outer world as a symbolism to express subjective moods. The greater the subjectivity, the less the imitation. Though perhaps there is always some imitation" (L 607). Yeats' wavering at this point is characteristic. He develops next a commonsense view, but common sense was hardly his strong suit in aesthetic matters.

> The element of pattern in every art is, I think, the part that is not imitative, for in the last analysis there will always be somewhere an intensity of pattern that we have never seen with our eyes. In fact, imitation seems to me to create a language in which we say things which are not imitation.
>
> At the present moment, after a long period during which the arts had put aside almost everything but imitation, there is a tendency to over-emphasise pattern, and a too great anxiety to see that those patterns themselves have novelty. [L 607]

Novelty, originality, individuality—those motives did not interest Yeats, especially when they left out, in poetry, the dramatic and the pictorial and when, in visual art, they led to the rhetoric of the abstract. Nine days later he wrote to his father on Cubism as evident in the work of Wyndham Lewis:

> You ask for examples of "imitation" in poetry. I suggest that the corresponding things are drama and the pictorial element and that in poetry those who lack these are rhetoricians. I feel in Wyndham Lewis's Cubist pictures an element corresponding to rhetoric arising from his confusion of the abstract with the rhythmical. Rhythm implies a living body, a breast to rise and fall, or limbs that dance, while the abstract is incompatible with life. The Cubist is abstract. [L 608]

In part, Yeats concedes, artists like Lewis were reacting to the passivity of the Impressionists and their acceptance only of the instinctive and unconscious. The violent reaction of the Vorticists and their contemporaries in France and Italy and Russia was in principle reasonable but in practice disastrous:

> It was the impressionists' belief that this arrangement of the subject should be only unconscious and instinctive that brought this violent reaction. They are right in believing that this should be conscious, but wrong in substituting abstract scientific thought for conscious feeling. If I delight in rhythm I love nature though she is not rhythmical. I express my love in rhythm. The more I express it the less can I forget her. [L 608]

Yeats saw the modernity of Lewis as antipathetic to the essential motives of art. Pound could, in "The Game of Chess," feed upon David Bomberg's abstraction but Yeats could see nothing there that would work for his art, nor in Lewis and, later, Brancusi.[5] Modernity denied the richness of nature, and it denied perhaps above all the shaping that came from a love not of art only but of art as an embodiment of knowledge spiritual in form and not otherwise accessible. Cubism, Vorticism, Imagism—these were all limiting, not liberating to the spirit.

During the period from 1900 to 1917, Yeats had many and scattered preoccupations, but when he returned to his poetry in lyric form he found himself discontented with the work for all his increased technical proficiency and for all his effort to bring into his poetry more definite outline and less of the blurring that cloaked the lyrics through *The Wind Among the Reeds*. He sought freedom from overelaboration, but he could not extend himself into a world of free verse and mere horizontal reference. Such a world would have left too much out.

He wrote during that time some wonderful poems, but the danger was very real that he could have become a poet of sentiment commemorating a personal past and a body of legend that, in "The Two Kings," was redeemed from Tennysonian reflection only by his own obsessive feeling for strangeness and the supernatural. In Yeats' own classification, he came to write lyrics that were rough and comic or at best tragicomic, inhabiting a world of feeling that had no resiliency or rich suggestiveness, as in "The Three Beggars" or "The Hour Before Dawn." From his own point of view, I imagine, poems like "A Memory of Youth" and "Friends" and "The Cold Heaven" and "That the Night Come" were granted to him far too seldom. He was more likely to discover himself reacting to the external, even in so fine an occasional poem as "September 1913," and not bringing forth poetry growing from and articulating a passion that permitted sharing the deepest human nature.

Beginning with the 1917 edition of *The Wild Swans at Coole* and continuing through his life, Yeats would move past the limits of sentiment that afflicted even the 1917 volume, some of the farewells to Maud Gonne degenerating into sentimentality. His poetry ceased to be, as at its worst it sometimes could be, merely personal, and he moved toward a more certain grasp of his experience and of the world that impinged upon him in his later historical poetry. As his understanding of the world increased, he came to see modernity in art as part of the historical breakdown that his system clarified. Perhaps enough has been said about his edition of *The Oxford Book of Modern Verse*, hardly a monument to clear perception of poetic quality and merit. The recent edition of the 1925 text of *A Vision*, however, grants something more than idiosyncratic omissions, inclusions, and commentary that seems motivated more by pique than reasoned judgment. The text edited by Harper and Hood (AV-A) with the body reproduced by photolithography provides the section on the modern world that was excised in later editions, and there we can see a full and reasoned treatment of modernity in art as part of the modern world. Without that material, Yeats had seemed lazy and irresponsible in many of his judgments or merely self-assertive and arbitrarily personal.

The "Dove or Swan" section was the last part of the book finished, at Capri in February 1925. At its conclusion he shapes an image drawn from experience of the art of his own time. For someone schooled in Yeats' sense of the spiritual and sacred, this is an art cut off from ecstasy, joy, passion—all that he associated with personality as distinct from character, that social construct, and individuality, that denial of social role. The art that he sees is an art of abstraction, not merely in the technical sense, but in a drawing away from the human and sacred, even a drawing away from love and contemplation. The art of the late nineteenth century prepared the way, lacking force and consequently the capacity for choosing preferences in life as in art, growing passive before its own activity: "synthesis for its own sake, organisation where there is no masterful director, books where the author has disappeared, painting where some accomplished brush paints with an equal pleasure, or with a bored impartiality, the human form or an old bottle, dirty weather and clean sunshine" (AV-A 210). Such works (he is specific only about Flaubert's *St. Anthony*) carried "synthesis . . . to the utmost limit possible, where there are elements of inconsequence or discovery of hitherto ignored ugliness" (AV-A 210). They foreshadow yet another and more abstract age, going beyond even the possibility of any shared knowledge, so that the intellectual justification of any scientific view is rendered impossible.

Against this historical background he can see the last quarter of the Christian era moving toward its close, and he sees its qualities "in certain friends of mine, and in writers, poets and sculptors admired by these friends, who have a form of strong love and hate hitherto unknown in the arts. It is with them a matter of conscience to live in their own exact instant of time, and they defend their conscience like theologians" (AV-A 210–11). They assert the dogma of the temporal, and everything that mattered to Yeats in the human spirit was shunted away:

They are all absorbed in some technical research to the entire exclusion of the personal dream. It is as though the forms in the stone or in their reverie began to move with an energy which is not that of the human mind. Very often these forms are mechanical. . . . I think of the work of Mr Wyndham Lewis, his powerful "cacophony of sardine tins," and of those marble eggs, or objects of burnished steel too drawn up or tapered out to be called eggs, of M. Brancusi, who has gone further than Mr Wyndham Lewis from recognisable subject matter and so from personality. [AV-A 211]

We have returned in more fully articulated form to the arguments that Yeats made in writing to his father some nine years earlier. The subject matter of art and life he sees violated by historical necessities to which the artist need not surrender except by conscious choice. Yeats was too deeply involved, or mired, in his personal and public life to look upon such a choice with envy. And he saw that these artists and their associates could not remain happy with a choice so antithetical to what Yeats took to be the essential motives of art. They would come to hate the abstract:

> I find at this 23rd Phase which is it is said the first where there is hatred of the abstract, where the intellect turns upon itself, Mr Ezra Pound, Mr Eliot, Mr Joyce, Signor Pirandello, who either eliminate from metaphor the poet's phantasy and substitute a strangeness discovered by historical or contemporary research or who break up the logical processes of thought by flooding them with associated ideas or words that seem to drift into the mind by chance. [AV-A 211]

Yeats himself used historical or contemporary research, but his fantasy was present and controlling, and the logical (by which Yeats means, I think, "consecutive") design refracted the imagination. Modernity as he saw it was unduly restricting. He could not be confined by the comedy of social character, the assertion of reactive individuality, the barrenness of technique used only to see where it might go; the false purity of the mechanical, the surrender to chance rather than choice, the physical fact used in its full inertness. Against that he presented, in his peculiar sense of the term, the personality with its passionate perceptions, its capacity for seeing things as they are in their full suggestiveness, its acceptance of the formal restraints against which the imagination evoked its energy, its capacity for ecstasy rather than passivity, its inevitable moving beyond pleasure to joy, its participation in a world of spirit that the art and life of his own age could not conventionally accept.

For Yeats was in the deepest sense of the term a traditional poet. When the modern world impinged on his work, it took its form from the social and political disorder that he knew all too well in the microcosm of modern Ireland. He objected to modernity in art because its limits would make his own art impossible. He was peculiarly immune to fashion, for he was absorbed as person and poet by the work his experience and tradition required. He was, to put the matter simply, a great poet working in the modern world, maintaining the dignity of his permanent role.

Reprinted from *Yeats: An Annual of Critical and Textual Studies*, Vol. III (Ithaca: Cornell University Press, 1985).

Abbreviations

AV-A   *A Critical Edition of Yeats'* A Vision (1925). Ed. George Mills Harper and Walter Kelly Hood. London: Macmillan, 1978.

E&I   *Essays and Introductions*. London and New York: Macmillan, 1962.

L   *The Letters of W. B. Yeats*. Ed. Allan Wade. London: Rupert Hart-Cavis, 1954; New York: Macmillan, 1955.

VP   *The Variorum Edition of the Poems of W. B. Yeats*. Ed. Peter Allt and Russell K. Alspach. New York: Macmillan, 1957.

Notes

1. "The Later Yeats," *Poetry*, 4 (May 1914); rpt. in *Literary Essays of Ezra Pound*, ed. T. S. Eliot (New York: New Directions, 1968), pp. 378–81; hereafter cited as Pound.

2. Unpublished letter, Humanities Research Center, University of Texas at Austin. I am grateful to Dr. John S. Kelly and the Oxford University Press for permission to quote from Yeats' unpublished letters, the full text of which will be included in their forthcoming edition of *The Collected Letters of W. B. Yeats*.

3. "The Fault of It," *Collected Early Poems of Ezra Pound*, ed. Michael John King (New York: New Directions, 1976), p. 207.

4. Unpublished letter, 8 March 1913, Henry W. and Albert A. Berg Collection, New York Public Library, Astor, Lenox and Tilden foundations.

5. *Personae: The Collected Shorter Poems of Ezra Pound* (New York: New Directions, 1971), p. 120.

Some American Poets

15

Robert Lowell: *For the Union Dead*

It is no longer possible for any member of my generation to approach a book like *For the Union Dead* with genuine freshness or innocence, as we could *Land of Unlikeness* or *Lord Weary's Castle* when they first struck our attention. It would take a more elaborate artifact than seems to me worthwhile to give the impression that Lowell—whatever "Lowell" is—had not been central to my awareness for a long time. There are, however, certain growing platitudes that I should like to squelch from the outset. Lowell, for people who came to maturity during the Second World War, was not *our* poet in the way that Eliot and Auden and Thomas and even Archibald Macleish was "our poet" for a large body of people. It makes me uneasy to hear the period from c. 1945 to the present referred to as "The Age of Lowell"—the phrase has a tinny fabricated sound. Lowell was something we reacted to and against, but there was never a sense of coziness about the whole thing, especially if one met it, except briefly, in cool print. He was, rather, an other and representative reality. One reacted to what he represented, religiously and aesthetically, as much as to whatever it was that he was. And finally he sent us back to his constituents, so that he hardly seemed an individual force but a literary figure, that is, a complex type. He embodied various elements and gave them a special uneasy bond. There was a basic instability in his work precisely because of the incompatibility of the orders it accepted.

Taking only one example: that generation, and it is really a generation now with children and defined intellectual contours and tastes and powers, held a vision of itself as politically radical while practicing and admiring art that is culturally conservative. Wisdom should have warned us that confusion lay in that direction, and *The Mills of the Kavanaughs* is a monument to that confusion. Those of us who have remained alive to pressures of being, learned painfully and fully the results of such confusions. Lowell was a reminder of pain. He dramatized, not knowing it himself any more than the rest of us, that pain was normal for our generation because of the irreconcilabilities we had chosen as our substance, and then the ultimate numbness that great pain imposes. It always surprises me to contemplate how many of my contemporaries carry lead or the weight of prison sentences or the shock of the violence of the state in its many forms as part of their physiology. The experience of depression, war, and cold war was violent and constricting, so that when Lowell writes of

> . . . pain
> suffering without purgation,
> the back-track of the screw. . . .

he says cogently what was at the base of the matter. Pain was what we expected society to impose, and all our cultural conditioning has led us to associate purgation and genuine suffering with that pain.

Hence Lowell's painful poetry was accepted for the moral and emotional orders it sanctioned. Now with *For the Union Dead* he has written a book that carries this painfulness one step further, and he has written a genuinely popular book—people who wouldn't otherwise read poetry read it. At the same time I find it very hard to defend *For the Union Dead* on poetic terms. It is possible to say all sorts of nice things about it as part of an oeuvre and on, once again, representative terms. We can assert its equivalence to the freedom that Lowell has earned in his theater pieces, and we can place it in relation to *Life Studies* as a continuation of the relaxed tone and feeling for a tradition of the self started in that book. We can move out into comments on confessional poetry and the sentiment of release engendered by Sylvia Plath and Anne Sexton. In the larger history of American poetic idiom it extends the poetic world of Williams and others so that our tradition can be defined more clearly. Only folly or malice could deny the biographical and historical function of the book.

Beyond these generalities, other qualities in the poems are compelling as subject matter and inescapable images, especially the crucial metaphor of the animal. The poetry does in the movement of its imagery do more than make a sentimental claim on the audience by referring to other poems in the Lowell canon and the contours of his life. Domesticated animals are monsters. Beasts associated with men become more or less than beasts—dogs, rats, chickens, pigs are all revolting as ideas, however charming any single specimen may be. They are parodies and realizations of our natures. *For the Union Dead* is full of animals that have been made monstrous by human tones and cagings. The muskrat that slices the poet's thumb and smashes a wooden crate to pieces in its furious frustration is not an animal but a being made monstrous by human impositions. When Lowell urges us to pity the monsters, he is in effect asserting that we are in some sense responsible for their monstrosity, our perception has made them extra-natural, even though our perception is not natural. In this book there are no innocent animals because there are no innocent human relations to animals. The animals in themselves do not represent human traits; they evoke them, become the occasions for self-degradation and disgust. Men may be sovereign but they have abused their power to the point of lessening themselves and all in their custody.

Thematically the animals relate to the fallen, even collapsed, state of the protagonist, who lives again through paradise lost. Heaven, paradise, nature, youth, the past which has real youth that no present can ever have had—these are all losses in this book, so that the personal life effectively goes through the processes of the racial. Animals in our world have been monstered by human action as much as the free beasts of the pre-lapsarian state were monstered by the primal crime. That crime has, in the background of the poetry, been re-enacted. The poems are post-Christian; even more than that: they are poems of a world that has denied its second and would deny a third chance by taking the whole matter out of the hands of any god at all. Men really are as gods; they really can control their environment at all levels, tidal, meteorologic, cosmic; they can destroy it, this being the ultimate control, just as violence is the ultimate ratio. Reason and measure are simply not relevant terms.

The poetry shapes most powerfully a world of feeding and devouring in which life can be resolved to the purest of force, no more, no less than force. Submarine or strangling in a false element, lives become archaic like paleontological reminders of witless disaster, immobilized in gestures that have fragile lost meanings like those of statues whose social motive is exhausted now or was false from the start. The animals complement the statues, and the architecture has as much and as little meaning as beast and human imitation.

"This might be nature," he says wistfully—two water-towers in New York? The claims of tenderness that the poem makes won't stand up under the data, so the poem is not finished. There is a kind of savagery operative, not the famous savagery or vindictiveness of tone that is the physical voice of a Lowell poem, but the sophistical savagery that denies the art that it practices. It won't do, the kind of evasion that says this or that poem is about poetry or about the impossibility of finishing even the poem that one is working on at the very moment. We should ask what it is that the poetry refers to that *makes* it poetry or impossible to be poetry.

With this book it seems to me that Lowell has moved past the pain and disgust of his earlier work toward impatience. This may be our great collective psychosis right now, and once again Lowell has taken on himself a representative role. But with impatience, which won't do in art or science, comes the more specifically poetry-destroying force of futility and guilt. Whatever the personal position of the man writing poetry, poetry is not guilty; the author may hold what attitude he will, the poem has to be free, innocent. The poet may, as Wordsworth did, as Yeats did, doubt the efficacy of his enterprise; the poem cannot. Guilt and futility are bound together, and if they had been present to any degree in *The Divine Comedy,* then it would have been neither divine nor a comedy; and their presence in the structure of "Among School Children" is enough to cloud even so brilliant a poem. What happens in *For the Union Dead* is that so long as guilt and futility remain subjects, even attitudes, the poem can take care of itself; when they become the poem, the entire process breaks down. Then the poem is warranted by the momentum of the book, and since the linear movement has pace and direction, the book doesn't suffer.

The poem does. The kind of operation involved in taking, as I am arbitrarily doing, a book separated from an oeuvre is drastic (e.g., there are lots of animals in other books by Lowell), and excising a poem from a book is even more radical surgery. Books of poetry, let me plead, are books of poems, and if this common sense judgment can be kept free from academic notions of form, it has legitimacy. There is a danger that in reacting against the doctrine of the autonomous poem, current poetics is putting in its place the autonomous book and eventually the autonomous man. And, looking at the books so engendered and encouraged, one sees a facile vindication of the lax and shoddy. Poets should and do compose books—only lunacy could suggest that mature writers should not know what they are doing or have any notion of larger design. The books should be books of poems.

Even granting the power of the dramatic spectacle of *For the Union Dead,* its least ingratiating qualities are evident in the structures of individual poems. The general architecture seems grand, but the main difficulty is within each poem, structural. The temptation of the poems is to make violent resolutions by language that is not accurate because literary or excessive: "my child exploding into dynamite" doesn't make sense, and the poems often make such resolutions that sound proper only because of their rhetorical violence. This extreme of tension is matched by another extreme of passive laxness: "beginning in wisdom, dying in doubt." As an ending of a poem, this is unforgivable as measure even if right in judgment, and it is the ends of poems, their conclusions, that do not conclude but stop, run down. Frost said once that any damn fool can get into a poem but it takes a poet to get out of one. These poems just end. Hence the deliberate flatness, the rhetorical questions, the return at the close to the phrasing of the opening. Wherever the poem would take the poet, he won't go. At these points, in the texture and structure of the verse, imaginative control wavers or cannot maintain itself, and they account for the sense of many earnest sympathetic readers that the poems don't live up to their promises, their subjects and feelings. Interjections of irrelevances, however powerful, don't let the poems follow out their limits. The subject of "The Severed Head," from Hawthorne's butterfly on, is the imagination, and the alter ego of the poem is the poet objectified to his terror and disgust, so that when it says "Sometimes I ask myself, if I exist," the result is genuine terror since the narrator's existence is entirely dependent on that of the alter ego. Yet when the basic subject of the poem is ready to be seen freshly, the poem in effect takes back its full vision and substitutes for it domestic trouble: "Her folded dress lay underneath my head" asks us to consider all that we have found in the poem of the claustrophobic imagination and the self-feeding animal world and effectively explain it away. Ernest Jones on Hamlet is hardly more devastating than that concluding line. And the poem's data are inexplicable by this intervention.

I have deliberately chosen one of the most powerful and attractive poems to make this point. Any commentator on this book finds it hard to be particular without ending with an argument ad hominem. It's hard to imagine, for instance, that a line like "where the fish for bait were trapped" is really justifiable, and equally hard to say that the poet who wrote "Those Before" or "Eye and Tooth" could write this line without full intent. One comments on Lowell rather than on the book, and one resents this imposition, not for fear of offending poet or fashion but because one is judging (is driven to judge rather than explore) twenty years at hard labor and asking if this is all. There are few poets among Lowell's contemporaries who require such severe questioning, and even fewer who survive it.

Such questioning is then a form of praise. To return more positively to the large dramaturgic question, the person in history is the main subject, and it is good to see poetry treating the moment where person and history meet even without maximum continuous concentration. Retrieving from the novel this subject matter has been a steady obsession of poets for over half a century now. The local data of Lowell's poems, even when irritating, remind us of what those historical problems are, as do his themes and images. Closely related to the book's larger problems are the details of language.

Poets may begin emotionally and thematically anywhere, but they really end in language. Lowell's language in this book offers invitations to corruption that are quite serious. "My old flame, my wife!" Well, yes, every one feels this as being in some depreciatory sense right, exact, and still false. Old flames are jokes, and sure, there are no old flames, not even that for *le soldat inconnu* or John Fitzgerald Kennedy. So we know from the start that we are being jollied, as is the apostrophized woman. The tone is that of indolent play, fun and games, but fun with questionable rules and premises. "Reading how even the Swiss had thrown the sponge / in once again . . ." They hadn't; scaling the Himalayas is not, has nothing to do with, a boxing match, and the poem makes nothing of the metaphor; we are presented with limited cleverness. And so with "long-haired Victorian sages accepted the universe"—not really, what is involved is a joke by one of the sages against a silly woman, and the depreciation of even that common currency is redundant. Why write a poem on the cliché expression "killing time" and prove it impossible? Are we to take seriously this language as we might the experience rendered? And if the experience is limited to this language, what are we to make of it, what *can* be made of it?

Nobility, tranquillity. These are not proper to these poems and would destroy them. Surely the world of their reference, I concede at once, neither possesses nor admires those qualities, and denying the conditions of life is a form of moral suicide. The language Lowell uses as his base, like the syntax of Berryman's *Dream Songs,* has lost the capacity for resisting, probing against, the world it posits. It is not a language that permits genuine tension, and tension is a basic aesthetic premise that the poetry nowhere else questions. If a poet like Gary Snyder uses such language, we know where we are because his poetry denies the aesthetic and psychological primacy of tension as ordering force. But with Lowell we are asked to accept dramatic but not linguistic tension, at least until the language reaches the level of metaphor. This accounts for, even promotes, the appearance of impotence, especially since the poetics, unlike that of Snyder, is not sequential and processive. With Lowell it is not a matter of fine indifference or recklessness; the poetry takes no pleasure in its processes, meaning the continuities break down. Many of the poems are narrative and dogged in tone, anecdotal, reminiscent, as if only that procedure could be trusted to move from point to point. Hence the very bald repetitions, so evident that they are taken to be the results of conscious will rather than imposed by the chosen idiom—the poetry loses its freedom.

This is important not only for Lowell's poetry and its heavy influence by example on all our poetry but as index to the state of the arts. Behind the grander modern authors, who are now our classics, was a nineteenth-century knowledge, and it was knowledge felt along the bone, of design that transcended the human. Lowell's mentor Allen

Tate still participated in that knowledge, and it was the reason for his otherwise incomprehensible railing against solipsism (it would be interesting to read his comments on *Being and Nothingness*). Orders and laws and permissions that grew from a paramount structure that human will or perception could propitiate but not substantially change—these were accepted as possible by Eliot, Lawrence, Yeats, and their work was to realize them in structured language. It is Pound's ambivalence and Williams' deep philosophical indifference that makes them seem more likely models for the young. Indeed for our young, the only agreed transcendent paramount structure seems to be the United States Constitution, an admirable document but still premised on an order of transcendent natural force. Without such sanction it becomes a matter of opinion expressing a taste and style. The principle of prior order means that the medium of art is not its essence but an inescapable material, and the art of the past twenty years represents first a surrender before media and second a surrender before a man-made order.

The abortive Catholicism of both Lowell and Tate was an effort toward evading or solving or protecting themselves against this very problem. The frantic anti-humanism of many of our best and most admired classics comes from this struggle to transcend a society controlled by the very worst of the merely human motives, the principal one being greed. Moral resistance against this is very fine, and Lowell holds the hard-earned position of being one of our primary moral consciousnesses. It may be that we respond excessively to his earnestness, his moral charm, his personal integrity, and not enough to the aesthetic surface of these poems. After all, a distinguished writer who can publicly and quietly rebuke Lyndon Johnson, without fury, rudeness, or bad taste, has something working for him. The question is whether the poems are equal rebukes to the order, if we can call it that, of a society that makes even Johnson seem sometimes adequate.

The language of *For the Union Dead* often brings to my awareness the surface of pop art. Admirers of pop art stress its reference to an objective world and contrast it with the inner reference of abstract expressionism; and we are already reading fairly laborious accounts of poetry as confessional with Plath, Sexton, Snodgrass, and Lowell adduced as exemplars, the point being that here is a poetry that frankly takes its position as referring to something outside its language. Yes, how could poetry do otherwise? What is impressive, though, in both the poetry and the visual art, is the fact that the quality of the humanity is not queried, as it must be by the premises of the art. Poets accepting the confessional burden as their subject are also asking for the confessional judgment, willy-nilly, and criticism doesn't seem equipped for the priestly role thus forced on it. Painful, honest, naked, and parallel terms are used as implied honors. Are they necessarily so? The quality of realized experience is surely much more at stake, and the audience defined by this quality. Taking mock-comic strip art as a norm, what it asks its audience to be is at once superior to and willing to relax into a world that it knows to be less than their best beings can entertain. Art can be judged, perhaps must finally be so judged, by what it asks its audience to become, and pop art and confessional poetry coerce their audience into postures that I find not at all edifying. Poets that we take to be confessional—Whitman, Baudelaire, Yeats—are often not at all confessional but artists freely constructive in intent and effect. They require something more than relaxation from their audience. They present a being more or less invented.

If we meditate on human nature, what we are composed of, most of us will agree that our nature hardly exhausts itself by what happens to it and that what is called confession is not that at all but a more or less systematic evasion and fraud. Being honest is artificial; being sincere is an invention—the skills required for art are not moral except in a final sense. Whatever is confessed in Donne or Herbert resolves itself to a complex type of humanity and is hardly individual. The drag toward individuality in confession is out of place in poetry as in religion. Carpaccio is more sincere and honest than Warhol. Passivity before events means a lack of involvement in the process that creates the ground for events, in art as in life.

In pop art and in *For the Union Dead* (insofar as it participates in the merely confessional mode), the age of anxiety evolves into an age of panic and ultimate helplessness. Action in Lowell's book becomes possible only in memory personal and historical; elegiac separation from experience, from doing anything about it, is the norm. The frequent topographical poems are related to the sense of helpless personal aging. Literary and historical analogues are muted commentaries that vindicate an air of wastefulness in the entire book. The visionary poems leave the seer perplexed, isolated, unchanged by the vision, unfit for the life that the vision presents as he is unfit for the life it takes him out of. Helpless panic—it seems to suit the tone of these very bad years where explosive action creates hopeless apathy and social action of the most dangerous and often pointless sort is followed hard upon by artificial paradises and communities "created" by lapsed papists in their sad role of spoiled priests. Collapsed morale, lost heart, gone mind—how much of our art has its only validation in a world where those qualities prevail.

So once again we are back with Lowell as representative figure. It is hard to deny or even question his expressive integrity. It would be silly to thrust aside the moral and personal charm of the poems. Only a large talent like Lowell's urges that we ask whether expressiveness and integrity are quite enough. The book has as its continuous subject the poetic sensibility in a world that is over-humanized, bleared and smeared with pointless and devastating toil, the legacy of wasted power and emotions, the corruption of meaning with false and irrelevant symbols. "Were it in my hands," Diane di Prima once wrote, "The atomic war would be past history." Lowell himself, in his incidental comments in interviews, has remarked on the danger that lies in the American sensibility, and in his own, in wanting total drastic solutions to the human condition. These poems, however, present a human condition to which there is no solution. All literature does. It may be wisdom on our part to admit that there are in experience as well as art insoluble problems, even that we are freshly creating problems that have as their chief characteristic built-in insolubility. Where this leaves us, *For the Union Dead* suggests. Artistically, even if this is so, it seems necessary to assert that expression, integrity, and representativeness are not in themselves valid. Art is a shaping spirit.

Reprinted from *Robert Lowell, A Collection of Critical Essays*, ed. Thomas Parkinson (Englewood Cliffs, N.J.: Prentice-Hall, 1969), and from *Salmagundi*, Spring 1967.

16

Robert Lowell: The Final Phase

The preceding chapter was written shortly after the appearance of *For the Union Dead* and bears the weight of a topical essay that at once reviewed Lowell's work to date and pointed to problems that the direction of his work indicated. The troubles suggested proved to continue and develop in later books. Lowell himself was concerned by the essay and when we met in Rome in 1970, he insisted on discussing the problems that I had raised. We had met only a few times before, so that there was nothing personal, just business. He flattered me by taking my comments so seriously, and at the same time made me wish that I had expressed more fully my admiration for certain of the poems in the book, especially the title poem.

Now Lowell has died, more peacefully than he lived, and he has left behind him the fond memories of friends, a large and representative body of work, and a growing amount of commentary. In the commentary, two books stand out because they present most fully the problems raised by the enterprise of Lowell's poetry. Ian Hamilton's *Robert Lowell, A Biography* documents with great thoroughness the events of Lowell's life but seems to me deficient because the poems themselves are not treated as events and Hamilton has an inadequate sense of what it meant to Lowell to be an American poet, taking his origins in Emerson and having as his mentors the complementary figures of Allen Tate and William Carlos Williams. His index does not mention Steven Gould Axelrod, whose *Robert Lowell: Life and Art* treats Lowell's poetry as a set of events in the process of American poetry. He discusses very little of Lowell's personal life; his subject is the relation between life and art as they are evident in Lowell's work. The result seems to me a surprisingly mature and extremely thoughtful and sympathetic rendering of the merits and problems of Lowell's work. Hamilton's book presents a figure in society; Axelrod's presents a figure in history who at once embodies and transcends his country at a troubled time. Biographies must treat personal troubles; the advantage and dignity of sound literary critical study is that the only troubles that concern it are those faced and posed by the poetry. This does not make such study abstract; in fact, it forces the author toward the definite and indestructible and not merely passing. In Hamilton's work many of the figures in Lowell's life—especially Elizabeth Hardwick—compell any sensitive reader to admiration and wonder. At other times, the book seems to make Lowell into a figure of high society.

I should rather follow the example of Axelrod. His work shows the attraction of Lowell to critics and students of poetry. Lowell commanded a dazzling poetic vocabulary, drawn from his studies in the literature of Western Europe, especially that of England and America. He was, in spite of the interruptions documented by Hamilton, a tireless worker, happiest when pondering and reworking the poem under his hand. And like Yeats and other serious poets, he was not satisfied with the praise and accolades that came with his work. His passion was poetry. Further, as Axelrod so persuasively presents the matter, his poetry was American in the widest and most detailed sense of the term. Americans are heirs of all the ages and at home in none. For Lowell and his contemporaries, their own age was certainly not home but an alienating presence. As poets they were deprived of what gave Yeats so substantial a base, that is, the sense of functioning in a growing cultural ambience. Whatever Yeats's difficulties with Catholic mercantile society, he could always consider himself, in a metaphor that he prized, a coral insect living and dying to create a permanent cultural reality that extended beyond himself; hence his work in the Abbey Theatre and the Irish Senate. Lowell hardly considered himself in that light, and his relations with American society tended to be indifferent, negative (as in his refusal to attend Lyndon Johnson's cultural gathering at the White House) or fraught with despair. His relations with American history past and present were quarrelsome, from the Puritan-Indian Wars to Viet Nam.

Some of Lowell's political attitudes were questionable, and many were right. From his concentration on problems posed by small wars and social injustice came two of his more compelling poems, "For the Union Dead" and "Waking Early Sunday Morning." Axelrod construes the latter poem as at least in part a later commentary on Wallace Stevens's "Sunday Morning," but with an inversion of Stevens's ultimately benign acceptance of the lovely natural scene that has been the norm and salvation of much of American life. There is no joy to be seen in a planet that, from the point of view of the American governing forces, must be policed, leaving within this country "our monotonous sublime." The contrast with Stevens is intended and present in the poem, but the texture of the verse is reminiscent of the meditative political poems of Auden contorted by the violent rhetoric that intervened in so much of Lowell's work, partly as his legacy from Allen Tate. The result is a poem with justified political agony, coming as it does when the presidency was leading the country away from whatever hope it had of peace beyond the borders and the construction of a more fair and just society within the borders. Following the lament so richly expressed in the title poem of *For the Union Dead*, this lengthy poem marks a time of pointlessness. In the book in which it appears, *Near the Ocean*, Lowell is clearly marking time, translating from Juvenal, Horace, and Dante, and writing his poems of personal occasions that had become the standard Lowell poem. He could no more be satisfied with the point his poetry had reached than with the conditions of national and planetary life.

Lowell manifests the two major strains in American poetry, represented in his own work by his main mentors, Allen Tate and William Carlos Williams. Tate in their intimate and friendly association brought fully to his attention the traditions of English Renaissance poetry and the analytic approach to poetry that marked what came to be called, unfortunately, The New Criticism. In that remarkable body of work by Ransom, Richards, Winters, Burke, Blackmur, and Tate himself the novelty came from two sources, first the refusal to accept merely historical and biographical data as adequate explanations and descriptions of poems, and second an insistence on the epistemological validity of verse and imaginative writing generally when compared with science. The models for critics were to be found in the writing of Eliot especially, and the poetic models were drawn from Donne, Herbert, Yeats, Frost, and other Renaissance and modern poets. The French Symbolists were in the background, but the New Critics were genuinely post-Symbolist and anti-Romantic. Except for Winters, whose earlier practice and theory grew from the Imagist movement and who delighted in the work of Williams, the American tradition that grew from Whitman through Williams and onward was shunted aside.

When Lowell found the poetics on which he had been nurtured inadequate to his experience, he turned increasingly to an idiom less restrained, less formally repetitive in rhyme and linear form, and growing more overtly from experience. There were two main difficulties that came with this change. Lowell never learned to think in free verse; it was not his poetic cradle language, and he came to it relatively late. The complaint that free verse is arbitrarily chopped up prose could never be made against Lowell; what he takes to be free verse is very close to the traditional line of five major stresses. By the time he came to *Life Studies* and the later work, his mind thought in the traditional line. The second difficulty that kept him from working fruitfully in the tradition of Whitman and Williams grew from the conditions of his life, the state of his environment and polity, and the fact that he had no coherent view of an alternative cultural set of possibilities. Williams had worked toward more than the full use of colloquial language; his love of the rhythms of American speech conformed with his belief in the possibility of a fresh design of human culture growing from ordinary life. At times Williams seems to negate the traditional civilization; Lowell in many ways was precisely that civilization. Whatever their friendship, and it was genuine, and however much they may have admired each other's work, in fact they were basically involved in irreconcilable processes.

The point where they come together is the intimacy of their verse. They differ in their impact. Williams seems to be talking directly to us; Lowell brings us into his life. The later poems of Lowell, those after *Near the Ocean*, seem more intimate because they drop the habit of rhetoric, so that the poems no longer seem to be attempting to convince Lowell or his audience but simply to permit them to share experience. The poems seem to be overheard.

Lowell at his infrequent best manages in the long sequence of fourteen-line poems that forms the bulk of his later verse to bring the main modes of American verse into an uneasy union. For his complete work, perhaps *The Uneasy Union* would shape an informing title, referring to both his poetic method and the condition of his country. Taken as a whole, this verse offers an effortful attempt to embody in one person an entire age. This is done with full self-consciousness, unlike the verse of a poet from so different a culture as Ireland, so that when we look carefully at Yeats, we see not any attempt to place a person fully on record but to confront the problems of living the creative life in a culture in the process of defining itself with many blunders and bypasses, and always with the traditional artistic aim of shaping an artifact cogent, beautiful, and full of wonder. The wonder of Lowell's later work is that it did in fact get written.

Hamilton records the difficulties of Lowell's life, his deteriorating marriage, his divided loyalties between his family that he leaves, as he leaves his native land, and his new family, in England; his continued difficulty in controlling his mental health, his attempt to involve himself one final time in the public politics of the Eugene McCarthy campaign, so sad and feckless, and his continuing hatred of American foreign and internal policy; his searching through his past friends and his poetic and artistic contemporaries for meaning that would parallel and validate his enterprise, and his reminiscent search for design and pattern in his experience that would parallel that of his country and his art. It is the record of an individual quest for meaning in the history of his soul and his civilization.

Clearly Lowell's is no small undertaking. I speak of him in the present tense because his poetry is so very much among the life of his citizens. Ehrenpreis spoke of him under the rubric "The Age of Lowell" and Helen Vendler's editing of *The Harvard Book of Contemporary Verse* grants Lowell the central place in poetry since 1945 along with his colleagues and students. In the process, she manages to leave out practically an entire significant tradition, including the only one of Lowell's contemporaries who might be legitimately placed at the center of contemporary poetry with Lowell because of the large reach of his work and its technical brilliance, that is, Robert Duncan. I am not playing the ridiculous game of "My poet is better than your poet," but merely pointing out the grip that Lowell has on intelligent critics, so that they are blinded to qualities that are not those of his design and his associates.

Why do some critics have difficulty with Lowell? It is not a matter of denying the importance of his enterprise. Nobody could deny the representative quality of his many books. The extent of his oeuvre alone is formidable. He wrote in a life shortened by mental illness and by death at sixty-one an amazingly large set of poems. He was one of the best translators and adapters of a period rich in excellent translations. Some of his plays, notably *Benito Cereno*, are very stageworthy and have weight and eloquence. If his essays and interviews were collected in a single book, the result would have qualities of cultivation and intelligence that are rare and admirable.

I think my difficulties with Lowell can best be elucidated by an analogy with visual art. In 1985 the British Academy held an exhibition at once beautiful and illuminating. Its title was "The Age of Vermeer and de Hooch," and it filled that substantial set of galleries. The paintings held to a high level of quality throughout and they composed a world. Their world permitted only horizontal reference, that is, it took the visible world for real, and its mothers were not virgins and its babies not the Son of God. The world of the painting was domestic, commercial, agricultural. The paintings were on a scale that would have made them welcome on the walls of relatively small houses, and they would have been lost in the palaces and churches that housed Titian, Tintoretto, or Rubens. They were bourgeois paintings, and they were a credit to the burghers of Holland.

The art taken as a body was the art of a generation, an age, in the specific ambience of Holland. The paintings represented that age, and the conventions of that age granted them a high level of accomplishment. Then, at several points, one would discover a painting that was highly individuated, going quite beyond the style of the age; these paintings were usually by de Hooch and Vermeer. Finally, there would be the transcendent work that went beyond the style of the age and even beyond the individual style, that seemed to be part of the permanent universe, notably Vermeer's "Woman Holding a Balance."

The exhibition taken as a whole can be used as a prototype of the problems presented by any large body of art, whether the art of a style and age or the art of a poet or painter. Lowell attracts comment because his work treats the problems of the age and employs the major devices of that age in its iconography and prosody and sense of dramatic spokesman. His work is clearly individuated in its style. But in reading individual poems, I find that what matters is not the ultimate glory of the artifact but the style of the age and the expression of the individuality of the poet. Poetry with this stress has been called "confessional," but it is difficult to think of confession without any formal structure of forgiveness, and to ask for that from a poem is to ask the impossible.

The result in the books that range from *Notebook 1967–68* through *Day by Day* (1977) is a body of poetry that has genuine attractiveness, in its conversational intimacy, its fluency, its frequent felicity of phrasing, its candor and cogency. Read consecutively, the poems in *History* (1973) grant access to a sensibility of high order, so that the reader's and poet's minds become a single being. The state reached, when the poems are operating most fully, is one of communion, so that the reader and writer become one. This happens often enough that the work is rewarding. But it never seems to attain the kind of fullness that the best of Stevens and Yeats do. Comparing the most successful of these poems with "Sunday Morning" or "Nineteen Hundred and Nineteen" or "When Lilacs Last in the Door-Yard Bloom'd" leaves a sense of dissatisfaction. The counterargument is that Lowell is writing books rather than single autonomous poems, and that even the finest of modern poems are not satisfactory and complete in themselves: "Nineteen Hundred and Nineteen" requires some sense of the idea of progress, some awareness of the actions of the Black and Tans, even Yeats's note on Lady Kyteler. Whitman's great poem depends at least on some awareness of the differing versions of the poem. The idea of the autonomous poem seems in that context merely a pedagogue's dream of neatness, requiring poetry isolated to some range totally lucid through careful searching of the Oxford English Dictionary.

If biography and history are excluded from criticism of Lowell's poetry, the surfaces, even of the most fluently discursive later poems, remain inscrutable. The advantage that he takes is the advantage that Yeats took in his treatment, for instance of Maud Gonne or Lady Gregory, so that the sequence on *Harriet and Lizzie* extracted from the *Notebook* has a narrative structure that raises what is superficially personal to a level where the biographical persons become complex types with wide reference that can be taken into the lives of readers. What Lowell managed in his later work was to see his experience as not his own, so that he could employ it for genuinely objective purposes.

The question of whether these poems manifest social and biological good sense simply does not apply. The experience treated is taken as a painter would take pigment, as given for the purposes of the work of art. Poetry takes precedence over life. Decorum in poetry means the appropriate word functioning in the poem as a whole.

This is the aesthetic argument taken to the ultimate extreme. And there can be no question about the richness and integrity of Lowell's work in the later years. What can be questioned, however, is the quality of individual poems. In his earlier work, individual poems stood out and endowed books with special qualities, even salvaged them, as did the title poem of *For the Union Dead*. *The Mills of the Kavanaughs* was redeemed by "Falling Asleep over the Aeneid," and *Life Studies*, like *For Lizzie and Harriet*, shapes an identity through the poet's associations in familial and professional aspects, and in his role as husband, lover, and father. The fourteen-line blank verse poems that comprise the bulk of the later poetry have charm and are on occasion moving, though none of them seem to have the redeeming power of earlier poems by Lowell. The level is irregularly maintained within individual poems, so that fine opening lines are followed by turgid rhetoric, and the personal becomes obscure when lines clog and pivot on references that the syntax does not make clear.

The last book published during Lowell's lifetime, *Day by Day*, is a representative book, in its achievements and in the general habits of its rhetoric. The poems enrich each other, and still there are few points where the individual poem comes fully alive on the page and in the reader's mind and heart. The first poem, "Ulysses and Circe" promises substance and reality, and it may be the best poem in the book. Lowell manages to give subtle and rich reverberations to the return of Ulysses, and the line, varied free verse, works as speech, meditation, and description. The form of Ulysses's works and wanderings gives the poem balance, so that the concept of ten years to and ten years fro works to give Ulysses a position at once static and moving. The poem is that of a heroic wanderer, changed by his journeys yet constant in his person and attachments. The poem has a basic tone of elegiac love that will not be wasted, and it sets one of the basic themes of the book.

The poem benefits from its known structure, but that structure is also enlivened by a fresh and compelling understanding. It is Lowell at his best, not as translator but as creative imitator and carrier of a tradition. The following poem, "Homecoming," denies the applicability of the design of Ulysses to the life of the poet, who is exiled and unrecognized and finds his early associates themselves unrecognizable, his early love clumsy and irretrievable, and himself no longer part of the lost world, for "No dog knows my smell." No Argos will give this wanderer even a feeble welcome.

The first two poems complement each other, but from there the first section of the book becomes random, though the elegiac tone persists to the point of pathos. Even the swans of "Last Walk" do not permit the poet to see possibilities beyond nostalgia with no real hope for any home. "Suicide" intervenes with its confession of trouble without resolution, and "Departure" concludes the first section of the book with its tone of hopelessness. The poems seem more and more, as the book progresses toward the third and title section, to be poems written day by day, living and suffering as the experience requires. The second section is obsessed with death, as is the entire book, and the elegiac becomes the funereal, except in the memory of Robert Penn Warren at Louisiana State during Lowell's youth where the tone become celebratory. Broken loves, broken minds, and hearts that reach out but never genuinely touch—these are at the center. The poetry does touch, however, for the heart of the poet reaches out in language that is both affective and pathetic. He may be "three parts iced over" but he continues his struggle with life and language. The struggle is doomed to defeat, but the struggle becomes heroic because of its very pointlessness.

The poet becomes an existential hero in these notes that assume an unwritten autobiography. Human marriage seems fragile, fraught with illness in man and in woman, and the only security and stability is in the ultimate "marriage with nothingness." The best season is autumn, possibly because it does not last. Even the gold of summer appears, finally, counterfeit. Reality is illness, physical and mental, what husband and wife share and what separates them. With physical illness, pain isolates the sufferer and violates the partner until he turns almost with relief to mental illness. Throughout the process, the poet moves back in memory to earlier and crucially formative events, his relations with his parents, his love and envy of his grandfather, his memories of early friendships and adolescent humiliations, childhood tantrums and slyness. All this is presented in an immediate context of current drunkenness, mania, and depression, and the result is the presentation of a life limited in its moments of solitary and shared pleasure and extensive in its uncomprehending and inevitably passive suffering.

Yeats, following Matthew Arnold, believed that passive suffering was not a proper subject for poetry. This judgment has aroused some ire because Yeats used the proposition to justify his exclusion of Wilfred Owen from *The Oxford Book of Modern Verse*. Yeats looked on the argument as a traditional and reasonable one, and Arnold went so far as to ascribe the argument to Aristotle (inaccurately). The obvious answer to the argument would be that its logic, followed out completely, would rule out the suffering of Prometheus as subject. By excluding his *Empedocles on Etna* from the 1853 edition of his *Poems*, Arnold believed that he was simply following out the principle that no poetical enjoyment could be derived from it and similar subjects

> in which the suffering finds no vent in action; in which a continuous state of mental distress is prolonged, unrelieved by incident, hope, or resistance; in which there is everything to be endured, nothing to be done. In such situations there is inevitably something morbid, in the description of them something monotonous.

Arnold seems far from current preoccupations, and it is hard to imagine his reaction to much of recent literature. Certainly, he would find *Day by Day* morbid and monotonous. He would be wrong, for there is variety in *Day by Day* and the tones shift and change. Only when the book is taken as a whole does Arnold's stricture seem pertinent, but the book does ask to be taken as a whole.

When the book is seen as a whole, the centers of value reside in Homer's *Odyssey* as present in the first poem and in Flemish burghers, an odd note in a poet so negative about contemporary bourgeois values. The family photograph of Lowell with his new and pregnant wife and her three small girls from another marrage ends with a description of the disorderly boy who will emerge from Caroline. Then Lowell turns to Van Eyck's *Arnolfini Marriage* and the beauty of the portrait that seems to live in a visitation of the airs of heaven. Even at the end of describing this beatific secular painting, Lowell returns to his obsession with his own death, for Giovanna will outlast Giovanni by twenty years.

In the "Epilogue" to *Day by Day*, Lowell turns to Vermeer.

Epilogue

Those blessèd structures, plot and rhyme—
why are they no help to me now
I want to make
something imagined, not recalled?
I hear the noise of my own voice:
The painter's vision is not a lens,
it trembles to caress the light.
But sometimes everything I write
with the threadbare art of my eye

> seems a snapshot,
> lurid, rapid, garish, grouped,
> heightened from life,
> yet paralyzed by fact.
> All's misalliance.
> Yet why not say what happened?
> Pray for the grace of accuracy
> Vermeer gave to the sun's illumination
> stealing like the tide across a map
> to his girl solid with yearning.
> We are poor passing facts,
> warned by that to give
> each figure in the photograph
> his living name.

Vermeer's accuracy is imagined and illusive. His paintings are not imitations compelled by the desire to create the illusion of accuracy but renderings of reality, a reality that is no mere passing fact in any sense but permanently, even eternally, present. The solidity of yearning in his "girl" comes from the blessèd structure of the painter's artistic treatment. Passivity before the data would never have given us the intimate greatness of Vermeer or de Hooch. They do not merely say what happened.

In spite of the strictures that Arnold would have applied to this book and my evident sense that they would be at least in part valid, I still find *Day by Day* a moving as well as troubling book. A genuine talent is present, and even the failure of the talent moves and disturbs any sensitive reader. The book shows what became the growing intent of Lowell, to present directly and fully the being of a person in the America and Europe of the years that comprised the Great Depression, the terrible Second World War, the Cold War and the disintegration of the British Empire as evident in the fate of the country house Milgate, and the anguish and terror of his native country moving through a series of small wars and increasing moral corruption. Perhaps in such a set of events, a "continuous state of mental distress" might be inevitable. Certainly in Lowell we are privileged to see fully what such a state of mind can do to limit and qualify a man with great poetic gifts and singular training and learning. Lowell is certainly one of the finest poets of the early twentieth century, and even his failures have in them an exemplary quality.

17

The Untranslatable Poetry of Yvor Winters

Until recently, the poetry of Yvor Winters was not completely available. The 1960 edition of his *Collected Poems* (still in print) and the 1966 edition of *The Early Poems of Yvor Winters, 1920–28* taken together did not form a complete poems. Now, a new volume edited by Janet Lewis Winters with an introduction by Donald Davie—and unfortunately also called *Collected Poems*, to the confusion of bibliographers—comes very close to being a complete poems. Some poems are omitted, but they are trivial and can provide material for hard-pressed assistant professors in search of discoveries. The book was printed by Carcanet Press in England (1978), published here by Swallow Press, and is being distributed by Ohio University Press; to increase bibliographic confusion still further, the Swallow Press cover and dust jacket announce *The Poetry of Yvor Winters*, while the title page retains the Carcanet title of *The Collected Poems of Yvor Winters*. In ordering the book, readers should be certain to specify the Carcanet printing, which includes twice the number of poems in the 1960 *Collected Poems*.

Arthur Yvor Winters was born in 1900 and died in 1968. In his maturity, Yvor Winters thought of himself under the modest rubric of "poetic technician." He wrote a great deal of criticism that has been rather widely misunderstood, but he looked on criticism as part of his self-elected role, describing procedures that were, to his poetic imagination, helpful or harmful to the current practice of poetry. In his introduction, Davie asserts that reading poetry as reflection or justification of the poet's criticism is "an eccentric and impoverished and mean-spirited" way of reading any poet. This is especially true of Winters, who believed that poems have paraphrasable content but that poems are not ideas. They are rather the embodiment in language of important sets of human experience, so that the reader should trust the poem rather than what the poet says about poetry. The better the poem, the less susceptible it is to translation into any other language than its own. The concept of untranslatability has its classical phrasing in book twenty-two of Coleridge's *Biographia Literaria:* "The infallible test of a blameless style, its untranslatability into other words of the same language without damage to its meaning."

The basic advice is to take the poet literally, assuming that he means what he says and what he says is what he means. Davie points out that a poem by Winters is a "considered utterance"—not considered *before* the fact but considered *through* the language of the poem and its technical articulation. This does not mean that the language is given free rein rather than conducted along certain intended directions (including in the later Winters accentual-syllabic lines and stanzaic structures), but that the language itself and the structures of line and stanza have public lives, independent of the single writer, that enrich the utterance beyond any cerebral intention. I say "cerebral" rather than "rational" because I want arbitrarily to extend and qualify the term "rational." The accentual-syllabic line of Winters' later work, rhyme, and stanzaic pattern are intrinsically anti-cerebral because anti-syntactical. The rationality of a poem is greater than the merely cerebral, including as it does the imagination, heart, emotions, even kinesthetic reactions. To identify the paraphrasable content as the meaning of a poem by Winters, whether in free or traditional measure, is as fruitless as it would be to read Winters' ideal, Baudelaire, in so reductive a manner. How are we to paraphrase or, better, translate into more appropriate language this brief poem:

A Leave-Taking

I, who never kissed your head,
Lay these ashes in their bed;
That which I could do have done.
Now farewell, my newborn son.

This later poem has the compression that was the aim of Winters' early poetry in the imagist mode. Like Pound's "A Fan Song: For Her Imperial Lord" the poem implicates the action outside the poem in the simple clarity of stated action. The first two lines get much of their impact from the common gesture of kissing a baby's fragile head, here never consummated; the cradle of this child is the earth. The rhyme of "head" with "bed" grants the lines a wider extension because they have no cerebral connection; the connections go into a deeper realm of feeling than the merely paraphrasable content. The term "newborn" is in one sense merely denotative, but this child was evidently stillborn or lived very, very briefly. If we did not know that the author was a modern skeptic, we should read "newborn" as orthodox optimism. The author is being, as he is throughout the poem, objective in describing the action, so that the literalness of the term newborn is even more emotionally affecting. Easy words like ambiguity or irony cannot touch this reality. The helplessness of the third line has a stoic finality that qualifies the tender thwarted affection of the concluding line: "Now farewell, my newborn son." He could not write as Ben Jonson did "On My First Daughter" that the child's soul would subsist in heaven, while "This grave partakes thy fleshly birth. / Which cover lightly, gentle earth." In Winters' poem the earth is the final resting place.

I am not comparing the poem to one of Jonson's greatest works in order to elevate or depreciate it. Winters is treating a moment common to many people, with restraint, dignity, tenderness; he is neither imitating Renaissance poetry nor following a simple idea. He is taking a considered human reaction to the common difficulty in which he finds himself. Similarly, the comparison to Pound is not frivolous. Winters grew up in the imagist tradition, and at the age of twenty-four he wrote what was at once the most important articulation of the living essence of imagism (what endures) and the basis of his own poetics ("The Testament of a Stone").

This becomes clear now that a relatively complete edition of the poems is available with Winters' introduction to the early poems. The introduction can and does speak for itself. Anybody interested in the life of poetry in this century will want to read it and will be rewarded by it. One general point that emerges from that brief compact statement along with the early prose (*The Uncollected Essays and Reviews of Yvor Winters*, ed. Francis Murphy) is that Winters knew little about the history of poetry in English before he entered Stanford in 1927. He wanted first of all to write his own poetry, study his contemporaries, and do formal work in the Romance languages, which he did at the University of Chicago in his freshman year, during his three years in the Southwest fighting tuberculosis, and in the three concentrated years at the University of Colorado (Boulder), where he earned a master's degree in Romance Languages. During his first years of teaching at the University of Idaho (Moscow) his main courses were in Spanish and French language and literature. In 1926, when he and Allen Tate began their correspondence, Winters had not yet read *Paradise Lost*, and his depreciation of Shakespeare was affected in part by his participation in the anti-mimetic prejudice but caused mainly by the lack of any youthful introduction to the wonders of Shakespeare's language. His view of Shakespeare is not odd when one considers the traditional French reaction to him. He did not read Chaucer before becoming a graduate student at Stanford.

Although Winters disavows any direct connection between his entering graduate school at Stanford and the change in his poetic theory and practice, the change became evident within a year after William Dinsmore Briggs introduced him to the poetry of the Renaissance. Until then, the oldest poets he mentioned directly in his public essays and reviews were Hardy (who did not die until 1928) and Dickinson (who was a relatively recent figure, considering the late publication of her poems). His heroes were Rimbaud, Baudelaire, Corbière, Hardy, Dickinson, Robinson, Stevens, Williams, and Crane. The translations in the new *Collected Poems* indicate his passionate concern with Medieval and Renaissance French and Spanish poetry. The intense study of the English poetic tradition from Chaucer to Swinburne affected him deeply, and some of Winters' dedication to the tradition grew from that shock and joy.

His habit of judicial criticism began at that time. His first negative review (of the *Fugitives* anthology) appeared in May of 1928. That is also his first review in which the tradition of English poetry is invoked for a negative purpose: to decry the Websterean blank verse of T. S. Eliot and his followers and to propose that Hart Crane was wiser in choosing Jonson and Marlowe as models. Briggs would have approved.

After that point, a great deal changed, but until 1928 his important work was experimental and in the imagist mode. The initial volume, *The Immobile Wind* (1921), is very soft Imagism—what Pound would call Amygism—and *The Magpie's Shadow* (1922) is an experimental *jeu d' esprit*, written mainly when he was in Sunmount Sanatorium under treatment for tuberculosis. Unable to concentrate his energies for full poems, he invented a six syllable poem, using as epigraph for the book Rimbaud's *O saisons, ô châteaux!* Winters' poems written from 1921 through 1926 and collected as *The Bare Hills* in 1927 compose his first mature and complete book of poetry.

Of the forty-five poems in *The Bare Hills* only twelve were preserved in the 1960 *Collected Poems*. The book is complex in its organization, so that rather than going into that problem, I should like to confine myself to considering only two characteristic poems, both written in winter of 1926, both favorites of Winters, neither poem singled out for praise by Hart Crane or Allen Tate (though Crane quoted two lines favorably from one of the poems), both omitted from the 1960 *Collected Poems*.

THE DEAD: MAZDA WAKE

Hard chair and table
skeleton of feelings
carved away by glassy light

> condensed in
> grief the old man
> walks beside the bed or
> lifts the flamepure sheet
>
> to see this
> woman: jagged grip on Space
> deposited by life
> a thought made visible
> in wrinkle upon wrinkle
> not to be forgotten
>
> but now done and gritty
> gathered at his feet.

The poem is in many ways characteristic of the book, the compact free verse, the literalness of the details ("Mazda"—a trade name for electric light bulbs), the glassy light, the table and chair's being hard, carved to skeletal form by the electric glare, the futile loneliness of the old man, the harsh definition of life as "a thought made visible," the ultimate futility as the once living and still wrinkled unforgettable being becomes gritty dust. The book is very bare, as are the hills of the Rocky Mountain states—Colorado, Idaho, and the mountainous sections of New Mexico where almost all the poems are set. The poem is followed by a poem on survivors:

> THE GROSBEAKS
>
> The beauty of
> these hard
> small birds is
> clean as scattered seed—
> dry penguins
> of the cliffs of light!
>
> Along crushed hills
> they flutter watching men
> who drag the earth
> and lengthen
> into wrinkles
> above thickening frost.
>
> They leap into
> the air and
> gather,
> the blown chaff of
> stony ground, and
> so are gone.

These were two poems Winters especially liked when he was preparing the volume for the press. We might say that birds are not "hard," but Winters is speaking of both the toughness of these small birds in a hostile environment and their beauty. The comparison or rather identification of them with penguins at first seems not appropriate—a grosbeak is a small fraction of the size of a penguin—but the identification is also a contrast between the bird overlooking the rich sea and the bird perched on the harshly lit cliffs of a barren countryside. They flutter above men harrowing the earth of infertile lands with unpredictable frosts. The birds become so identified with the soil that as they rise and gather, they seem like chaff from a stony ground, tough beauty in these hills crushed by massive movements and erosions of the earth.

There are better poems in *The Bare Hills*, but these are among the chief poems that Winters liked at the time (along with "The Rows of Cold Trees" and "The Barnyard"). The poems have a tense integrity, and although I have stressed two poems that are harsh in image and situation, the book has genuine variety. In a strange sense, the book is better than the sum of its poems, has an impact that is neither charming nor engaging but stirring in a manner that few other poets of the 1920s achieved. *The Bare Hills* asks to be read as a book, not as a collection of poems accidentally cast together. As for the general tone of the book, Winters was extremely susceptible to the effects of his immediate environment, so that the concentration on the seasons, the insistence on rock and spare vegetation, and the persistent sense of cold and fire are natural products of living in the unpredictable climatic changes and the harsh beauty of New Mexico, Colorado, and Idaho. The speculations, often ironic, on Christ and God and literature are reminders of a cultural bareness that fit the geologic bareness of the hills, and the sudden intervention of the love poems beginning with "March Dusk" and ending with "Midnight Wind" brings unsettling passion and affection into the inhospitable world.

The same qualities appear in the *Fire Sequence* (selected from poems written from spring of 1926 through autumn of 1927), both in subject matter and measure. Winters wrote mainly in free verse with occasional deviations into the prose poem. The notation remains spare. There are more poems in the dramatic monologue form and the solitude of the poet is not so severely stressed. These two volumes seem to me excelled only by the then current work of Williams and Crane (the sections of *The Bridge* that make it an extraordinary poem, not the three sections written after "The River" in 1927). Leaving aside the work of the expatriate poets and Stevens, who was not writing or publishing at the time, these poems certainly compare favorably with those of Jeffers, MacLeish, Tate, and other contemporaries. They would ultimately not satisfy Winters, and in fact, *The Fire Sequence* is an accomplished book but a dead end. Winters had done what he could do with the measures used in these two distinguished books, though his sense of the unit of poetic notation, the image, would remain constant in his later work.

Hence *The Proof* of 1930 is genuinely transitional, for at least three of the poems (possibly more) were originally part of *The Fire Sequence* in its manuscript form as Crane and Tate read it, and only with "The Moralists" in the summer of 1929 did Winters commit himself completely to accentual-syllabic lines. Most of the poems that are thought of as the characteristic work of Yvor Winters follow that date. For readers who think of Winters as a minor follower of Robert Bridges there is no hope (largely because those who mock the poems written by Bridges through 1900 must be barely literate or have tin ears or both). But Winters did not write like Bridges any more than he wrote like Jonson or Dickinson. Winters was a thoroughly modern poet, treating in a very modern manner the recurrent problems of mankind. Whatever use he made of traditional measures was conditioned and qualified by his thorough immersion in modernism. The fact that he remained skeptical about certain directions and tendencies of our poetry, especially since 1912, merely indicates the depth of his engagement.

In the current *Collected Poems*, the poems from page 115 through page 188 demonstrate an integration of the modern with the traditional that bears comparison with any of the modern writers of lyric and meditative verse. It is not merely funny that Winters should have said of Robert Graves that he showed a certain engaging boyishness in his verse; it happens, alas, to be all too true. Winters wrote a genuinely mature poetry. For those who are willing to give Winters an even break, good poems to start with are "The Slow Pacific Swell," "The Marriage," "On a View of Pasadena from the Hills," the poems on classic myths ("Apollo and Daphne," "Alcmena," "Theseus: A Trilogy"), the poems on the frontier ("John Day, Frontiersman," "John Sutter," "The California Oaks," "On Rereading a Passage from John Muir," "The Manzanita"), "To the Holy Spirit." At first, it might be wise to leave aside the occasional poems, though they often have a more than passing interest (notably the poems on the David Lamson case). But I should like to conclude this brief review with a poem that I have read and cherished for years and which seems daily more poignantly beautiful:

AT THE SAN FRANCISCO AIRPORT
To my daughter, 1954

This is the terminal: the light
Gives perfect vision, false and hard;
The metal glitters, deep and bright.
Great planes are waiting in the yard—
They are already in the night.

And you are here beside me, small,
Contained and fragile, and intent
On things that I but half recall—
Yet going whither you are bent.
I am the past, and that is all.

But you and I in part are one:
The frightened brain, the nervous will,
The knowledge of what must be done,
The passion to acquire the skill
To face that which you dare not shun.

The rain of matter upon sense
Destroys me momently. The score:
There comes what will come. The expense
Is what one thought, and something more—
One's being and intelligence.

This is the terminal, the break.
Beyond this point, on lines of air,
You take the way that you must take;
And I remain in light and stare—
In light, and nothing else, awake.

There is so much merit in the poetry of Yvor Winters, both in what it conserves and what it suggests, that the American literary community disregards it at great risk. There is such hard work, such integrity, such accomplishment in his *Collected Poems* that for many it may present a revelation of poetic possibility and achievement, these apparently simple, untranslatable poems.

Reprinted from *Georgia Review*, 1980.

18

Kenneth Rexroth, Poet

Many readers have difficulty in disengaging Rexroth as poet from Rexroth as social critic, Rexroth as man of letters, Rexroth as poetic warrior carrying on a vendetta with those who do not see the world of poetry as he does. One distinguished writer remarked scornfully in my presence that he did not consider Rexroth a poet but a politician. In the interests of dinner table decorum I didn't bother to press him to a clearer definition, but the remark was so pejorative in tone that it was hardly necessary. Now the poetic community has before it the *Collected Shorter Poems* and the *Collected Longer Poems* from New Directions, and the matter is there to be explored afresh.

I say "explored" deliberately, because magisterial criticism seems to me impertinent to most current literature, and because the poetry of Rexroth is special in the contemporary canon: because it gives a world to explore, it is not predicated on convention or a break from convention, it is not tuned to the sequence of fads that absorbs so much energy better invested. In an age of fashions without style, this body of work has style. There is integrity of manner because there is integrity of vision that is not clouded by polemics or confined to the merely aesthetic. The poetry articulates, often overtly but more often by example, a devotion to the contemplative life. Insofar as it is a record of events, it records the anguish and reward of pursuing the contemplative life in a world of spiritual, religious, environmental, and economic agony. When the world intrudes on the quest it is sometimes met with fury and invective, scorn, sarcasm, contempt, and hatred.

Style is a by-product. Writers of stature do not say, "I must develop a style," and then go about deliberately seeking mannerisms that will set them apart from their contemporaries and past convention. Style is a by-product of an habitual disposition toward experience. The man who devotes his life to an art or to the arts does so because he has a love for the medium of that art and what has been accomplished through that medium, and he has an intuitive and often secretly arrogant belief that he has something to do with or say through that medium, something of importance. He is persuaded (with little objective reason persuaded), with the fatality of birth, that there is something he can do that no one else can do, and that the art is his work. He has a vocation. How many people have felt that persuasion and then, after disappointment and neglect, sometimes justified, have turned to some other mode of being. Henry James said once that a man can be taught the techniques of an art but he cannot be taught the one necessity, courage. To be an artist at any time demands courage; to be an artist in California from 1927, when Rexroth first established himself in San Francisco, through the Reagan regime, when Rexroth resettled in Santa Barbara, demands heroism.

And he will have something to do with or say through that medium. The implied distinction sets Rexroth apart from, say, Ezra Pound. When Rexroth writes of the Revolution of the Word, he is saying something very complex. Certainly he has in mind the *logos*, and there is an underlying religious motive. Certainly too he is thinking of the revolution of the word that began with Baudelaire and Whitman, continued through Pound and Apollinaire, and is the heritage of the modern age, the attempt through changing the medium of verse to change sensibility and hence in effect the structuring of society. But he also means the revolution *through* the word, and his affection for the poetry of D. H. Lawrence is revealing (for Eliot was quite right in saying that in Lawrence's poetry at its most transcendent one is not aware of the poetry but of what one is seeing through the poetry). Like any poet, Rexroth is concerned with what he can do *with* the medium, but his stress is on what can be done *through* words. He uses as epigraph for his *Collected Shorter Poems* a translation from an anonymous Provençal poem:

> When the nightingale cries
> All night and all day,
> I have my sweetheart
> Under the flower
> Till the watch from the tower
> Cries, "Lovers, rise!
> The dawn comes and the bright day."

Poets growing up between 1920 and the present have used Ezra Pound's early poems as the best working out of poetic problems. Rexroth knew this, and his incidental comments in conversation on Pound's prosody set all those young associates, as I then was, wondering. Pound rendered the same person:

> When the nightingale to his mate
> Sings day-long and night late
> My love and I keep state
> In bower
> In flower
> 'Till the watchman on the tower
> Cry:
>> "Up! Thou Rascal, Rise,
>> I see the white
>>> Light
>>> And the night
>>>> Flies."

Here is a difference.

The Pound version is a pedagogue's delight, and that was one of Pound's functions. He instructed an entire generation of American poets. Seldom has the poetic game been so nakedly given away; the leading of vowel tones that Duncan talks about mysteriously is not one bit a mystery here. The diphthong *ai* takes control, and finally the diphthong *ai* dominates and concludes. The poem is formulated in circular design—it is all there, evident. Who can not like it, teacher, student, or poet? Rexroth knew all that, and deliberately set about determining the motive of his collected shorter poems by denying it.

The Rexroth version does not point to itself but to the experience. Anyone who thinks that this is an accident has very little sense of the recent history of poetry—the Pound version points to itself, to its fine shadings, to its subtleties, to its movement and recoil and ultimate satisfaction of expectations established in the opening line. Irresistible. I admire it gratefully—any pedagogue would—but there is something lost to the experience in the Pound version. Rexroth appeals to the common experience of the dawn song, Pound to the overt artifice of his special treatment.

The Pound poem makes a convention new: the Rexroth poem attempts to recreate a traditional experience. The difference represents in miniature Rexroth's definition of his poetic function. Conventions irritate him to the point of indifference, so that he is not even interested in destroying them. Traditions, the core experience of the race, as embodied in wisdom whether poetical or philosophical or historical or religious—these are the substance of his concern. He writes poetry to discover and render wisdom. Wisdom is useless knowledge, knowledge after the fact, and the fact never recurs in precisely that form. It is not paradoxing to say that genuine wisdom is unique in the same way that a genuine poem is. It makes a generous accurate statement about the special form that a universal recurring problem, and an insoluble one, takes. The human effort to be good, the hunger for righteousness, is its sad area for contemplation.

This is why, after the first two books, *The Art of Worldly Wisdom* and *In What Hour*, Rexroth settles into a relatively fixed mode of prosody, normally syllabic in structure. Although sympathetic to innovative writing, he publishes few experiments with language because of his basic persuasion that what poetry lets us see is more important than its texture, that verbal process is only incidentally revelatory, that knowledge, experience, understanding are the materials. His admiration for Tu Fu, Catullus, Baudelaire, Lawrence, and Stevens shows his own motivation. That is the lineage of the visionary and moral traditionalist.

But Rexroth has his special particular tone, that of the civilized man in a barbarous world, self-conscious and socially aware, speaking in an urbane ironic voice. Of art and letters, girls and wine, food and politics, children and music, nature and history, the conversation of a club that never existed on land or sea. Perhaps, thinking of the poetry, the hardest thing to comprehend is just that tone—all one can do is listen, for its modulations, its sudden surge to anger, its suave inversion of its own plausibility, its tinge of sadness, its rage against insensitivity. It goes on talking, talking, a reminder of possibility in the darkening years.

This was the ground of his appeal, especially with the poems from *The Phoenix and the Tortoise* on to the present. Nobody else was thinking of writing poetry in just those terms. Nobody else had the boldness to define his poem's subject as so large and inclusive:

> . . . And I,
> Walking by the viscid, menacing
> Water, turn with my heavy heart
> In my baffled brain, Plutarch's page—
> The falling light of the Spartan
> Heroes in the late Hellenic dusk—
> Agis, Cleomenes—this poem
> Of the phoenix and the tortoise—
> Of what survives and what perishes,
> And how, of the fall of history
> And waste of fact—on the crumbling
> Edge of a ruined polity
> That washes away in an ocean
> Whose shores are all washing into death.

It could have been written yesterday; it was published in 1944. Rather than talk about the two formidable collected volumes, I should prefer to look closely at the volume that for me still embodies the reasons for my admiration and indebtedness to the poetry of Rexroth.

II.

I have several copies of *The Phoenix and the Tortoise*. One of them is worn from reading. The binding is broken. I don't know how many times I have read it. Except for books used in teaching, very few books in my library show equivalent wear.

> The seasons revolve and the years change
> With no assistance or supervision.
> The moon, without taking thought,
> Moves in its cycle, full, crescent, and full.
>
> The white moon enters the heart of the river;
> The air is drugged with azalea blossoms;
> Deep in the night a pine cone falls;
> Our campfire dies out in the empty mountains.
>
> The sharp stars flicker in the tremulous branches;
> The lake is black, bottomless in the crystalline night;
> High in the sky the Northern Crown
> Is cut in half by the dim summit of a snow peak.
>
> O heart, heart, so singularly
> Intransigent and corruptible,
> Here we lie entranced by the starlit water,
> And moments that should each last forever
>
> Slide unconsciously by us like water.

I have been reading this poem for twenty-five years with deepening pleasure. It is not a pleasure that comes from recognizing new relations within the poem that had evaded me before but instead a joy that grows as my experience grows, makes the poem more true because I have, at least quantitatively, more opportunity for knowing what the truth is or might be. The quietness of notation, the directness of knowledge, the attentiveness that lets us see in what fullness it is that the natural world lives on without assistance or supervision, the rightness of the perceptions. Perhaps the poem has conditioned my experience so that it has become difficult to distinguish between the two, but if so its power is dual, the power to alert the sensibility, the power to vindicate.

There are others of the short poems that show the same kind of imagination at work. The view here shown, of the break between man and nature, the adoration of a natural structure that has an integrity and beauty of design beyond human touch or apprehension, the elegiac realization of human separation from such an order, its failure to *be* in a way analogous to the biological and astronomical order— there is great poignance in it. The poem immediately following it shows the same basic biological design:

Now, on this day of the first hundred flowers,
Fate pauses for us in imagination,
As it shall not ever in reality—
As these swifts that link endless parabolas
Change guard unseen in their secret crevices.
Other anniversaries that we have walked
Along this hillcrest through the black fir forest,
Past the abandoned farm, have been just the same—
Even the fog necklaces on the fencewires
Seem to have gained or lost hardly a jewel;
The annual and diurnal patterns hold.
Even the attrition of the cypress grove
Is slow and orderly, each year one more tree
Breaks ranks and lies down, decrepit in the wind.
Each year, on summer's first luminous morning,
The swallows come back, whispering and weaving
Figure eights around the sharp curves of the swifts
Plaiting together the summer air all day,
That the bats and owls unravel in the nights.
And we come back, the signs of time upon us,
In the pause of fate, the threading of the year.

James Broughton once said about the reputations of Bay Area artists, whether poets or film-makers, that they suffered in relation to those of New York artists because they were interested in, believed in, natural and aesthetic beauty, were not at all bashful in reacting to it or trying to make it. The beauty of this poem—and it is beautiful—parallels the beauty of, grows from, the natural order of the world. The poem has faith in that order, even to the weaving and unweaving of flight patterns by swift, swallow, bat, owl. The subject is old. In the Mediterranean spring and summer, whether in Italy or California, I am moved by the changing of the guard when the swallows suddenly seem to diminish and move more clumsily because the bats have taken over— there is a poem dimly in my memory on the subject. It must be one of the genuinely classical human observations.

The poem's faith in the almost military regularity of nature, the breaking of ranks by the cypress trees, the swifts' changing of guard— this is not an aesthetic but an experienced order: "The annual and diurnal patterns hold." The vocabulary of nature is limited but endless; the human entity is more varied but has a definite term, is not irreplaceable, as the fog necklaces on the fencewires are. There is pathos here without self-pity, and the curious thing is that this poet who speaks so frequently of personality as necessary to poetry, as inevitable, and does so sometimes with rancor and vigor that seem excessive to the subject, should himself become in these poems more type than person. Nobody else could have written such poems, but the style, as I have already asserted, is more the way of expressing a complex disposition toward experience than the assertion of personal uniqueness. These poems stand as refractions of general design, parts of the universe rather than expressions of a separate individualism.

The term "classic" keeps forcing itself on my attention as I contemplate this body of work. At times Rexroth exhibits that enviable gift of getting to the ground of experience that one sees in the poetry of Lawrence or Yeats when they are at their least effortful. The theme of these two poems is close to that of "The Wild Swans at Coole," but the poems are much more selfless than Yeats' moving lyric. For in one of its aspects, Rexroth's poetry strikes the same nerve as "I have a gentil cok" or "The Maidens Came," poems that are not often part of critical discussion because there is nothing much to do but admire them. His feeling toward nature has none of the egotism that afflicts Keats or Wordsworth or, to take the really egregious example, Hopkins. Perhaps this is because Rexroth has lived closer to wilderness than to what Europeans call "nature"; it is one thing to listen to a nightingale on Hampstead Heath and something very different to walk in the hills of Marin County or lie by a dwindling camp fire in the Sierra. Wilderness has a way of putting human emotions in their proper place.

At the base of many of the shorter poems, then, is the recognition of an extra-human order, non-social, transcendent. Yet there is no sentimentalizing of nature, no infusion of it with human quality. It is a measure and norm, indifferent.

Among the other shorter poems are numerous erotic poems, something set in wilderness, sometimes urbanely Roman or Mediterranean. Rexroth seemed to fix on several qualities in his life in California that extended to analogies to other cultures and geographies, and his favorites were the Orient and the classic world of the Graeco-Roman tradition. His later work would result in his book of translations from Mediterranean poetry and his two books of poems from the Japanese and the Chinese—beautifully printed, lovingly rendered, these books have achieved the status of ideal Christmas presents. Their tone was already present in the translations that conclude *The Phoenix and the Tortoise*, and it infused the style of the entire book. Somehow he discovered among the dreary stretches of Ausonius the one poem surely by him and genuinely fine. From the medieval *Carmina*, he chose the brilliant "Rumor Laetalis." They are adaptions—the tone is what mattered to him.

The special quality of this poetry, however, is pleasure in the language and in the experience. The pleasure grows from the clear fact that the poet knows what he means, he says what he means, and he means what he says. Sometimes the poetry appears declarative, what is sometimes disparagingly called the poetry of statement, as if cogency and fullness of statement did not in themselves have suggestion and overtone enough:

> . . . I have only the swindling
> Memory of poisoned honey.
>
> Poetry and letters
> Persist in silence and solitude.
>
> . . . In ten years
> The art of communication
> Will be more limited.
> The wheel, the lever, the incline,
> May survive, and perhaps
> The Alphabet. At the moment
> The intellectual
> Advance guard is agitated
> Between the Accumulation
> Of Capital and the
> Systematic Derangement of
> The senses, and the Right
> To Homosexuality.

These several statements, the cheated lover, the neglected poet, the saddened intellectual—all of them have the overtone of their voice, one that is widely diffused. They are characteristic, and compared to other verse of the period they have a quality of sustained judgment, of ultimate good sense, of wry factualness, that is extraordinary. The capacity for making judgments appear factual, to reify the moral imagination, is not so frequent that one can take such poetry lightly. It is not just that this was the way things were, but the way they are, their continuousness, and alas, their permanence.

III.

The long poem. Since 1912 the quality and quantity of poetry in the United States has steadily grown. Looking at the recent output of a small press sent to me for review, I find myself murmuring Yeats' words about the Rhymers' Club, "I don't know whether any of us will become great or famous, but I know one thing—there are too many of us." The very growth of poetic technique and skill, however, had for a long time a deleterious effect. First, the exploration of new methods turned the poet's attention from what he could do through words to what he could do with them—a very salutary thing for the art. The novelist knew no such inhibitions, and from Gertrude Stein and James

Joyce on, novelists incorporated the new poetic devices into their work until, finally, the novel had become so Alexandrian as to lead literary historians to declare that *Finnegans Wake* was the novel's funeral.

At the same time there was a determined effort to reclaim from the novel much of the ground lost by the modern poem's tendency toward the compact, the elliptical, the privately symbolic. These efforts are well known, and the line from the *Cantos* of Pound through Williams' *Paterson* to Olson's *Maximus* poems is clear to see. Crane's *Bridge* does not fall entirely outside that line of development, but its use of closed forms seems to shunt it toward another line of development.

The Bridge, The Four Quartets, The Phoenix and the Tortoise. The sequence does not seem exactly right, but it seems to me more appropriate than placing Rexroth's poem in the Pound-Williams-Olson lineage. In fact, Rexroth stands outside both lineages, but it might be helpful to see his poem in conjunction with the *Four Quartets,* which were written and published, except for the first of them, during the Second World War. For the *Quartets* are in effect war poems, poems written to celebrate the religious and historical continuity of England when that continuity seemed most menaced, poems also designed to place the poet's religious responsibility for the spiritual state of his world. *The Phoenix and the Tortoise* is also a war poem but written from outside the war, and from outside any state or national loyalty. Its loyalties are placed in another realm. At the same time, it is a religious meditative poem on history, on what abides and what perishes, on the place of man in nature and the cosmic resonance of individual responsibility.

"Meditations in a cold solitude." The cold in this line is physical, night by the sea, and the solitude of the poem comes from the contemplation of tragedy. Remote on the Pacific shore, there is nothing to sustain except what in the cultural imagination gets across the Sierra. His memory broods over, ruminates on, what makes for historical continuity as he stands

> . . . here on the edge of death,
> Seeking the continuity,
> The germ plasm of history,
> The epic's lyric absolute.

He can find that absolute in love, in the sacrament of marriage, in sexual abandon, in the imperious remoteness of geology, in courtesans and trivial survivals: the baby, the rose, the pear tree, the coin that outlives Tiberius, vulnerable mere data. Tragedy—

> . . . beyond the reach
> Of my drowsy integrity,
> The race of glory and the race
> Of shame, just or unjust, alike
> Miserable, both come to evil end.

History apart from irreducible values of biology and personality (in a sense not at all conventional) he sees from an Augustinian perspective. History, the public articulation of human energy, is evil and at best tragic, and the state is the organization on massive scale of the evil motives of men. In the midst of the Second World War, this isolated clear look has an austerity and compassion that are unique and, now, all the more accurate:

> Men drop dead in the ancient rubbish
> Of the Acropolis, scholars fall
> Into self-dug graves, Jews are smashed
> Like heroic vermin in the Polish winter.

Christianity, when its communal and metaphysical sanctions give out, places an intolerable and even paralyzing burden on the believer. Eugene O'Neill's life is one bitter monument to that fact. There are many others. Christianity cannot accommodate tragedy; all its habits and drifts are toward ultimate resolutions, and the insoluble it cannot admit. If one maintains the ethic of Christianity without belief in its rituals and dogmas, then all that sacrifice, repentance, and prayer are self-flagellating. The Augustinian doctrine of history without a Day of Judgment leaves one caught in a world of pointless cruelty. After describing some of the horrors of the Second World War, Rexroth shifts the burden to his own shoulders:

> This is my fault, the horrible term
> Of weakness, evasion, indulgence,
> The total of my petty fault—
> No other man's.
>
> And out of this
> Shall I reclaim beauty, peace of soul,
> The perfect gift of self-sacrifice
> Myself as act, as immortal person?

He walks on, through the light of nature, clouds, and sea, as the sun rises:

> My wife has been swimming in the breakers,
> She comes up the beach to meet me, nude,
> Sparkling with water, singing high and clear

Against the surf. The sun crosses
The hills and fills her hair, as it lights ,
The moon and glorifies the sea
And deep in the empty mountains melts
The snow of winter and the glaciers
Of ten thousand thousand years.

The answer is love, is sacramental marriage. In the terms of Rexroth's preface, "I have tried to embody in verse the belief that the only valid conservation of value lies in the assumption of unlimited liability, the supernatural identification of the self with the tragic unity of creative process." This is to be achieved by the movement from the self to the other, and through that other to universal commitment.

Rexroth claims no individual credit for the idea, citing Lawrence and Schweitzer as predecessors:

The process as I see it goes something like this: from abandon to erotic mysticism, from erotic mysticism to the ethical mysticism of sacramental marriage, thence to the realization of the ethical mysticism of universal responsibility—from the Dual to the Other. These poems might well be dedicated to D. H. Lawrence, who died in the attempt to refound a spiritual family. One of the poems is a conscious paraphrase of one of his.

The Phoenix and the Tortoise is an attempt to portray the whole process in historical, personal and physical terms. I have tried to embody in verse the belief that the only valid conservation of value lies in the assumption of unlimited liability, the supernatural identification of the self with the tragic unity of creative process. I hope I have made it clear that I do not believe that the Self does this by an act of will, by sheer assertion. He who would save his life must lose it.

Unlimited liability is a product of the imagination. If a president who declared an aggressive war intervening in the lives of remote and innocent people had to conduct it by personally strangling each man, woman, and child of the "enemy," there would be no such wars. But since he has no personal responsibility, he can allow and even threaten and encourage actions that would make slow strangulation a welcome death.

One difficulty is that the people endowed with imagination are the ones most deeply hurt, in the moral sense. To live in the twentieth century with full imaginative sensibility operative at the highest level is to have a molecule painfully cut out of one's body each second of each day, as some peasant dies from fragmentation bombs, as some black chalks up another hopeless second in the concentration camps that are called corrective institutions, as some baby dwindles away from his possibilities in some disease-ridden hut or tenement. And those who are doing the cutting believe in their righteousness. "Why should we pour our money into the rat-hole of some slum? If you've seen one slum you've seen them all."

So the title poem of *The Phoenix and the Tortoise* stands in its integrity as a witness to the love of true righteousness, of mercy, of pity, of love, of knowledge and understanding. How can one be good in an evil world? the classic traditional question that never leaves us, our moral doom.

The poem seems to me the most perfect artistically of the long meditative poems of the twentieth century. It cannot be reduced to a series of barren meditations relieved by occasional bursts of lyric felicity. The texture is even in its interest and appeal. Rexroth can think in verse, and unlike so many of the large established poetic imaginations of the twentieth century, he is not a truncated man, a literary specialist with some cranky notions about economics or language or religion or history. He knows the fashions of his age, and he knows what is faddish and impertinent in them. He is not taken in by the thought of the moment that is there only to feed an empty desire for false novelties. The only comparable poems are Eliot's *Four Quartets,* and to choose them over Rexroth's poem strikes me as a foolish act. *The Phoenix and the Tortoise* is a saddening poem *not* because it doesn't shape a valid artistic form—it does—but because even the world of 1944, the agonies of that terrible war, seems more possibly habitable than the world that has come out of the post-war years. Now it would be hard to say that the annual and diurnal patterns persist, power is so heavily concentrated and so savagely misused.

IV.

I have insisted on talking of Rexroth as poet and concentrated on a single book in so doing because economy requires some selectivity. What I have said of *The Phoenix and the Tortoise* does not "cover" his poetry, which is diverse and rich beyond the limits of any single book. *The Collected Shorter Poems* and *The Collected Longer Poems* provide a massive body of work for exploration. The whole seems to me unique and overwhelmingly useful. Utility, beauty, integrity, fullness of vision, and a knowledge of the world that extends beyond the latest critical book on Mallarmé while including it. To Rexroth poetry envisions and embodies life on a scale and grandeur that none of his poetic contemporaries has attempted to reach. At the same time he has not neglected precision of observation, clarity of articulation, verbal play and prosodic invention.

In a curious way, for his fellow poets, and especially those younger ones who take him with appropriate seriousness, he doesn't tell us much about poetry. His later work, from *The Phoenix and the Tor-*

toise on, settles into an adaptation of Apollinaire's revivifying of the eight syllable line in French, with variations, and of modern poets in English Rexroth seems to have profited most from the study of Apollinaire. Still, if one wants the experience of Apollinaire's qualities, better to go to him directly. If one wants to learn the rich vocabulary of forms that is the heritage of the modern period, Rexroth has less to offer than Stevens, Neruda, Pound, Williams, Desnos, Eluard, Rilke, Yeats, even Auden. Rexroth offers something else, a model for emulation that one can neither imitate nor loot because it is all of a piece, a fully ordered design of a recognizable universe to which one can give imaginative assent. I don't know what the term *major* exactly means, but if the body of Rexroth's poetic work is not a major achievement, then we can forget the term.

Reprinted from *Ohio Review*, Winter 1976.

19

Reflections on Kenneth Rexroth

Kenneth Rexroth was born in South Bend, Indiana in 1905 and died in Santa Barbara, California in 1982. He spent practically all of his mature years, from about 1927 on, in California. Both of his children are California natives, as are most of his books. He was a relatively popular poet, although his critical reputation never, to my mind, equalled his accomplishment. There are many reasons for this. He published more than he should have, especially in his later years, and although he was a steady contributor to *The Nation* and *Saturday Review*, so that he had a national audience especially for his shorter essays, he did not have an altogether amiable relationship with some of the nation's cultural powers, partly because of their conviction that Indian Territory began on the west bank of the Hudson River and partly because of his volatile cantankerousness in matters of literary and intellectual politics. And he was a very difficult and unpredictable person. Alfred Kazin once described him as a "beatnik," thus expressing an unrelieved hatred and a perfectly awe-inspiring ignorance of Rexroth's work and his mind when it was functioning at its best, as it did most of the time. But then, Kazin gave the Berkeley campus one of its heartiest laughs when, in a state of panic, he asked his assistants for a large course in American literature, "How many of those students do you think are members of the John Birch society?" In 1963? And Kazin really meant it.

Rexroth's association with the beat writers has been much too heavily stressed. He was friendly to them, but then he was invariably friendly to young people concerned with the arts, as he had been with William Everson, Philip Lamantia, Robert Duncan and others in the period from about 1944 through 1950, in some instances promoting their work in published essays and through his influence with James Laughlin at New Directions. If he had not written an essay on writing in the San Francisco area in George Woodcock's *Now* Magazine, *Horizon* would not have published Philip Lamantia's dreadful essay, and I should not, in a moment of anger, have sent Stephen Spender a long poem to prove that I did not write like William Cowper (as Lamantia had said), and my "September Elegy" would not have been printed and accompanied by praise from Spender. I do not bring this up from egotism but to indicate the kind of impact Rexroth could have and perhaps to suggest something more important, that for many people Rexroth was a central figure in their intellectual and artistic development, not only for the beat writers. It is true that Rexroth was receptive to Ginsberg when he first appeared at his home in 1955, and sent him to talk with me. One night at his apartment I met an intense young man who immediately thrust a poem on me, and that young man was Michael McClure. After reading the poem ("Point Lobos: Animism") I told myself that no matter what else he did, Michael should be trusted as an artist—he had written one wonderful poem. Aside from those experiences, the writers associated with the beat movement became known to me because Allen Ginsberg's little cottage in Berkeley, where I met Kerouac, Snyder, and Whalen, was at 1624 Milvia Street and our old farm house was at 1610 Milvia, so that while Allen was writing "Howl" he was also taking a special course with me in Whitman's prosody and was in and out of our house as a welcome guest. Kerouac was, as a manic lush, not welcome, and I heard at the time that Rexroth also barred him from his home. For one thing, he bewildered and frightened our young daughters.

Rexroth responded to the beat writers appreciatively; they certified the continuance of the revolution of the word and, like Duncan and Everson before them, presented alternatives to poetry growing out of and returning to a set of conventional assumptions that Rexroth found irrelevant to the state of the art and of the world. I avoid the term "academic," which Rexroth could enunciate with an unmatchable vitriol, partly because he did admire the poetry of Yvor Winters while disliking his criticism. In fact, Rexroth had typed out the early and inaccessible poetry of Winters from Library copies and had the poems bound in a folder. He had an equal admiration for the work of Janet Lewis. But he had little use for the Fugitives and little sympathy for writers machining their suburban poems while on Fulbrights. Rexroth was anti-establishment not out of resentment or envy but because he believed that the political and artistic establishments of the country were destructive to human freedom and to the truth. So he worked with some of the beat writers. He and Ferlinghetti read their poems to the accompaniment of jazz bands, though there was always an odd disjuncture between Rexroth's cleanly made poems on the Sierra and the sea and the dark smokey crowded rooms and the noise of jazz. There was in fact something a little droll about it. Ferlinghetti was much more in tune with that milieu. No matter how Rexroth might have wished it, he was no MacOrlan or Prévert.

He also wrote essays that promoted the beat writers' work, and he was very generous with his time. Eventually he came to feel that Kerouac was impossible, and that Ginsberg and Corso were entirely too avid for publicity. Something in him allowed him to keep an ultimate and absolute divide between poetry and public relations, no matter how much he wanted good popular poetry that came from social awareness and went directly back into the public consciousness. The beat episode was brief and by no means central to the enterprise that was Rexroth's career as poet and man of letters.

Poet and man of letters. It is in those terms that I like to think of him. And with Rexroth gone, there is a considerable gap in American literature that may never be closed. Malcolm Cowley and Kenneth Burke remain as monuments to that great tradition, but they are octogenarians, and neither of them was ever the imaginative writer that Rexroth was; neither wrote a book of poetry of the stature of *The Phoenix and the Tortoise.* That is the grand, accomplished book, though all of the books have attractive and often profound qualities. There are also the essays, especially those in *Assays* and *Bird in the Bush* and the brief evaluations of the classics of world literature that appeared in *Saturday Review* for several years and the review essays in the *Nation.* Nobody writes like that now, and nobody like him writes in such publications. A glance at the descriptions of contributors in any American magazine shows as much: _____ is (assistant, associate or just plain) Professor of _____ at _____ University. There are reasons for this concentration of ability in universities, but it is not entirely healthy to have the literary life of the country in the hands of people who have done nothing from the age of five except go to school and teach in school. One loss has been the familiar style. Malcolm Cowley sometimes publishes in magazines along with distinguished figures from the academy; the stylistic difference is immense and, as critical style grows farther from the spoken language, the loss makes the distance between literary thought and any literature non-academic audience practically unbridgeable.

Rexroth's best commentaries on literature were like his conversation, direct, colloquial when appropriate, frequently eloquent, always factually based. Some of the essays, notably the introduction to the *Selected Poetry of D. H. Lawrence,* are models of clarity and incisiveness; the Lawrence essay, like Cowley's introduction to *The Portable Faulkner,* changed perceptions of an important figure in world letters. Good as it was, Rexroth's prose work was generally written for money and out of love. It echoed those concerns that underlay his vision of life and art. He was a philosophical anarchist, modelling his thought on that of Prince Kropotkin. Isolated as he was, he had a strong drive toward community and a deeply concerned religious sense. His long experience of the plains and mountains and seaboard of the western states gave him a deep love of the natural world and a passion for natural order. Like Kropotkin, who directed the geodetic survey of Russia, he saw and passionately admired an order in nature that transcended the human and gave it a model. He had a strong feeling for ritual, finding ritual orders in nature, the passage of seasons and the designs of animal activity, and he had a deep and, in this age, by no means easily satisfied urge toward social and religious orders and rites that would fulfill basic human needs. At his best, he was the most civilized of men and his work had a civilizing mission. He was also remarkably funny, often in unrestricted language, as in his memorable description of a pompous and stupid literary figure: "Why, I've been farther around the shit-pot looking for the handle than he's been from Harvard Yard."

He embodied all this in his person, his prose, his verse. I have written in the previous chapter on his poetry. This is perhaps the most cultivated body of poetry written by an American, with an enormous range of subject and feeling and method. Some of it is trivial, and in his later years he seems to have lost the kind of concentration and economy that distinguished his work through about 1960. His later work falls into a design that touches too many poets, always excepting the very large writers, Goethe, Yeats, Chaucer. Only specialists can take seriously the later Wordsworth, and the old Swinburne is a great embarrassment. Whitman's health gave out; Arnold stopped writing poetry. Rexroth in his late years gives the impression of writing pale versions of Rexroth poems.

He had a wonderful productive time, however, and that should not and will not be forgotten. There is a genuine integrity to the large body of the best work of one of this country's few poets who was also a fine man of letters.

There was Rexroth, the public man, the poet and the man of letters. Then there was Kenneth, probably the most exasperating, unpredictable, contumelious, and abusive person that I have ever known. People who did not have close relations with him looked on him as a lovable curmudgeon on the model of H. L. Mencken or as a boorish Major Hoople. At times his private nature imposed on his public work, so that Alfred Kazin had some objective reason for his unmeasured judgment of him. There were times when the civilized veneer cracked and the original sinner emerged, rude, nasty, malicious, with a diabolic sense of what would most deeply hurt and offend his victim.

He was not always like this. He could be completely charming and generous with food, wine, conversation. It was a joy to take walks with him in natural surroundings, partly because of his evident joy in the weathers of the hills and partly because of his precise and wide knowledge of the flora and fauna. Walking with a highly trained entomologist once, he picked up an insect and said casually, using the Latin name, "This insect simply doesn't belong in this region," and walked on. The entomologist lagged behind and discovered that the insect was of a species that had never been reported within two hundred miles of Marin County. Part of the joy in these walks came from the fact that physical activity liberated his physiology, drained the adrenalin, eased his bleeding ulcer and relieved him from his sedentary and often unrewarded toil. And he enjoyed being with people in an atmosphere that was totally free from any sense of intellectual tension or competition. A few weeks after astonishing Hamilton Tyler with his identification of the improbable insect, he picked an argument with Tyler at his own home on the Potrero Hill. The subject was the Spanish Civil War. Rexroth was splitting kindling at his fireplace, and when Tyler (who had fought with the Lincoln Brigade and deserted toward the end of the war when he saw what the Stalinists were doing to the Catalan Anarchists, hiking away over the Pyrenees) offered some comments, Kenneth was furious. The little fact that Tyler knew the war at first hand and was every bit as anti-Stalinist as Kenneth did not stop Kenneth from flying into a rage, calling Tyler every nasty political name he knew (and he knew them all) and, in the process, chopping up a sizable piece of his fireplace. It was funny and neither Tyler nor I took it seriously. Kenneth forgot it almost immediately and had no idea what had happened to the fireplace until his wife, Marie, explained it later.

He had no idea what had happened. After a few disturbing episodes with Kenneth it occurred to me that he had a discontinuous personality that made him morally unpredictable. If one wanted the rewards of Kenneth's company, the company of the best-stocked mind and the most willing pedagogue and brilliant conversationalist that I have known (possibly excepting Robert Duncan) among literary people, then there was a price to pay. If the price got excessive, one could always leave. In a week's time, he would not remember that in the middle of an amiable conversation he had suddenly, on my getting up to stretch and standing briefly at my full height of two meters, said in a tone of boundless contempt, "You freak" and then gone on with the conversation as if nothing had intervened. He knew with part of his mind that he had expressed rancor (and envy) but that part flickered on and off, as it had with Tyler. Some people took the abuse from physical fear. From some points of view Kenneth may have looked large, but he looked easy enough to handle from my point of view, and there were moments when I came pretty close to showing him just how easy it would be. But what do you do with a discontinuous personality? You can't change it. Sometimes the events were not accidental but consciously intended, and of course at those times one would respond, often with explosive results. But such instances were infrequent.

Sometimes they were serious: all of his friends had longish periods of estrangement from him, and by the end of his life none of the friends that had known him for years would go near him. The last time I saw him, his wife Marie (by then his ex-wife twice removed) was present and she said brightly, "Isn't it strange that Tom is the only one of your old friends that still comes to see you?" He fixed that by spreading the bloody lie that I had stolen his letters from Dylan Thomas, a slander that would not have helped the reputation of a man whose major scholarship is based on the use of manuscript material by modern poets. Well, he had an awful sense of how to get at the jugular. That was enough for me.

Others had parallel experience and can speak for themselves. They almost certainly will, but it is my sincere hope that people will learn to put the breaks in this discontinuous personality in perspective. Looking back on my years of knowing Kenneth, I discover an affectionate amusement and profound gratitude, so that the irritations diminish in any considered view. It was enormously amusing, for instance, that Kenneth should have given his annual forgiveness party on his birthday near Christmas when he would invite all the people he had insulted during the year so that *he* could forgive *them*. That night his home was always crowded. Gratitude is another matter. Kenneth was the greatest natural teacher that I have ever seen, and I learned more from him than from any other single person, even those college teachers who gave me so much of themselves and of their knowledge, even my friends and contemporaries among the poets and my gifted colleagues at Berkeley. There was a grand scope and ambition to his knowledge. One poem in *In What Hour* is titled Gic to Har, and in the poem he is once again idling through the Britannica, bored with what he already knows, tired of knowledge and committed to it, when he comes across a picture of a grosbeak. He undergoes a Proustean moment that evokes his first grosbeak and he becomes once again a boy who could experience the glory of the bird and its song. Not one of his best poems and easy to parody, but the truth is that Kenneth's knowledge was encyclopedic. Sometimes I would get a little weary with the knowall tone and what seemed like pretentiousness, but whenever I knew a subject very well, Kenneth's knowledge was amazingly accurate and inclusive. One came to trust it. The fact is that Kenneth really did read the Britannica through, and whenever a subject engaged his attention he got it up. He was self-educated but rarely showed the horrors of unskilled labor and he should not have let the job out—he did it very well. He knew what many holders of higher degrees (he never graduated from high school, he liked to brag) do not know: he knew how to learn, which is all that education can give us and seldom does.

Kenneth represented something very important in the world of knowledge and learning. For younger people like myself, and I was barely twenty when I first met him, knowledge can be a passion and learning a primary concern, equivalent to sex or religion. They have intellectual passion, and in Kenneth they found a kindred and validating spirit. He had grand appetites. What seems to be missing in so much of current intellectual and artistic life is precisely that grandeur. It was perhaps fortunate that the great artists and thinkers of the modern world were not, until after the Second World War, subjects of systematic academic study. Kenneth's evenings at home were informal seminars in modern social and artistic and intellectual concerns.

This essay has already become too much of an intellectual autobiography, but that was the kind of shaping impact Kenneth could and did have on many people. When did one break with Kenneth? I never broke with my father and Kenneth was only fifteen years older than I was, more an older brother than father image. And, like the Turk, he would bear no brother near the throne. When younger people ceased to be dependent on him and reached any sort of personal achievement that was publicly recognized, the rupture was almost sure to come. And he was the efficient cause.

Sometimes I think that California's three best poets were not beneficially affected by their isolation, that it encouraged them in a kind of self-indulgence close to intellectual solipsism. Jeffers certainly was deleteriously affected by both his isolation and the sycophancy of the second-rate minds of Carmel, and Rexroth would have benefitted from the presence of comrades and equals. But when they emerged among the younger figures of the area, he would not accept comradeship or equality. Winters in his poetry was not affected negatively, but his criticism might have had a better balance if he had had more access to minds like Cowley's or Tate's; the immensity of his correspondence with Tate indicates such a hunger, and it was unfortunate that Kenneth Burke's residence in California came too late to affect Winters as benignly as it might have. But he was supported by a stable family life and children and by his obligations to students and colleagues. Most of the institutional supports that are necessary to grant a social identity were not there for Kenneth until too late in his life. By then his character was fixed.

These reflections are just that, some takes on Kenneth with no pretension to exhaustiveness. He had the essence of greatness in him and he partly brought it to embodiment in his work. If there was waste, pointless excess, occasional failure in human relations, how many of us can claim immunity to such dangers? He has left behind him a body of considerable work that will have permanent interest and the gratitude of many, readers and those fortunate enough to have been personally associated with him. He was in no way a saint but he was a man memorable and grand in many ways.

Reprinted from *Sagetrieb*, Winter 1983.

20

Robert Duncan's *Ground Work*

Robert Duncan's *Ground Work: Before the War* is his first extensive book from a national publisher since his *Bending the Bow* of 1968. Segments of the book have appeared from small presses ranging from San Francisco to New York to France and Australia. His work has been the subject of a critical book by several hands, and the essays in *Robert Duncan, Scales of the Marvelous* include extensive comments on some poems included in *Ground Work*. Duncan is fortunate in his critics, especially Jayne Walker, Michael Davidson, Thom Gunn, Ian Reid, and Sean Golden. The essays testify to the fact that Duncan's poetic work, taken as a whole, has a grandeur to it that is complemented by the scope and intelligence of his theoretical and practical work on the life of the poet. By "life" I mean here the continuing vigor and spirit of the work, and Duncan is a working poet, a maker, and as his admired predecessors are, part of a process that is at once natural, historical, and spiritual. Hence language and life become identified while remaining autonomous, so that they do not exclude or substitute for each other. The most extended and revealing appearances of his critical and theoretical work remain scattered in the numerous publications of sections of his *H. D. Book*, which reminds me more of Coleridge's *Biographia Literaria* than any other nineteenth- or twentieth-century work.

I do not compare Duncan and Coleridge accidentally or in order to grant Duncan high prestige. From all accounts, Coleridge's conversation was rather like Duncan's, and his extended prose shows, as does Duncan's, a remarkable appetite for being and for all forms of knowledge that can be subsumed in the poetic. The primary difference between the two resides in Duncan's playfulness, with language, and consequently with experience, that varies from the often magisterial seriousness of Coleridge. Duncan continuously experiments without conclusion, so that if a conclusion is drawn, that becomes in turn the occasion for fresh development. Nothing is "finished," both in the sense of intellectual and historical development and in the sense of the work of art, so that Duncan follows Whistler in that respect as he follows so many other American artists. Finish and accomplishments are not the ends of art, though they occasionally occur in the work. Keeping the imagination of possibilities matters more than any finality.

Duncan embodies many other qualities of the American poetic tradition, based in turn on the American political and philosophical traditions. Merely to pun on William James, his concern with the varieties of religious experience is validated by his pluralistic humanism and his espousal of radical empiricism rather than vicious intellectualism. As Dewey took James for a master Duncan in turn accepted both James and especially the Dewey of *Art as Experience* as part of his pantheon. Jefferson and Adams became mentors and he shared the anti-Hamiltonism of his immediate poetic masters Pound and Williams. And his beloved Whitman was always present as releaser of possibilities.

I stress the immediate American intellectual and poetic backgrounds because they rest quietly below the exotic, the Egyptian and Hermetic, the cabalistic, the Renaissance rhetorical poetics, the Dantesque, the Homeric, the French surrealist, in short, the Grand Collage which is at once the universe and the great continuous work of the world's artists. Duncan talks of himself as an imitative and derivative artist, but this seems to me his way of describing himself without pretension, even with ironic self-depreciation, as a traditional rather than conventional artist. He derives from the past, initiates and innovates for the future, and maintains a coven of contemporaries. The artistic community knows no break.

Continuity and tradition do not mean repetition. Originality for a poet like Duncan means getting at origins, finding the ground from which the images of the work arise and to which they return. Whether he is working from Dante's prose, Renaissance meditative poems, or Thom Gunn's *Moly* sequence, he works *from* them and *to* what they leave open or unexamined, so that the implications of Southwell's "The Burning Babe" extend to napalmed children in Vietnam, martyrdom enriched by and commenting upon martyrdom. I use the term "enriched" in a quantitative sense and with some ambiguity: the children are at once magnified and granted a wider human extension into a permanent horror that only love can counter and endure. As images they are enriched; as children they cannot be healed or saved.

The construction that Duncan forms around the Southwell instigation takes first the consuming greed of jealousy from his own experience and then contains the consuming impersonal military violence. The personal failing can through the image of the babe reach an alchemical balance. Southwell's vision is a trial to the soul, a difficulty, a judgment, that, revealing the unconsumable detritus of the person that is the bitter core, can bring a purging fire to the heart:

Robert Southwell, The Burning Babe

As I in hoarie Winters night stoode shivering in the snow,
Surpris'd I was with sodaine heate, which made my hart to glow;
And lifting up a fearefull eye, to view what fire was neare,
A pretty Babe all burning bright did in the ayre appeare;
Who scorched with excessive heate, such floods of teares did shed,
As though his floods should quench his flames, which with his teares
    were bred;
Alas (quoth he) but newly borne, in fierie heates I frie,
Yet none approach to warme their harts or feele my fire, but I;
My faultlesse breast the furnace is, the fuell wounding thornes:
Love is the fire, and sighs the smoake, the ashes, shames and scornes;
The mettall in this furnace wrought, are mens defiled soules:
For which, as now on fire I am to worke them to their good,
So will I melt into a bath, to wash them in my blood.
With this he vanisht out of sight, and swiftly shrunk away,
And straight I called unto minde, that it was Christmasse day.
[St Peter's Complaint with other Poems, April 1595—following his martyrdom
in the Roman Catholic cause by edict of Queen Elizabeth on February 21st,
1595, at Tyburn, after three years imprisonment with rack and torture]

from ROBERT SOUTHWELL'S *THE BURNING BABE*

The vision of a burning babe I see
doubled in my sight. The one
alight in that fire of passion that tries the soul
is such a Child as Southwell saw his Christ to be:

This is not a baby on fire but a babe of fire,
flesh burning with its own flame, not toward death
    but alive with flame, suffering its *self*
the heat of the heart the rose was hearth of;
    so there was a rose, there was a flame,
    consubstantial with the heart,

long burning me through and through,
    long time ago I knew and came
to a knowledge of the bitter core of me,
the clinker soul, the stubborn residue
that needed the fire and refused to burn.

Envy of the living was its name, black jealousy
    of what I loved it was, and
the pain was not living, it was ashes of the wood;
the burning was not living, it was
    without Truth's heat,
a cold of utter Winter that refused the Sun,
an adversary in the body against its youth.

In this I am self possesst of such a hoarie Winter's night
    as Southwell stood in shivering—
a shivering runs me through and through.

O Infant Joy that in Desire burns bright!
Bright Promise that I might in Him burn free!
His faultless breast the furnace,
my inner refusal the thorny fuel!

All the doors of Life's wounds I have long closed in me
break open from His body and pour forth
therefrom fire that is His blood
   relentlessly

"Who scorcht with excessive heat, such
   floods of tears did shed"

—it is no more than an image in Poetry—as though

"his floods should quench his flames,
   which with his tears were bred" until

tears breeding flames, flames breeding tears,
I am undone from what I am, and in Imagination's alchemy
   the watery Moon and fiery Sun are wed.

The burning Babe, the Rose,
the Wedding of the Moon and Sun,
wherever in the World I read
such Mysteries come to haunt the Mind,
the Language of What Is and I

   are one.

Duncan's imagination transforms the energy derived from Southwell into terms at once personal and international, so that the cosmic powers of "The Burning Babe" metamorphose into a Christ that sees suffering without purgation, the main horror spiritually and socially of the modern experience:

"A pretty Babe"—that burning Babe
   the poet Southwell saw—
a scorching, a crying, that made his cold heart glow,
   a fuel of passion in which
the thought of wounds delites the soul.
   He's Art's epiphany of Art new born,
a Christ of Poetry, the burning spirit's show;
He leaves no shadow, where he dances in the air,
   of misery below.

Another Christ, if he be, as we are,
Man, cries out in utter misery;
and every Holy Martyr must have cried
   forsaken in some moment
that from Christ's "Why hast Thou forsaken me?"
   has enterd our Eternity
or else is not true to itself. But now

I am looking upon burnd faces
that have known catastrophe incommensurate
    with meaning, beyond hate or loss or
Christian martyrdom, unredeemed. My heart
    caves into a space it seems
to have long feard.

I cannot imagine, gazing upon photographs
    of these young girls,   the mind
transcending what's been done to them

    From the broild flesh of these heretics,
by napalm monstrously   baptised
    in a new name,   every delicate and
sensitive curve of lip and eyelid
    blasted away,   surviving . . .
    eyes? Can this horror be calld their
fate? Our fate grows a mirroring face
    in the accusation beyond accusation
    of such eyes,
a kind of hurt that drives into the root
of understanding,   their very lives
    burnd into us   we live by

Victor and victim know not what they do
    —the deed exceeding what we would *know;*
the knowledge in the sight of those eyes
    goes deep into the heart's fatalities.
And in our nation's store of crimes   long
    unacknowledged, unrepented,
the sum of abject suffering, of dumb incalculable
    injury increases
the sore of conscience we long avoid.

What can I feel of it? All hurt
rushes in to illustrate that glare
and fails. What can I feel of what was done?
All hatred cringes from the sight of it
and would contract into self-loathing
to ease the knowledge of what no man
can compensate. I think I could bear it.

I cannot think I could bear it.

Even in the other sections of the Renaissance Suite, Duncan does
not follow the same procedure; the works evade categories. Moving
from Southwell and Jonson and Herbert to Dante creates another set of
possibilities, as do the marginalia to Gunn's *"Moly"* suite and the de-
signedly disparate and inconclusive series of *"Passages"* and the "Structure of Rime." The book sounds a bravura chord, exhibiting a range of
tones and voices, in a mode that Duncan mocked with playful seriousness in the first of the *Letters* of 1956 (published 1958):

Lists of imaginary sounds I mean sound signs I mean things
designed in themselves I mean boundary marks I mean a
bounding memorizations I mean a memorial rising I mean
a con glomerations without rising
1. a dead camel
2. a nude tree
3. a hot mouth (smoking)
4. an old saw (rusty edge)
5. a copy of the original
6. an animal face
7. a broken streetcar
8. a fake seegar
9. papers
10. a holey shawl
11. the addition of the un
    planned for interruption:
    a flavor stinking coffee
    (how to brew another cup
    in that Marianne Moore-
    E.P.-Williams-H.D.-Stein-
    Zukofsky-Stevens-Perse-
    surrealist-dada-staind
    pot)   by yrs R. D.
12. a table set for break
    fast

Duncan deliberately situates himself at the center of American and
European modernism, vintage 1924 or 1925 (the date wavers), including all his American coven and his contemporaries, especially those
first encountered through the pages of *Origin* magazine and known immediately at Black Mountain College, most notably Olson and Creeley.

"Post-modern"—the term comes to mind almost automatically,
which should serve as warning: Duncan does not ease into categories.
He admired and emulated Pound and Williams, but he loved the
nineteenth century, and although Eliot is not mentioned in this 1956
list, he too was one of Duncan's honored ancestors, as was John Milton, and Duncan's love of Whitman is much more unequivocal and
passionately informed that that of Pound or Williams. Whitman was
much too oratorical and operatic for Williams, and for Duncan the high
rhetoric and the over-arching arias of Whitman were both invitations
and satisfactions. Where Eliot and Pound qualified their enthusiasms,
narrowing their openings to poetry and reality in the process, Duncan
proposed reckless devouring appetites. He would not follow Eliot,
Pound, Moore, and Stevens in "the contraction and even the retraction
of sympathies" that he saw growing from their "sense of what respectable educated opinion is, the tolerance and intolerance of schoolmas-
ters of English Literature and Philosophy the world over." So he saw

them, however briefly, in *The Truth and Life of Myth,* his essay in essential autobiography of 1968. His exclusion of H.D. from the list of the squeamish is, in the context, clearly intentional, for she does not speak or think as modernist but as embodying and instigating what Duncan himself seeks, participation in primal creation that is artistic and religious; he is not making a religion of art or an art of religion but finding in the reality of experience and signs, especially linguistic signs, the reality at once in and of the universe that is many.

The universe that is many—that may seem a semantic solecism. What I am attempting to express is that for Duncan's poetry a belief underlies that artistic enterprise, a belief in an unfinished, unknowable but penetrable mystery that can be realized and momentarily stabilized through art. The way to exploration runs through multiple myths through which in turn the soul and the world undergo transformation and realization. This is a frame of being in which, as in the work (and universe) of Freud, there are no mistakes, even the slightest apparent error being a revelation and transformation.

The aesthetic that accompanies inevitably Duncan's sense of the ground and the work troubles commentary. In the preface to his "Dante Études," he says of the moment of writing, and of reading Dante, "What we took to be a stream of consciousness, we take now to be a light streaming in a new crystal the mind ever addresses. Dante again enters my thought here—even as I digress—and I feed upon prime." There are no digressions possible to this universe in which nothing is casual and there are no accidents. Later in the "Études" (Book Two) the poem is interrupted by the parenthetical statement:

(thank you, Jack Clarke, for sending me the Latin)

meaning the original form of Dante's *De Monarchia.* By definition what seems at first glance to be part of the stream of consciousness becomes a fusion of writing the poem and reading Dante, "a light streaming in a new crystal the mind ever addresses." Jack Clarke's place is justified as are those of Pound, Olson or Shelley, being necessary to both ground and work. The poet's mythopoeic faculty makes him part of the work.

Allusions in the modernist poetic bear the risk of attaining the onerous status of poetic diction in the eighteenth century which Gray celebrated in his letter to Mason because of its total separation from the language of prose. Duncan in his omnivorous way takes all proper names and all language of poetic tradition and everyday life as part of an unending vocabulary of potential forms. Duncan extends the possibilities of the modernist poetic to a field without bounds.

I deliberately invoked the "field" and with it Duncan's carefully unified and structured book *The Opening of the Field* because *Ground Work* presents a differing set. With *Roots and Branches* and *The Bending of the Bow*, *The Opening of the Field* paid obeisance to the modernist concept of the book, Yeats' *The Tower*, Eliot's *Four Quartets*, Stevens' *Harmonium*, Williams' *Spring and All*—the list is indefinitely extendable, but all these works can be subsumed under the notion of the intended and integrated. *Ground Work* does not so insistently stick or hang together. *Ground Work* fulfills the resolve made by Duncan in 1972 when Sand Dollar printed the new edition with preface of *Caesar's Gate*: "I do not intend to issue another collection of my work since *Bending the Bow* until 1983 at which time fifteen years will have passed." The inclusive book *Ground Work* collects collections and composes an aggregate or conglomerate. There is reason also to doubt that this is a collection of fifteen years of poetry, Duncan being naturally prolific and most of the poems centering around the period from 1969 through 1974.

Ground Work indicates several directions. First, there is the quality of the book itself, its vigor and range, and the one element in it that the book's aesthetic forbids comment on, that is, the unevenness of the poems and this discontinuity. Second, there are the implications of that very problem for the tradition that Duncan embraces and continues, the tradition that he (very properly) sees in Whitman and the line from Pound, Williams, and H. D. through Zukofsky and the Objectivists to Olson and Creeley and their associates. Basil Bunting's defense of the *Cantos* concedes what critics consider their unevenness and then asserts their value in his expressed contempt for negative reactions: "Fools! These are the Alps." The problem with the aesthetic involved in the tradition that Duncan carries onward resides in distinguishing Alps from molehills, or as Williams wrote to Pound in momentary annoyance with college students concerned with poetry, he wished they would be interested in poems. The autonomous poem can become a conventional notion justified only in pedagogical situations, but for Williams it remained a valid concept, so that even an Alp should be a mountain. His practice does not always suit the idea of autonomy from poem to poem, and his later and most influential writing holds to dramatic and narrative strains rather than the isolated or isolatable lyric. *Ground Work* pushes the notion of the serial poem beyond that incorporated in Duncan's preceding books, and it raises major poetic questions. Duncan is a grand poet, large in aspirations, omnivorous in appetite for experience, greatly learned and ideologically complex. His poetry can, accordingly, hardly be called modest.

Ground Work is a trial work, for Duncan a movement away from and beyond his preceding books. It would have been easy for him to avoid this shift and troubling of the image of his work, but the risk was to go on and become the imitator of Duncan. Instead he chose a break-ing point. The book also places the tradition that is Duncan's on trial. The recent study of *The Modern Poetic Sequence* by Rosenthal and Gall is uneasy with that tradition and manages to leave Duncan out of consid-eration. Without him the tradition is not only incomplete (it will always be incomplete) but will appear almost blandly secular, for Whitman, Pound, and Williams are Enlightenment figures and Duncan is a heterodox mystic in the heroic mold of Blake, as the variations on Southwell suggest. With H. D. he could admire Freud because he saw that the childhood of the individual was the childhood of the race, and form his mythopoeic imagination on that order.

Ground Work, then, has symbolic or symptomatic stature in the de-velopment not only of Duncan's poetry but of the American imagina-tion. The poems range widely in mode of reference while maintaining unity of tone. Readers coming to Duncan for the first time or after ear-lier but not full readings will find the following poems good induc-tions, and to my mind among the best work now being done in the art: "Achilles' Song," "A Song from the Structures of Rime Ringing As the Poet Paul Celan Sings," "Bring It Up from the Dark," all the *Poems from the Margins of Thom Gunn's* Moly, readings in the "Seventeenth Century Suite" and the "Dante Études," especially "Book Three," and the con-cluding poems beginning with "The Missionaries."

In addition to the poems, the prefatory *Some Notes on Notation* grows from the fact that this text has been prepared by Duncan himself as typist and photographically reproduced, so that the notation of this book is as accurate to the poet's imagination as can be. Duncan is a genuinely expert typist and for years made his major income by typing scholarly manuscripts or what work came to his hands. The prosodic problems posed by Duncan's poetry parallel those growing from the work of Whitman, Pound, and Williams, and Duncan indicates his mode of settling a way of noting the dance of language. The day may come when poetry returns through sophisticated electronics to its orig-inal vocal being; then the written or printed poem will be, in all senses of the term, a score. Notation of verse outside the syllabic and accen-tual modes has been puzzling and unsatisfactory, and the modes of verse that seem, at least superficially, measurable are hardly satisfac-tory, partly because of the often irrelevant application of the concept of the prosodic foot as unit.

Duncan's notes on notation are eminently sensible, and although they reflect his specific practice, they grow, as does the practice, from careful and reasoned participation in the imaginative modes of modern verse. These notes seem to me essential movements toward a rationale of verse that will bring into proper emphasis the basically kinesthetic nature of all poetry, its weights, measures, and silences. Poetry grows from the body and its being in the universe and returns through language to the body in its finest articulations. *Ground Work* accomplishes this grand intent, showing forth in the poems means of being and in the brief theoretical (and practical) notes on notation suggesting linear and syntactical rationales. Only greed would ask for more.

Reprinted from *Southern Review*, Winter 1985.

21

Yes, Beautiful Rare Wilderness!

My title comes from one of the rarest poems of our age. It is a poem of history, love, and the soul, and it has the advantage of being itself beautiful, dense and rich in its reference to the world of history and the world of desire. By now, Robert Duncan's "A Poem Beginning with a Line by Pindar" is the sort of anthology piece that runs into danger of being destroyed by its success, so that the next generation beyond my children might find it part of schoolwork. At least now it is not that, and citing it or thinking of it forces those who care about poetry to see their lives freshly.

It has many curiosities. There is Goya, Apuleius, Whitman, the political history of the American quest. It even seems caught by the kind of fatality that haunts Whitman's art, as if so much passion and hope had gone into the poetry that it has magical properties. Is there a terrible prophecy in the litany of bad presidents after Lincoln that makes the poem now, after the multiple assassinations, seem the expression of a desolate expectation? The poem asks, "What / if lilacs last in *this* dooryard bloomed?" Duncan might not, almost certainly does not, approve of Kennedy politics—but what of the poem itself, appearing at the time of the 1960 election? For it is a poem deliberately at the center of the American consciousness:

> Solitary first riders advance into legend.
>
> This land, where I stand, was all legend
> in my grandfathers' time: cattle raiders,
> animal tribes, priests, gold.
>
> It was the West. Its vistas painters saw
> in diffuse light, in melancholy,
> in abysses left by glaciers as if they had been the sun
> primordial carving empty enormities
> out of the rock.

The legends here enumerated and the melancholy grow even from the very force that will be accepted and evoked later in the poem, that of the beautiful rare wilderness.

The poem is too complicated to let any part of it stand for itself. There has for over a century been so much talk about organic form as to amount to too much—but this poem really is an organic form. To violate it requires a higher interest; wilderness is that interest.

II
"Those terrible implacable
straight lines . . ."

Yeats wrote once of "Those terrible implacable straight lines / Drawn through the wandering vegetative dream." He might have had in mind the Italian Gardens that would later be so finely and lovingly described by Georgina Masson, and to the point would be her illustration 133 of the gardens of Villa Dona dalle Rose at Valsanzibio. To an American eye, this photograph is downright frightening. There is no tincture of melancholy in it but the white blatant conqueror's arrogance, marble, gravel. The only relief permitted comes from the caption that indicates that the garden is now "an entirely green garden of deciduous trees and evergreens." To someone like me who loves the landscape of the Veneto almost as passionately as my native landscape and who prizes the elegant geometry of Palladio even more than the grotesquery that his designs permit as ornamentation, the garden sets tremors of doubt in action. There is no point in considering the concept of wilderness in looking at this vast implacable construct; nature, perhaps; cultivation, yes; artifice, above all. The garden is not really beautiful. The Renaissance attitude toward the natural world was not beautiful any more than Renaissance art was genuinely pleasant. Perhaps there was too much conflict between art and nature, between the triumph of illusion and the defeat of what was represented, nature being put in its place, and that a subservient one.

Is nature really a wandering vegetative dream? Does art have always to assert a contentious relation to nature? The sense of tangle and pointlessness that Yeats considers might well lead one to dislike both nature and art. The rectilinear mind; the designless clutter. These are not alternatives but menacing boundaries of possibility. Even the abstractions of the Renaissance mind that still coerce the imagination were violated by the demands of the great artists, so that Spenser and Shakespeare discover worlds beyond such bounds, as did Giorgione and Tintoretto. Yet the force of the later Renaissance was probably greater than its best products, so that the Cartesian view still prevails, as it does in the torturing lines from Yeats. This may be why the art of the twentieth century wanders off, why it bullies, why it dreams badly, why it terrifies whether through control or through messiness.

Taking the concept of the dream to another context, it is a mysterious psycho-physiological idea. What it seems to be is a re-ordering of forces, at once a release of energy and a fresh organizing. The nervous system lies at rest and prepares itself for new tautness; it even creates fresh intentness and resolve for its own protection. It siphons away what it takes to be waste and loss and substitutes gratifications for despairs. It pounds at limits and creates entire cities of trouble. The body excretes, turns, cramps, stretches with the mind. Controls are imposed and forgotten; bright unknown creatures compete with sad and altered friends or lovers. The body and mind become identical until the world calls, the cry of a bird, branches creaking against the roof, fog-horns sounding, the swish of automobile tires on morning dew. The identity of physical and psychic is broken; adrenalin pumps through the veins, and the biological clock declares that it is dawn for the body. The dream ends. It may be three o'clock in the morning with a cloaked moon. Momentarily the eye is still caught in its dream. Earth has changed. It is minutes before the chronological alarm will go off; it may be hours; the body and mind have conspired to take the human entity out of chronology. The person is ready to live.

Often very badly—dreams are not uniformly benign. Where the force for life, the direction of all that energy, its control, derives from is impossible to determine. Even if the reduction to libido is allowed as explanation, libido, its quality, its emotional worth, remains unexaminable. The dream at once expresses and issues into action, a social realm. The implacable straight lines are themselves superimposed dreams; the dream has design that is not random, is sometimes vulgarly self-indulgent, is sometimes a lofty complex of experience that is transcendent, but it hardly vegetates or luxuriates on its own. The more profoundly it incises, the more energy it releases or depresses, the more impersonal it seems, the more it asks to be watched on its own, independent, the apparent product of others that in some unalterable way concerns the dreamer. Concerns him: has important content for him; makes him concerned; touches, and more than touches, moves; yet and perhaps most important, maintains its own stability, is an other, a non-self.

In his Tavistock lectures, Jung italicizes his definition of the source and function of dreams: *Dreams are the natural reaction of the self-regulating psychic system.* The definition is peremptory yet tallies essentially with any psychoanalytic definition that has come to my attention.

Depth psychologists are further agreed that dreams are hallucinatory, they compel the suspension of disbelief in a commanding, even coercive, manner. They condense material in ways that are elliptical and deny rational order and connectives: they defy syntax. They distort material and effect a free placement of new relations; the result has symbolic force, suggests a missing context, and has affective power not limited to its structure. They promote the emotion of absurdity, and their ambiguity defies rational consideration—the temptation for those making analytical study is to substitute an entirely different structure for the dream itself. They are consoling and painful, often both at once in puzzling ambiguity. And they are guileless.

Much remains to be considered, but on contemplating even this selective outline of the dream's structure, it is no wonder that such critics as Frederick Crews and Franz Politzer turn their attention increasingly to psychoanalysis; for the critic, not to mention the teacher with his problems of transference (yet another realm for literary study that remains untouched), is in the position of the analyst facing the hallucinatory, condensed, distorted, symbolic, absurd, painful and pleasant, ambiguous and guileless object that is the artifact. For it is increasingly clear that the entire world, once placed within the power of men, is a dream or perhaps more accurately, a series of more or less related dreams, that experience is by definition experience of artifacts. The act of drawing boundaries around Yosemite National Park is an artificial action that forms and identifies shapes and beings into a relation that without the actions and refusals of men, would not exist, would effectively be destroyed.

Literary people until recently tended to accept Jung more readily then Freud. Freud's positivism, his Comtean theory of history, his relegation of spiritual and artistic experience to realms governed by powers other than their own, his abstract rationality—this was offensive because reductive. Even those scholars and critics not at all squeamish about sex, willing to accept the Freudean insight into the personal and social, were made uncomfortable at the reduction of art and religion to neuropathic or psychopathic symptoms. They were more cheered by Jung's acceptance of the "Big dream" as having a legitimacy beyond the merely personal dream of the neuropath. The big dream was symbolic beyond single troubles:

> The dream is the small hidden door in the deepest and most intimate sanctum of the soul, which opens into that primeval cosmic night that was soul long before there was a conscious ego and will be soul far beyond what a conscious ego could ever reach. For all ego-consciousness is individualized and recognizes the single unit in that it separates and distinguishes, and only that which can be related to the ego is seen. This ego consciousness consists purely of restrictions, even when it

stretches to the most distant stars. All consciousness divides; but in dreams we pass into that deeper and more universal, truer and more eternal man who still stands in the dusk or original night, in which he himself was still the whole and the whole was in him, in blind, undifferentiated, pure nature, free from the shackles of the ego. From these all-uniting depths rises the dream, however childish, grotesque, or immoral.

A great deal of mockery has been directed against Jung's primitivism, his love of the "dark" and irrational. I suppose objections to be drawn against this passage should stress this element in it; after all, when one returns to the original being, if that is possible, one returns to primal light. There is no reason, except Jung's self-acknowledged distrust and fear of the natural, for using such metaphors of blindness, darkness, and general messiness as distinguish this crucial passage. For it is crucial; it is an abstract statement of the very particular dream that, from the age of three or four, obsessed Jung's life and that accounts for much in his thought (the dream is described in his *Memories, Dreams, Reflections*). Sunnier minds would extend and alter this epitomizing passage. More decisive minds would shudder at the undifferentiated oceanic feelings here offered. They would be right to do so; just as one would be right not to repress giggles when reading Gutheil's *The Handbook of Dream Analysis:* "Most dream material is selected from recent experiences, but the experiences influence the dream plot only to the degree that they cause in it an echo of deep-seated personal complexes." By the time Gutheil gets through interpreting a dream, it is a wonder that any patient could recover from the insult.

The quality that Jung speaks to in his crucial definition is the quality of the big dream, the artifact that can be objectified to public reality: the dream of poet, architect, designers of aesthetic and political policy. Such dreams bring men together in a psychic community that unites while diminishing restrictions. In the presence of the big dream of Chartres, these conditions prevail, without the darkness of Jung's ambiguous vision, so that one's life is exalted and made common at once. And bad big dreams, the characteristic new Hilton Hotel, diminish and make common. *Those* terrible implacable straight lines assert nothing but the denial of the universal, the imposition of the neuropathic human ego. And what is true of aesthetic badness can also be true of the political badness of such public figures as Glenn Seaborg, chairman of the Atomic Energy Commission or Eric Hoffer, that smug wind-bag who once wrote of his ambitions for the earth:

One would like to see mankind spend the balance of the century in a total effort to clean up and groom the surface of the globe—wipe out jungles, turn deserts and swamps into arable land, terrace barren mountains, regulate rivers, eradicate all pests, control the weather, and make the whole land mass a fit habitation for man. The globe should be our and not nature's home, and we no longer nature's guests.

The ignorance here expressed is unmatched in my experience. It makes no difference that clearing jungles, as dreary knowledge accumulated in South East Asia has demonstrated, creates a phenomenon known as lateration that turns the cleared land into pure brick after a few years of exploitation and that the same results would occur in such areas as the Amazon Basin. Nor does it matter that the attempts to eradicate all pests have resulted in the eradication of substantial food supplies, so that the Monterey sardine has disappeared, the California crab is clearly on the way out, and such useless creatures as pelicans are practically certain to disappear along with such minor pests as non-malaria bearing mosquitoes and annoying gnats. This is a dream, and so sterile and disgusting a one as to leave any one interested in the quality of human life trembling with rage. I turn with melancholy pleasure to the mind of an earlier happier time, when some human humility co-existed with scientific knowledge and common sense:

Why animals and plants are as they are, we shall never know, of how they have come to what they are, our knowledge will always be extremely fragmentary because we are dealing only with the recent phases of an immense and complicated history, most of the records of which are lost beyond all chance of recovery, but that organisms are as they are, that apart from the members of our own species, they are our only companions in an infinite and unsympathetic waste of electrons, planets, nebulae and suns, is a perennial joy and consolation.

The joy and consolation that William Morton Wheeler derived from his lifelong study of the social insects means nothing to the political dream of the Hoffers and Seaborgs of the world. Franciscans like myself would prefer it if Wheeler had left some room for permanent spirits with infinite sympathy, but certainly his world is more readily habitable than the purely human world.

III
Futurism

The idea of progress dies hard, and science fiction persists in believing in it. Kingsley Amis calls his study of science fiction *New Maps of Hell*, and a few works have a view of the future that is hellish. Even in those, however, the great evil of the destruction of the earth is taken with some jauntiness, and if the earth survives atomic war and becomes a claustrophobe's nightmare of crowded billions, the escape to free space is accessible. The physical and astronomical knowledge that makes Wheeler's affection for the plants and animals of the earth so poignant seems to have fallen into discard. In science fiction it is always possible to leave the solar system, thanks to the hyperspatial jump, and though my scholarship in the area leaves something to be desired, Isaac Asimov seems to be the mischievous character who devised this piece of faster-than-light nonsense. Recently at Berkeley one of the military men who teach ROTC courses sent his class reeling into disbelieving laughter when he said that the Air Force had broken the sound barrier and were not going to be stopped by the light barrier, in spite of Einstein. He couldn't understand their rudeness.

The greatest work of science fiction, as Amis rightly points out, is *The Space Merchants*, by Pohl and Kornbluth; in a real sense it is not science fiction but in the category reserved to *Brave New World* and *1984*. In many ways it is better satire than either one, as is the only other novel by Pohl and Kornbluth, *Gladiator-at-Law*. Pohl and Kornbluth have trashy minds; they are not hip to the latest, so that people who can take Anthony Burgess' shamefully simple theory of history in *The Wanting Seed* seriously are not the audience for the pop sadism and topical satire of *The Space Merchants*. At the same time, I should much rather have people reading Pohl and Kornbluth than Burgess, in spite of his intellectual credentials. I suspect that *The Space Merchants* is considered science fiction because it makes no real linguistic experiments and has no intellectual pretensions.

But Pohl and Kornbluth remain within the potentialities of our life, with its annual meetings of corporations and proxy votes, its advertising idiocies and increasingly crowded unlivability, the world where suburban developments (Belle Rêve) become rural slums (Belly Rave) and the really subversive elements are the conservationists (consies). Other writers like E. E. (Doc) Smith are not so confined: even one galaxy is not enough for him. His Lensman series covers five volumes, ending with *The Children of the Lens*, though there is some slight menace that those dreadful children will also have children. Like many of the extended series, projections into the future of current tensions, this series has a clear relation to the cold war, which it seems to take with a kind of seriousness that I had always thought reserved to ex-Marxists, whether Soviet or American. The books are chiefly distinguished by so humanity-centered a view as is hard to imagine. In spite of his Arisians' concern with visualizing the Cosmic All, Smith shows little respect for the cosmos. Planets are considered not as entities that have some claim to respect but as disposable items in an intergalactic struggle. In spite of the alliances between Velantians and Tellurians a persistent ethnocentrism shadows all the action. Some of the aliens have powers concentrated beyond those of men, and are willing to use them for good purposes, but finally humanity is the most intelligent, humanity is the most warm and feeling, humanity, to no one's surprise, is the most human.

The futurism of this series is pernicious in exactly the same way that Eric Hoffer's dream for the rest of this century is: it dreams of total human power that knows no mercy or concern for the claims of any other biological entity. It is, when the light emerges, anti-human in the same way that the first chapter of Genesis is anti-human, i.e., it grants human beings powers that they have no claim to, it destroys sympathy—genuine objective capacity for seeing and knowing what rights "others" have—and it promotes arrogance and self-congratulation.

Why should I care about Eric Hoffer and E. E. Smith, and why should I admire two works that are, in any serious evaluation, subliterary? I think they demonstrate in symptomatic form very clearly what is *under* our literature, what is likely to explode in such a way that the ignorance of literary people will find itself surprised into chaos. They represent the major assumptions that govern the world at present, and I am constantly astonished that in attacking the governing forces, so many literary people accept those very assumptions. Pohl and Kornbluth may have very meager dreams to present, but they are dreams that recognize the enemy, the implacable straight lines.

The concept that nature was man's enemy is the basis of the idea of progress and the desire to terrace the barren mountains, clean up the jungles, destroy all entities not immediately and obviously necessary to man's survival. The result is a world that threatens man's physical survival and certainly diminishes his psychological harmony. Matthew Arnold chided the nineteenth-century gentleman who wanted to live in harmony with nature as a "restless fool," but he did not deny the legitimacy of co-existing with nature; it remains for the idolators of technology to do that.

It is not to the present point for me to suggest alternatives to the world that creeps over the entire landscape of this country, though I have several. What matters, I think, is the realization that our country, the entire human world, is no longer in conflict with nature but uneasily occupying common ground with it, for if the natural world continues to be corrupted by human power, there will be no more humanity. The dream of wilderness in Duncan's poem will be gone, but so will the poem and all that goes with it.

How to describe the planet without bringing in the idea of processing it—perhaps it helps to see it as the substructure of human dreams, so that the wilderness is equivalent to that mysterious realm that Jung and others have tried to bring into language and into action, tried without hope beyond some faint adumbrations. For that realm is not inexhaustible; there is no guarantee that any evergreen and deciduous trees will remain to reclaim the acreage of freeways when they decay from unusableness. Nor are the few remaining areas that can be called wilderness (they are really just ordinary nature by now) any vague wandering vegetative dream—they tend to be austere, thin of air, windy, with spare furtive life eking out minimal substance on the arid and rocky. They are diminished reminders of the rich mammal possibilities of the continent. In many instances they are grand rock gardens on a Japanese rather than European model, though on an American scale.

IV
The Poem

Whitman thought that these States formed the greatest poem, thinking of them as the expression of moving dreams of freedom against the backdrop of intact wilderness constantly replenishing the dreams. This sense of things prevails in the best moments of the best Americans; but the senses become daily more outraged as that poem diminishes, some odd manuscript deteriorating, written over with violent and obscene commands of exploitation and lying. The dream within cannot stand up against the nightmare outside, so that the poetry of these states becomes irrelevant to their objective death-in-life. An enormous bad poem.

The greatest poem is the earth, planet, enormous space ship threatened by entropy: a mathematical expression of the degree in which the energy of a thermodynamic system is so distributed as to be unavailable for conversion into work. The irreversible tendency of a system toward increasing disorder and inertness. In self-conscious beings, a reversible tendency toward self-abuse, suicide, murder, war, sadism, masochism, hatred of all outside the self, inability to realize the interdependence of beings that are others, non-selves though persons. America is an entropic center; Russia is an entropic center; China is an entropic center: how do I join the fourth world? *Poets and gurus practice firing murderous weapons in Marin County, shooting at the fourth world, the kingdom of life.* The very thought is an abomination, it exists.

Alone on the earth we seek the fourth world, wilderness, the true poem, love, freedom, cities growing from our own order. The earth is the greatest poem.

Reprinted from Thomas Parkinson, *Protect the Earth* (San Francisco: City Lights Books, 1971).

22

The Poetry of Gary Snyder

Gary Snyder was born in San Francisco in 1930. Shortly after his birth, his family moved to a small farm outside of Seattle, where he early acquired his proficiency with tools and animals. When he graduated from high school, Reed College in Portland wisely gave him a scholarship, and his senior thesis, *He Who Invented Birds in His Father's Village*, exhibits his early professional interest in the anthropology and mythology of the American Indians. During his youth and in summers while in college, he worked with the Forest Service and in logging camps in the Pacific Northwest, increasing his knowledge of the remarkable Indians of that area at first hand and further developing his expertise in the outdoor life. His primary experience has come from India and the Pacific Basin, that is, the three Pacific Coast states and Japan. After graduating from Reed, he broke that pattern by studying at the University of Indiana; his subject remained the anthropology and mythology of American Indians. He then returned to the Pacific Coast and enrolled at the University of California at Berkeley, where he studied Oriental languages, with special emphasis on Japanese. He completed all requirements for the doctorate except for a thesis, but he decided not to continue his formal studies because that would commit him to, or at least afford the temptation of, an academic career. His true vocation was poetry, and his cultural assumptions extended beyond the Far East to include the Far West in a vision of a Pacific Basin Culture. His travels as a merchant seaman in the Pacific and Indian Oceans gave him some detailed geographical perceptions, and his several years spent in Japan, much of them while in residence at Zen Buddhist monasteries, gave him a rather full knowledge of Japanese culture and language. Unfortunately, during those years, access to China was almost impossible; India, as I read his *Indian Journals*, was a source of grief and pity as, ultimately, the ruination of the Japanese environment became.

These preliminary biographical notes should indicate that Snyder's world-view grew organically from experience and basic impulses. The fact that some aspects of his view should have been taken up by the unskilled and unknowing as fads and fashions should not depreciate his hard-earned and solidly based thought, for Snyder is not interested in fad, fashion, or convention: he is interested in tradition, and he is concerned with constructing a valid culture from the debris that years of exploitation have scattered around the Pacific Basin.

RIPRAP was Snyder's first book. The title means "a cobble of stone laid on steep slick rock / to make a trail for horses in the mountain." In the last poem in the book he wrote of "Poetry a riprap on the slick rock of metaphysics," the reality of perceived surface that grants men staying power and a gripping point.

> Lay down these words
> Before your mind like rocks,
>   placed solid, by hands
> In choice of place, set
> Before the body of the mind
>   in space and time:
> Solidity of bark, leaf, or wall
>   riprap of things:
> Cobble of Milky Way,
>   straying planets,
> These poems . . .

The body of the mind—this is the province of poetry, a riprap on the abstractions of the soul that keeps men in tune with carnal eloquence. Snyder's equation is one of proportions: poetry is to metaphysics as riprap is to slick rock. Things and thoughts are not then in opposition but in parallel:

> . . . ants and pebbles
> In the thin loam, each rock a word
>   a creek-washed stone
> Granite: ingrained
>   with torment of fire and weight
> Crystal and sediment linked hot
>   all change, in thoughts,
> as well as things.

The aim is not to achieve harmony with nature but to create an inner harmony that equals to the natural external harmony. There is not then an allegorical relation between man and natural reality but an analogical one: a man does not identify with a tree nor does he take the tree to be an emblem of his own psychic condition; he establishes within himself a condition that is equivalent to that of the tree, and there metaphysics rushes in. Only poetry can take us through such slippery territory, and after *RIPRAP* Snyder tried to find a guide in his *Myths and Texts*. *RIPRAP* was an engaging, uneven first book of poems. It is still in print and deserves to be so, but it lacks unity of impact and style, however proper its intentions.

Myths and Texts is a different matter. Although some of the poems were printed as early as 1952 and Snyder gives its date of completion as 1956, it is a world away from the first book. It has a genuine informing principle and coherence of purposeful movement, and the line has a life that is particular to its subject. The first two sections of the book are on Logging and Hunting, what men do to the earth; the third on Fire, why they do it. In this book appear in complex form the issues that compel the verse at its base. He wants to reach a prehuman reality, the wilderness and the cosmos in which man lives as an animal with animals in a happy ecology. This precivilized reality he finds embodied in Amerindian lore, especially of the Pacific Northwest and of California, and in Buddhist myth. He occupies the uneasy position of understanding this mode of perception and of acting, as logger and hunter, against its grain. This realization is the dramatic core of the book and holds it from sentimentality, granting it a kind of tension and prophetic force (evident in the pro-wobbly poems) that *RIPRAP* and much of his later work lacks. *Myths and Texts* is an elegy of involvement: to have witnesed, it was necessary to be one of the destroyers. His sense of involvement keeps him from invective, except against those exploiters who ordered the destruction of nature and at the same time denied rights to the workers who had the hard, nasty labor. The world that Snyder treats is part of his total fabric, and he cannot falsely externalize it. He cannot point with awe to the objects of his experience because they have become attached to him through touch and action. It is not even necessary for him to lament this world which, through his poetry, he has preserved. He moves fluently through this world as a local spirit taking the forms of Coyote and Han-shan and a ghostly logger. In these poems action and contemplation become identical states of being, and both states of secular grace. From this fusion wisdom emerges, and it is not useless but timed to the event. The result is a terrible sanity, a literal clairvoyance, an innate decorum. This poetry does not suffer from cultural thinness. The tools, animals, and processes are all interrelated; they sustain the man; he devours them. But the author of the book and the poet in the book are nourished by a web of being, a culture. To have the support of a culture you have to work in and respect your environs, not as one respects a supermarket (thanks for the grapefruit wrapped in plastic) but as one respects a farm, knowing what labor went into the fruit, what risks were accepted and overcome, what other lives (moles, weasels, foxes, deer) were damaged or slighted in the interests of your own.

One of the touchstone lines for modern poetry is Pound's "Quick eyes gone under earth's lid." It holds its unity partly through the internal rhyme of the first and final word, partly through the unstrained conceit of random association between eyelid and coffin lid, and the earth as dead eye and graveyard. Mainly, though, it has no waste, no void spaces, none of the flab that English invites through the prepositional phrase designs of a noninflected language. Solid poetry in English manages compressions that keep up the stress, and relaxations from that motive have their justification in the larger poetic unit of poem or book. The temptation of composition in serial form, the method of *Myths and Texts*, is vindicating the relaxed line in the name of a higher motive, the world view of the poet, the personal relevance. Snyder doesn't fall back on such flimsy supports. Sometimes, straining to maintain the stress he loses control: "fighting flies fixed phone line . . ." This is not only pointlessly elliptical but meaninglessly ambiguous and far too clogged. But in its excesses it demonstrates the basic prosodic motive, full use of consonant and vowel tone as organizing devices, reduction of connective words having merely grammatical function and no gravity.

Snyder himself thinks of this prosody as deriving from classical Chinese forms, and both he and Pound make severe and interesting variations on that line. But variations, and since Pound's *Cathay* and the Chinese Cantos, people like Snyder are compelled toward Pound's brilliant invention of a line using the Anglo-Saxon alliterative line in conjunction with a line of four and two main centers of stress divided by cesura or by line break.

I talk at such length of prosody because it is the main factor ignored in most recent discussion of poetry. Thanks to Donald Davie and Josephine Miles, attention has very rightly been turned toward poetic syntax, with fine results, and the extension to prosody is inevitable and right. New criticism (old style) placed heavy weight on suggestion and symbolic reference; now, as our poetry stresses drama and syntactic movement, vocality, it seems necessary to supplement the notion, and a pernicious one, that poetry functions through symbol mainly. Language functions symbolically and metaphorically, but poetry makes more precise and delimiting use of syntax through its prosodic measure. This is after all what Pound and Williams were agitated about: the dance of language. I don't want to hang everything on syntactic and metric effects and take a plunge into providing new mechanical vocabulary that will deaden poetic study from yet another perspective. What poets like Snyder, Duncan, and Creeley ask is that readers take the poem as indicator of physical weight. Until the day, not far off, when poems are related to taped performances as musical scores now are, the poem on the page is evidence of a voice and the poetic struggle is to note the movement of that voice so that it can be, as is music, followed.

> The groves are down
>   cut down
> Groves of Ahab, of Cybele
> Pine trees, knobbed twigs
>   thick cone and seed
>   Cybele's tree this, sacred in groves
> Pine of Seami, cedar of Haida
> Cut down by the prophets of Israel
>   the fairies of Athens
>   the thugs of Rome
>   both ancient and modern;
> Cut down to make room for the suburbs
> Bulldozed by Luther and Weyerhaeuser
> Crosscut and chainsaw
>   squareheads and finns
>   high-lead and cat-skidding
> Trees down
> Creeks choked, trout killed, roads.

The procedures of the line here are largely halving and coupling and the variations are relaxations that reach out semantically to other results:

> Crosscut and chainsaw
>   squareheads and finns
>   high-lead and cat-skidding
> Trees down
> Creeks choked, trout killed, roads.

The violence of the first four linear divisions creates a tension that is cumulative; the dangers of the catalogue are diminished by the prosody so that it is not a simple matter of adding item to item but of seeing each item as part of design and pattern, a concern of yoked energies. The final line leaves a single word uncoupled, a result, a relaxation into barrenness. The poem is a perversion of religious ceremony, the text of life against the myth of natural sacredness.

This book thus creates and denies one of the greatest of American experiences, that of a wild ecology. But it is not merely American; the human race really is on the way to destroying the planet, if not by some mad, outrageous single explosion then by steady, careless, greedy attrition of all those qualities that have over the centuries kept men as sane as they have been. Curiously, although this has been the overriding historical fact of the past generation, only one extensive book of poetry has tried to tackle this problem as subject and come to some prophetic stance. Yet there is nothing pompous or portentous about *Myth and Texts;* it is genuinely contemplative. It has received no prizes, but over the years it may well become, for those who care, a sacred text.

In 1965, Snyder published *Six Sections from Mountains and Rivers Without End,* part of a very long sequence of poems. The book has some fine matter in it, but much of it is taken up by poems that are not sufficiently concentrated, though they may serve a function in the whole sequence once completed. I shall concentrate on the poems that have power and represent important aspects of Snyder's world view.

Snyder has spoken often of the importance of the rhythms of various kinds of work for his poetry, and his sense of experience is largely a sense of work, of measured force exerted on the world. When he sees a second-growth forest, he wonders, looking at the stumps, what they did with all the wood; a city evokes in him the tough brutal labor involved, the carpentry and plumbing and simple excavating. His world is a world of energy constantly reformulating itself, and most often a world of human energy, exploited, misdirected, and full of pathos—he can't take it for granted but sees at its base the wilderness and fundamental man, and the products generated through history. This is why "The Market," full of dangers of sentimentality in tone, and mere cataloguing in technique, has an inner vigor that the hitchhiker poem lacks. This is not entirely a matter of mood but of conviction and of consequent drive. Technical considerations aside, poetry like all art comes out of courage, the capacity to keep going when reason breaks down. The equivalences established in "The Market" are equivalences of energy very roughly estimated.

> seventy-five feet hoed rows equals
> one hour explaining power steering
> equals two big crayfish =
>   all the buttermilk you can drink
> = twelve pounds cauliflower
> = five cartons greek olives = hitch-hiking
>   from Ogden Utah to Burns Oregon
> = aspirin, iodine, and bandages
> = a lay in Naples = beef
> = lamb ribs = Patna
>   long grain rice, eight pounds
> equals two kilogram soybeans = a boxwood
>   geisha comb.

equals the whole family at the movies
equals whipping dirty clothes on rocks
   three days, some Indian river
=piecing off beggars two weeks
=bootlace and shoelace
   equals one gross inflatable
   plastic pillow
=a large box of petit-fours, chou-cremes—
   barley-threshing
   mangoes, apples, custard apples, raspberries
=picking three flats strawberries
=a christmas tree=a taxi ride
carrots, daikon, eggplant, greenpeppers;
oregano, white goat cheese
   =a fresh-eyed bonito, live clams
a swordfish
a salmon

And the close of the second section shows the melancholy and weariness that accompanies the breakdown of reason before all this relentless, pointless, back-breaking labor:

I gave a man seventy paise
In return for a clay pot
of curds
Was it worth it?
how can I tell

The terrible concluding section leaves us with a vision of a totally human world, a world of monstrosity:

they eat feces
   in the dark
   on stone floors
one legged animals, hopping cows
   limping dogs   blind cats
crunching garbage in the market
   broken fingers
      cabbage
      head on the ground.
who has young face.
   open pit eyes
between the bullock carts and people
   head pivot with the footsteps
         passing by
dark scrotum spilled on the street
   penis laid by his thigh
      torso
turns with the sun

> I came to buy
> a few bananas by the ganges
> while waiting for my wife

Contemporaneous with this long-projected series of poems like an enormous Chinese scroll are other poems, more lyric and brief, and many of these have been collected and published this year by New Directions under the title *The Back Country*. Characteristically, the first two sections are called "Far West" and "Far East"; and Snyder's most recent essay is called "Passage to More Than India." The synthesis he is working towards, that obsesses his being, maintains its momentum:

> We were following a long river into the mountains.
> Finally we rounded a bridge and could see deeper in—
> the farther peaks stony and barren, a few alpine
> trees.
> Ko-san and I stood on a point by a cliff, over a
> rock-walled canyon. Ko said, "Now we have come to
> where we die." I asked him, what's that up there,
> then—meaning the further mountains.
> That's the world after death. I thought it looked
> just like the land we'd been travelling, and couldn't
> see why we should have to die.
> Ko grabbed me and pulled me over the cliff—
> both of us falling. I hit and I was dead. I saw
> my body for a while, then it was gone. Ko was
> there too. We were at the bottom of the gorge.
> We started drifting up the canyon. "This is the
> way to the back country."

This poem provides the title for Snyder's *The Back Country*, an inclusive collection, the longest and in many ways most representative book of Snyder's poetry. It includes poems written after the publication of *Myth and Texts* in 1960 and some earlier poems that did not fit the design of the three earlier collections. The book is carefully structured, with sections treating Far West, Far East, Kali (goddess of creation and destruction), Back (return) and translations of Miyazawa Kenji. The book is dedicated to Kenneth Rexroth, and many of the earlier poems have an apprentice tone, in particular the lovely elegiac poem "For the Boy who was Dodger Point Lookout." The poem is a nostalgic evocation of a casual meeting between the anonymous boy, Snyder, and his wife in the Olympic Mountains of western Washington.

> The thin blue smoke of our campfire
> down in the grassy, flowery,
> heather meadow
> two miles from your perch.

The snowmelt pond, and Alison
half-stoopt bathing like
Swan Maiden, lovely naked,
ringed with Alpine fir and
gleaming snowy peaks. We
had come miles without trails,
you had been long alone.
We talked for half an hour up
there above the foaming creeks
and forest valleys, in our
world of snow and flowers.

I don't know where she is now;
I never asked your name.
In this burning, muddy, lying,
blood-drenched world
that quiet meeting in the mountains
cool and gentle as the muzzles of
three elk, helps keep me sane.

The Back Country has the advantage both of variety and secure control of the medium of poetry. If it lacks the unified impact of *Myths and Texts*, it covers even more ground. The point of view remains constant, the wilderness as repository of possibilities and reminder of psychological richnesses that cities, notably "This Tokyo," pervert or destroy, the reality and importance of work, what a simpler age called the dignity of labor, while recognizing the horror of exploitation both of nature and of the working man.

Many of these poems are, like the hitch-hiking poem of *Mountains and Rivers*, the poems of a wandering man, wandering in his travels, wayfaring in his sexuality, solitary, exploratory, inconstant, seaman and bindlestiff, finding his true Penelope only in the world of poetry and thought. Like much of Snyder's work, these poems have the quality of a very good *Bildungsroman*. In fact, as narrative and description and characterization, they are far superior to the novels of the 1960s in this country. They are not tricked up, contrived, and in spite of their autobiographical content, they are not egotistical. They are articulations, not mere expressions. Their motivation is perhaps best expressed in essays written contemporaneously with the poetry: "Buddhism and the Coming Revolution," "Passage to More Than India," and "Poetry and the Primitive," printed in *Earth House Hold*.

"Poetry" as the skilled and inspired use of the voice and language to embody rare and powerful states of mind that are in immediate origin personal to the singer, but at deep levels common to all who listen.

The mercy of the West has been social revolution; the mercy of the East has been individual insight into the basic self/void. We need both.

The prose in *Earth House Hold*, parts of *Turtle Island*, *The Old Ways* and the forthcoming *The New Work* should be read not only as partial explanation of the poetry but as the record of an evolving mind with extreme good sense in treating the problems of the world.

Regarding Wave is best thought of as two books. *Regarding Wave* is both the title of the book and the first thirty-five pages of text. It is a unified work of art with some of Snyder's best poems, for instance, "Not Leaving the House."

> When Kai is born
> I quit going out
>
> Hang around the kitchen—make cornbread
> let nobody in.
> Mail is flat
>   Masa lies on her side, Kai sighs,
>   Non washes and sweeps
> We sit and watch
>   Masa nurse, and drink green tea.
>
> Navajo turquoise beads over the bed
> A peacock tail feather at the head
> A badger pelt from Nagana-ken
> For a mattress; under the sheet;
> A pot of yogurt setting
> Under the blankets, at his feet.
>
> Masa, Kai,
> And Non, our friend
>
> In the green garden light reflected in
> Not leaving the house.
> From dawn till late at night
>   making a new world of ourselves
>   around this life.

Unlike some of the poems in the sections that succeed "Regarding Wave," this poem shows Snyder in the grip of a major principle, so that he becomes the agent of a voice, that of common experience, and the personal and superficially exotic change to the general and present.

Snyder's most recent books, *Turtle Island* (poetry with some essays, notably "Four Changes") and *The Old Ways* reiterate his chosen themes and methods. Some critics complain that Snyder does not develop or change in any major way. Why should he? He has chosen a substantial body of thought and experience to explore. Poets change not through fad and fashion but through a realization that their idiom no longer fits their experience. When that occurs, change is valid, but Snyder's wide and varied idiom is adequate to his intense and rich experience.

Snyder has already written, published, read aloud, and generally made available a large and remarkable body of work. He is distinguished not only as poet but as prose expositor—he has a gift for quiet, untroubled, accurate observation with occasional leaps to genuine eloquence. He has taken to himself a subject matter, complex, vast, and permanently interesting, a subject so compelling that it is not unreasonable to assert that he has become a center for a new set of cultural possibilities. There are two kinds of trouble that readers experience with this impressive accomplishment.

The first is the Gary Snyder poem. I have already described this short, anecdotal, erotic, concrete poem set in the wilderness with Zen masters and Amerindian mythological creatures commenting on each other and on nature. There comes a time when tedium sets in, when the personal style seems to be carrying along for no particular reason except to carry along, keep busy in the act of writing. The poems then exist all at exactly the same level and seem to have interchangeable parts. Objects from one could be moved to another without loss or gain. The prosody retains the same tone. The surfaces are attractive and monotonous. Even though there are variations from high rhetoric to self-deprecating humor, the unanimity of the poems is restrictive. Too much goes along the surface, gliding. And often I get the impression that Snyder doesn't care about the art, that poetry for him is only one of a set of instruments in a spiritual quest, that the act of construction is not something that requires its own special resolutions. Like most writers with a coherent world view, he sometimes refuses to let his material be intractable, there is no sense of contention between subject and object, no dramatic struggle toward a new form. Then the poems do not seem *forms* but *shapes*.

I don't think this happens often or that it is a totally crippling defect; otherwise I shouldn't have troubled to write this essay. The complaints here registered could have been made against Blake, Whitman, and Lawrence. The second complaint, one that I have heard from students, especially those from large urban areas, is that Snyder does not face the problems of modern life. In this view, the great bulk of Americans live in cities and in an age of anxiety verging on total panic. The wilderness exists only in a mythical past or in the lives of those privileged by money (for pack animals and guides) or skills based on specialized work in areas remote from normal experience. Hence Snyder's poetry doesn't answer to the tensions of modern life and depends on a life no longer accessible or even desirable for men. A mystique of the wilderness based on the humane naturalism of the highly limited Zen Buddhist sect and the primitive insights of American savages can't satisfy the existential *Angst* of modern man. Everything is too simple, too easy, too glib, a boy's book in verse, Huck Finn on the Skagit, Innocents in Japan. The poetry is archaic, not in the sense that all poetry is, but out of tune with life in the current era.

But the argument that a poet must speak to the problems of the bulk of the people seems to me to support rather than undermine Snyder's work. Properly understood, Snyder's poetry does *speak to* basic current problems, but it does not simply embody them. A usually sensible critic recently praised a poet for writing what he decided was "The poem of the 60s." Now this is a mentality that I understand and abominate. It is the mentality that runs and ruins museums of modern art. Who would think of calling Catullus *the* poet of the sixties (B.C.)? At present commentators and curators seem intent on timely master-pieces, by which they mean representative documents. Qualitative judgments, relevance not to the contemporary limited box but to the continuously human—these do not seem pertinent. Prepackaged his-tory, projected museums, anticipatory anthologies for survey courses are all silly and pointless enterprises, admired and supported by people who pride themselves on being of all things, antiacademic.

Snyder's work is not part of that academy. It is rather part of another academy, an ill-defined and perhaps undefinable group of people, including historians, novelists, poets, artists, various scholars, and many others, who are seriously seeking some proper answer or at least a set of questions appropriate to the world in its current stage of history, but seeing that world against the vast background of all human possibilities. At present, human power, pure brute controlled energy, threatens the entire planet. Some norms have to be found and diffused that will allow men to check and qualify their force. Snyder makes this large effort:

> As poet I hold the most archaic values on earth. They go back to the late Paleolithic: the fertility of the soil, the magic of animals, the power-vision in solitude, the ter-rifying initiation and re-birth, the love and ecstasy of the dance, the common work of the tribe. I try to hold both history and wilderness in mind, that my poems may approach the true measure of things and stand against the unbalance and ignor-ance of our times.

He is calling upon the total resources of man's moral and religious being. There is no point in decrying this as primitivism; it is merely good sense, for the ability to hold history and wilderness in the mind at once may be the only way to make valid measures of human con-duct. A larger and more humble vision of man and cosmos is our only hope, and the major work of any serious person. In that work,

Snyder's verse and prose compose a set of new cultural possibilities that only ignorance and unbalance can ignore.

Reprinted from *Sagetrieb*, Spring 1984.

23

Lawrence Ferlinghetti

When the Beat writers emerged in the late 1950s in the San Francisco Bay Area, they were greeted with scorn as merely another aspect of American Bohemia: flashy, outrageous, bizarre in their social conduct, and in their poetry bombastic, sloppy, occasionally obscene. Most discussion of them stressed their anti-social conduct, and their literary efforts were scorned as unschooled Whitman, barbaric yawps by self-indulgent people.

Thirty years later, the entire matter is seen differently. In 1956 nobody could imagine Allen Ginsberg as a winner of the National Book Award, not that adolescent rebel with a habit of using then unprintable words in sprawling lines that had neither form nor any rational shape. Very few people could imagine Gary Snyder, described by one poet as a Buddhist Boy Scout, winning the Pulitzer Prize. As the years have passed, figures like Kerouac, Corso, McClure, and Whalen have become part of the American literary tradition, discussed seriously by academic critics in doctoral dissertations, articles, and books. And they have been widely read both in America and abroad. Ginsberg's first book *Howl* has sold millions of copies, and these writers became the primary reading matter for many young people throughout the world.

At the center of the Beat movement when it began, Lawrence Ferlinghetti provided in City Lights Bookstore a meeting place and mail drop. The store carried modern and very new poetry in English, French, and Spanish. After all, Ferlinghetti held a *Doctorat de l'Université* from the Sorbonne and was fluent in French and Spanish. He founded the publishing house City Lights Books which published work by the Beat writers, including his own translations from Prévert and his own early poetry, very witty and urban (not urbane) in the traditions of modern French poetry. His second book, *A Coney Island of the Mind*, has sold around a million copies, and in many ways it is the most satisfying single book by Ferlinghetti. But the best introduction to his work and the qualities of his sensibility is his selected poems, *Endless Life*.

Ferlinghetti is an engaging writer. He publishes perhaps too much, and though he is invariably interesting, *Endless Life* shows him at his consistent best. The most representative poem is called simply "Dog," and that dog "trots freely in the street" and really does see reality, this sad and serious and above all free dog who investigates everything with his unwavering objectivity and will not be muzzled. The dog is the poet, urban, curious, outspoken with his bark and poetry, democratic, questioning, puzzled by existence, hoping always for some victorious answer to everything. He is hopeful, then, and aware of all aspects of his urbanized world. Ferlinghetti is primarily the poet of cities: his doctoral dissertation was on the city in French poetry of the nineteenth century. His poem "Autobiography" begins with

> I am leading a quiet life
> in Mike's Place every day
> watching the champs
> of the Dante Billiard Parlor
> and the French pinball addicts.
> I am leading a quiet life
> on lower East Broadway.

The poem continues, for nine very funny pages. The setting is North Beach before it attained its current flashy commercial tone and was instead a cityscape inhabited by San Francisco Italians and Bohemians, where Ferlinghetti was at home.

His youth in New York, his university days there and in Paris, and his maturity in San Francisco give him urban settings and tones that he thrived on. When he went on travels to South America, the book was called *Starting from San Francisco*, and in the selected poems, the book is represented by a beginning poem on Machu Picchu but returns to San Francisco finally with a long hilarious work on "The Great Chinese Dragon," chief attraction in Chinatown's parade on Chinese New Year's Day.

The commitment to the city is evident throughout but perhaps most striking in "Reading Apollinaire by the Rogue River." Ferlinghetti has deep feelings for natural power and beauty, but he tends to use natural objects and processes for symbolic force rather than for their innate quality. The river becomes a snake that stands for doomed power, leading to reflections on the passage of time and ultimate destruction of all things, including the river and the poet equally. The poem concludes with a citation of Apollinaire's "Sur le Pont Mirabeau":

> As I sit reading a French poet
> whose most famous poem is about

the river that runs through the city
taking time & life & lovers with it
And none returning
none returning

Some of Ferlinghetti's poems may sound a little like E. E. Cummings, but that comes from the fact that they write in traditions established by Apollinaire and his French successors.

Ferlinghetti returns always to the city, so that when he sees wild horses in the Pacific Northwest he inevitably compares them to a watercolor by Ben Shahn. The strength of his obsession with the city is that it grows from an impassioned love of humanity that frequently extends to a love of the entire animal world and of the cosmos. Ferlinghetti is an engaging poet; he is also engaged in the issues of the world. The selected poems make him appear more purely literary (sometimes too literary in his allusions) than he is. Much of his poetry is topical and satirical. His politics are those of the American libertarian tradition, but he has traveled widely and knows a great deal about other societies. There is nothing precious, removed, or pretentious about his attitudes or his poetry.

Ferlinghetti, as poet and literary entrepreneur, is the kind of person that makes civilization possible. The work that he has done is well epitomized by this selected poems, and it reminds us that he and his contemporaries among the Beat writers have been consistently productive and responsible writers and human beings. The reverence for life that one sees in Ferlinghetti's poems of the city is present also in the rurally oriented poems of Snyder and the comic-cosmic plays of McClure. The final poem in this selected poems is also the title poem of the volume, "Endless Life." This work in progress continues the enterprise, in its wit, in its inclusiveness, and in its peculiar blend of the playful with the serious. The endless life here celebrated is not at all single, loveliness followed by horror, paradise by inferno.

Ferlinghetti remains absorbed in the processes and events of the life he sees, like his sad, serious, and funny dog. His hero is Charlie Chaplin.

So the Beat Writers have become part of the canon of American literature, each different, all sharing a certain sense of sad love for the life we knew. Was it a literary movement? Not if we accept George Moore's definition of a literary movement as "A group of people living in the same city who cordially hate each other." They were always friendly and remain so. What they did in the history of American poetry was to challenge the stiff ornateness of the poetry then dominant and bring poetry back to the realities of experience. They expanded the possibilities of the medium, by restoring Whitman to greater recognition, by using the experimental possibilities of William Carlos Williams and of the French and Spanish writers of this century. And they served to remind us that life is the origin and purpose of poetry. In that general set of aims, Ferlinghetti was, and remains, an important figure. *Endless Life* is a good book in itself and a good introduction to his considerable body of work.

Reprinted from *Poetry: San Francisco*, Summer 1985.

24

William Everson: A Poet, Anarchist and Printer Emerges from Waldport

My title suggests an event involving abruptness, drama, even a certain portentous explosion. What I really want to do is concentrate on those years from 1945 through 1949 when the poetry of William Everson became in the full sense public, and when he as a person brought the voice of his poetry to the reading rooms of Berkeley and San Francisco. I say "reading" rooms because there were several centers in private homes and apartments where the reading aloud of poetry was a matter of prime importance—Kenneth Rexroth's home on Potrero Hill, Leonard Wolf's apartment in south Berkeley, and Throckmorton Manor on Telegraph Avenue, a rooming house where for an important year Robert Duncan lived. The readings were by the poets themselves, including Richard Moore, Kenneth Rexroth, Philip Lamantia, Leonard Wolf, Jack Spicer, Robert Duncan, and William Everson. Duncan also organized a series of examinations of the main modern poets, none of whom was then taught in formal classes at universities, so that Williams, Yeats, Pound, Stevens, H. D., and Lawrence as well as others were presented by poets who found them especially important to their own life and work. In addition, Duncan organized an intensive seminar in *Finnegans Wake* that was held at George Leite's bookstore, Daliel's, which is now, symbolic of developments in Berkeley, occupied by the Eclair bakery. George also published *Circle* magazine, started to celebrate his admired Henry Miller, but ultimately to become an immensely successful experimental magazine, well produced and widely distributed. One issue came to 10,000 copies. There were ten issues in all.

When Everson emerged first from the C.O. camp at Waldport and then from the Treesbank farm of Hamilton and Mary Tyler, he came to a Berkeley that was extremely active in its extra-University life. The student population was dominated by the presence of the veterans of the war, the G.I. students, so that it was older and more independent than the usual student body of even so heterogeneous a university as Berkeley. And those students were joined by a good many who like Everson had passed the war in camps and prisons because of their "convictions." There were serious discussion groups that read and talked about various key anarchist texts, at Kenneth Rexroth's home and at Richard Moore's studio. Ultimately, in 1949, Lewis Hill, who had acted as a coordinator between the Friends and the government in the administration of the camps for conscientious objectors, with William Trieste and Richard Moore would found KPFA, the first listener-sponsored radio station, under the rubric Pacifica, and that rubric was not merely geographical. Poetically and philosophically, Everson found a large body of people who participated in or looked with a very friendly eye on anarcho-pacifism.

He found a personal welcome in Berkeley and San Francisco, and he found a body of poets who appreciated and admired his work. Before his arrival, the Tylers had introduced me to his poetry, and I had read the several books produced between 1935 and 1944, taking pleasure in his own printing and admiring the work. But I was not prepared for "The Chronicle of Division." Neither was the world outside the friendly environment in which Everson found himself. I wrote an extensive appreciation of his poetry and sent it to Theodore Weiss at the *Quarterly Review* because he had published and commented favorably on some of my own poetry. Weiss liked the essay and said that he would publish it if he could have some of Everson's poetry. This was arranged, the poetry was sent, and then Weiss changed his mind—my essay is now, so far as I know, lost, and "The Chronicle of Division" was too much for what was a fairly experimental publication for that period. Looking back on the matter, it seems to me symbolic of the general literary climate of this country. The extra-academic world in which we lived, the experimental literary and artistic climate—for those were also the palmy days of the San Francisco Art Institute—was perhaps only appropriate to the San Francisco area. It was at that point that I first defined San Francisco as The City at the End of the World.

Everson at that time was a modest, retiring, quiet man, and when I first met him at Treesbank, I had a sense of fellow-feeling, of comradeship, of being at home in natural surroundings with him. He had a printing press in the barn, and I walked out with him to inspect it. We were both poets, although he was eight years older and had published and written much more than I had. We did not have much to say to each other, but I did not feel awkward or uncomfortable, any more than I should have felt with the bears that sometimes emerged from the woods when I was logging in the Siskiyous. Everson was a great deal like the people I had worked with at Pondosa, and I am not trying to romanticize him as a primitive indigene. To put the matter simply, Everson was a working man. His work was his center, and his basic work was that of poet and printer. Because of his origins in the Central Valley and his work in the Oregon woods, he had an inner stability and the sense of being genuinely at home in the hills and valleys of Sonoma County. Without commenting on it or even being aware of it, we were simply of the same basic origins. We had both lived for protracted times in a community of males, though Waldport was not so free or so well-paid a community as Pondosa. We assumed that we lived in the same world.

In Berkeley, matters were different. I was no more prepared for "The Chronicle of Division" than I was for Robert Duncan's *Heavenly City, Earthly City*. Duncan and Everson were of a very special order, very different from others associated with the literary and intellectual sense of that time. It was not that Duncan was a tireless organizer with a passion for expressing and devouring knowledge, nor was it that Everson was a brooding temperament with occasions for rich sensual delight. There was a great substantial difference that they shared, whatever differences there may have been within that defining difference. Duncan and Everson were not social beings; they were natural forces.

"The Chronicle of Division" had an extraordinary impact on its audiences. Everson read it with great passion, and the effect was genuinely stunning. I mean that after one reading that remains in my memory, there was an absolute silence in the room. Nobody stirred, and my own feeling was—and is—that the reading left us paralyzed, caught in a world that was ours and not ours, so that we were transfixed by the familiarity and strangeness of the event. "The Chronicle" seen at this distant time and even when seen with detachment in 1946, does not appear a promising subject. Put simply, the chronicle records the departure of a man from his normal surroundings, his familiar home, his wife, and the landscape that was his to a distant camp where he is effectively imprisoned with a group of strangers who are unified only by their conviction that killing, in any cause, at any time, is wrong. To some of them it is a sin, to others a crime against life. They are thus divided from their previous being, from their women, and from their society, physically and morally. Each of them is further divided from the other and divided within himself. Enforced solitude in a violent and tragic world is the norm.

The "Division" of the central figure becomes magnified when he receives a letter from his wife, what military men of the period called a "Dear John" letter, telling him that she has taken up with another man. Divided from his normal life, he then becomes divided from love and memory. The situation seems doomed to promote bathos and self-pity, and this domestic problem hardly seems adequate to serve as a prototype for an entire world in the agony of the greatest war in human history. While 8,000,000 Japanese were dying in fire-bombings of their cities and in brutal warfare on the stepping stones of islands from Guadalcanal to Okinawa and Leyte, leaving aside the European horrors, the break-up of a marriage seems on the surface trivial and conducive to sentimentality. Yet the poem, for it really is a unified whole and not a series of notes, remains, even now, powerful to the point of being overwhelming.

Some of the power emerges from the fact that the sequence of poems shapes the education of the narrator, and each poem presents a fresh problem to his understanding of events and what underlies them. Nothing is to be taken as simple and final, but is instead an opening toward a further revelation. I am very skeptical about the notion that the process of forming the work of art is the work of art, but in this instance it is very hard to the point of impossibility to abstract the process of recording and evaluating from the texture of the work itself. Hence there is an intimacy that goes beyond the easy claims of sincerity and honesty that too often amount to excusing weaknesses in the interest of realities beyond art. If that poetics were operating in the chronicle, then the result would be confessional only.

What comes through the "Chronicle" is not a person but a presence, in Yeats' terms, more type than person, more passion than type. That type, in a sense, was "Division," so that the "Chronicle of Division" was the chronicle of Everson transformed into an embodied passion. When that passion is articulated, the result is a public reality, sharable as part of the human soul. A world at war is a world in division, country against country, the very air divided by power, the sea divided with threats from every direction, soldier divided from soldier, families divided and scattered, men divided from women, and over it all a tone of rigid categories with any human commonality shattered. This world at war is the overt context of the poem, and its power is enhanced by its participation in that general context.

I take the "Chronicle" as central to its time, yet it is amazingly enduring forty years later. The 1948 edition of *The Residual Years* was so arranged that without awareness of the earlier work, the entire theme and tone were set by the "Chronicle." The 1968 edition permits a clearer sense of the foreshadowing of this grave and troubling work. Many of the earlier poems create a norm of the natural ecology that is the object of the poet's love and trust and in which he moves securely. Many of the earlier poems bring into focus a violence, the control of which leads to the principled pacifism of the "Chronicle" and related poems. And the earlier poems also provide a context for the sexuality that remains an abiding problem throughout Everson's work, both before and after his Catholic conversion.

The themes of Everson's poetry were fairly well established by the time he emerged from Waldport, the themes and the problems. Sexuality was a violent force that had to be controlled and expressed. Solitude was a necessity and a burden, as was the poet's art. Nature was an alien blessing, a source of analogies and a rebuke to human personal and social failings, so that from the perspective of the Central Valley, the leaf on the bough, the lines of vineyards, man was the sick animal seeking his natural health that valley, mountains, and sea, and all the other animals had from their origins and without artifice.

The drama of the early poems of Everson would define a pattern that remained central to his later work. The fixed and rewarding relation with a woman, growing out of his awkward adolescence and involvement with an art that received little social approval, a feeling of reverence for life that found itself thwarted by national disorder in the economic depression and by international disorder in the world at war, a sense of isolation and dedication leading to life in a world of males isolated by belief and conviction. This pattern would be repeated in the later work, beginning with sadness, moving toward a Dionysian outburst, followed by a retreat again based on conviction to a male community, the continued reverence for natural order and beings, and the ultimate return to the world of sexual communion tempered by religious passion. There is a steady design that Everson came to learn and ultimately to control. The drama of the early poems, especially through "The Chronicle of Division" is the drama of learning.

The result is a body of poetry that has been central to the growth not only of Everson but also of many others who have seen in its patterns that answer to the designs of their own lives. For those of us who shared the years after the war and rejoiced in the brief period from 1945 through 1950 that released us from the weight of the war and opened possibilities that would be closed by the Korean War and the attendant period of repression that we associate with loyalty oaths and other insults to human freedom in the McCarthy years, the release of the arts in the San Francisco Bay Area was a spiritual reward of an extraordinary beauty. One of the centers, not an institutional but—as I noted earlier—a natural force, was the figure of William Everson. The extension of his poetry into the printing of *A Privacy of Speech* was an assertion of the continuity from person to artifact to public assertion.

I imagine that we all tend to look back toward the formative years of our lives, our main choices, our dedications to persons and our vocations, with often deceptive pleasure and satisfaction, but for me that period was a period of joy and one of the main sources of that joy was the person and work of William Everson. History impinged on all of us, and it is not merely an accident that the community of writers who gave Everson his cordial reception and learned so much from him should have been dispersed by the year 1950, by the recognition of vocations, by choices in marital loyalties, by political pressure. Jack Spicer thought that he was joking when he referred to the period as the Berkeley Renaissance, but the truth is that we all participated in an artistic and moral complex that was at once deeply serious, widely learned, full of sometimes outrageous fun, and extremely productive. There have been few atmospheres so conducive to understanding and comradeship and hard meaningful work. Everson was an essential part of that community, and as it broke under the forces that were inseparably personal and historical he went, as each of us did, towards a life at once chosen and fated.

I have been deliberately personal in treating this topic because I cannot separate Everson's work from my own work and life as a poet and scholar. He was and still is for me, a powerful poet and a splendid man. Once when my wife Ariel and I were spending an evening with Bill and Mary Fabilli, Lawrence Clark Powell came to pick up some of Everson's manuscripts that he had donated to the UCLA library. As he left, reverently holding the manuscripts, Lawrence Powell said in a voice clearly meant to be overheard, "Priceless, priceless!" At the time, the four of us thought it was pretty funny, Lawrence's way of paying for the manuscripts, but now when I think back on those days, I find myself repeating "Priceless, priceless!"

25

Reflections on Allen Ginsberg as Poet

Allen Ginsberg is a notoriety, a celebrity; to many readers and non-readers of poetry he has the capacity for releasing odd energetic responses of hatred and love or amused affection or indignant moralizing. There are even people who are roused to very flat indifference by the friendly nearsighted shambling bearded figure who has some of the qualities of such comic stars as Buster Keaton or Charlie Chaplin. And some of their seriousness.

His latest book, *Planet News*, grants another revelation of his sensibility. The usual characteristics of his work are there; the rhapsodic lines, the odd collocations of images and thoughts and processes, the occasional rant, the extraordinary tenderness. His poetry resembles the Picasso sculpture melted together of children's toys, or the sculpture of driftwood and old tires and metal barrels and tin cans shaped by enterprising imaginative young people along the polluted shores of San Francisco Bay. You can make credible Viking warriors from such materials. Ginsberg's poetry works in parallel processes; it is junk poetry, not in the drug sense of junk but in its building blocks. It joins together the waste and loss that have come to characterize the current world, Cuba, Czechoslovakia, the Orient, the United States, Peru. Out of such debris as is offered he makes what poetry he can.

He doesn't bring news of the earth but of the planet. Earth drives us down, confines, mires, isolates, and besides there is less and less earth available to perception and more and more artifice. The late C. S. Lewis might not have enjoyed having his name brought into this discussion, but his great trilogy that begins with *Out of the Silent Planet* and ends with *That Hideous Strength* demonstrates the same concern with the planet as Ginsberg's new book. Both of them see Earth as a planet, part of a solar system, part of a galaxy, part of a universe, cosmic. But where Lewis wrote out of hatred, indignation, and despair at the destruction of tradition by mindless technology, Ginsberg writes from sad lost affection. I think Ginsberg is our only truly sad writer, sad with a heavy, heavy world, and somehow always courageous and content to remain in the human continuum with all his knowledge of human ill and malice clear. He persists.

But is it poetry? This question is so often asked that it does require answering not only within the confines of Ginsberg's work but generally. I am not entirely sure what the question means, since it could legitimately be asked of Whitman or Hart Crane, and has been asked of them. What Ginsberg's work represents is an enormous purging and exorcising operation; it is in the area of religious and spiritual exploration rather than that of aesthetic accomplishment. In the dispute between Whistler and Ruskin over the concept of artistic "finish," Ginsberg's poetry would stand with Whistler's painting. He tends to use the term "poet" not as "maker" but revealer at best; at worst he accepts the notion that makes "poets" out of all confused serious persons who are genuinely unquiet about their souls and the condition of the planet. This is a widely embracing category. What troubles many readers of Ginsberg's work, if they are frank about it, is the continuous and consequently tedious reference to semen, excrement, masturbation, buggery, fornication, and the limited series of variations on such substances and processes. Who needs all the soiled bed-sheets? The only proper answer is that Ginsberg does—or did. They were reminders of the shame, guilt, and disorder that apparently afflicted his sexual life and obsessions; they needed to be purged and declared innocent, and the poems attend seriously to that very problem. To some readers they are frank, courageous, outspoken; others find them violations of the artistic principle of reticence. Both arguments seem to me trivial, having to do with civil rights or social formalities. What occurred in Ginsberg's work seems to me at once more rational and more historically determined than many readers seem willing to admit.

If Ginsberg is nothing else, he is a large contributor to the *Zeitgeist*. Legally and linguistically, he not merely reflects the drift of his time but diverts and channels it, not out of any sensational interest in so acting but out of the necessities that his being exacted from history. The coincidence of his particular hang-ups—and there is no other way to describe them—with the tabus of the society generate a freely inevitable kind of writing. For in addition to the concern for his own troubled being, he is involved in liberating his body and liberating his mind so that both can function properly: spontaneous me, I sing the body electric. In their most considerable work, both Whitman and Ginsberg are intent on destroying those cerebral bonds that impair their sympathy with their bodies and with others. For others appear only in the body. The irony in both writers is that their most rationally ordered poems are those that argue against the rational faculties. In fact, their real quarrel is with the misuse of cerebral power; they share this sense of imbalance with Blake and Lawrence. And there must be moments when Ginsberg would ruefully agree with Lawrence, who answered a correspondent who questioned his intellectual fulminating against the intellect by saying, in effect, that yes, he reminded himself of Carlyle, who once said that he had written fifty books on the virtue of silence.

When such paragraphs as the preceding one place Ginsberg in the realm of Whitman, Blake, Lawrence, and Carlyle, a certain uneasiness might justly prevail. I think that this is more a matter of habit than of perception. When the Epstein statue of Blake was placed in Westminster Abbey, I felt slightly miserable—it seemed that the British talent for retrospectively accepting the eccentric had over-reached itself. I don't want to see Ginsberg canonized because it would take the edge off his work. With contemporary poets, all question of relative evaluation with the mighty dead is impertinent. Some years back an acquaintance of mine was bad-mouthing Robert Frost and ended with what he took to be an unanswerable question, "Will he last?" and I tried to bring him back to biological reality by murmuring, "None of us will." What we can ask from our writers is a willingness to face up to the troubled planet.

Returning again to the sexuality of Ginsberg's work, I find that in this book, arranged chronologically, there seems to be a steady diminution of concern with the vocabulary and processes that bother many otherwise sympathetic readers. Several of the poems are among his very best work: Kral Majales; Who Be Kind To; Wichita Vortex Sutra; Wales Visitation. I can't imagine Ginsberg ever solving to his satisfaction the problems that have troubled his being for so many years; but he does seem to have undergone some profound religious experiences during the past five years that give his work a new density and fullness. He is one of the most important men alive on the planet. We should all be grateful for his presence.

But is he a poet? Again I find the question meaningless. He has written over a dozen first-rate poems; he has brought back to life, through his studies in French and Spanish verse, the Whitman tradition and informed it with a new pulse; he has served as a large part of the prophetic conscience of this country during its darkest period; he has been brave and productive. He has gone off on side-tracks; he has indulged himself publicly in some poems that seem better confined to note-books. But when a man liberates the sense of prosodic possibility and embodies in his work a profoundly meaningful spiritual quest that is compelling and clarifying to any reasonably sympathetic reader, well, yes, he is a poet. Only envy and spite could deny the title.

Reprinted from *Concerning Poetry,* Spring 1969.

26

Critical Approaches to William Burroughs, or How to Admit an Admiration for a Good Dirty Book

I want to begin by giving a retrospective view of my own relations to Burroughs. First, I saw both the *Yage Letters* and *Naked Lunch* before publication. In 1955 Allen Ginsberg lived in a little cottage four houses south of us on Milvia Street in Berkeley. He came to see me first in my office before we realized that we were neighbors, and he enrolled for graduate study at Berkeley. Kenneth Rexroth had advised him to see me, and together we worked out the best possible program that our graduate school would allow: required courses in bibliography and Anglo-Saxon and a special studies course in the prosody of Whitman. At first we talked incessantly about Whitman, and practically every day he came to the house and read Whitman aloud, and we discussed and argued. At that time Ginsberg was much taken with Richard Chase's book on Whitman and kept arguing for Whitman's sense of humor. At first I was amused and suggested that he could also write on intentional jokes in the *Faerie Queene*. Later we came to agreement, but I insisted he use the term *hilarity* rather than humor—a concept that I shall return to later. _

Ginsberg did not trust academic figures, but he gradually came to the conclusion that I was not really a bad sort and showed me some of his poems. I thought that those weak imitations of Andrew Marvell were pretty dreadful and told him so directly, advising him to follow Whitman. That came as a relief to him, and since that moment we have been good friends. He showed me parts of a long poem that he was working on, and he began talking about Kerouac and Burroughs. He showed me a typescript of *On The Road* and segments of what would become *Naked Lunch*. The long poem was *Howl*, which he would read aloud later in the year at several places in the Bay Area. The little cottage in Berkeley has since been torn down, but though it was extremely tiny, about fifteen by fifteen feet, Ginsberg lived there, Kerouac visited for periods, Phil Whalen was a constant resident, and, when Ginsberg lived for a week or more at a time in San Francisco, the only resident. Gary Snyder was a frequent visitor, and they often over-flowed into the old farm house—now torn down—where I lived with my wife and our first daughter. Mine is the melancholy fame of being the professor that the narrator of *The Dharma Bums* claimed to have scared the shit out of, with his customary elegance. The truth is that I threw Kerouac out of the house one evening because he was drunk, obscene, and was frightening my five-year-old daughter. In those days I stood six feet seven inches tall, weighed about two hundred and twenty pounds, was only 35 years old, quicker than most bears and as strong as some, and it would have been a pleasure to throw Kerouac physically out of the house, but he went mumbling away. Another piece of mythology about that period is that Ginsberg quit graduate school, though I encouraged him to stay, because Kerouac told him to quit. This is simply not true. Ginsberg on the way back from San Fran-cisco one night asked me whether he should leave graduate school be-cause, in his words, he could not twist his mind to work in the gram-matical categories of Anglo-Saxon and the systematic procedures of bibliographical study. I told him that if he tried to orient himself toward something alien to his being, he would be making a mistake. But he in-sisted that he could not let down some of the professors who had been kind to him, and I answered that perhaps he should think of his well being rather than theirs. Finally I lost my temper and told him that he was a grown man, should certainly know his own mind, and should get out of graduate school as soon as possible because he was only making himself miserable. Kerouac may have said something to him, but the day after our conversation Ginsberg withdrew from graduate school.

In 1957–58 Ginsberg spend several weeks at our house in London, where Donald Carne-Ross recorded the whole of *Howl* for BBC and I included part of it in a broadcast on American poetry. In spring of 1958 I met Burroughs in the hotel on 9 rue Gît-le-Coeur and found him charming, gentle, and kind. He had just returned to Paris from London where he had undergone the apomorphine treatment and was free of drugs, very calm and gently didactic in conversation with Ginsberg, who was deep in the writing of *Kaddish* and in one of the manic phases which affected him occasionally during that period. That was my only meeting with Burroughs, though I have followed his career with atten-tive respect.

In 1959 while writing my second book on Yeats, I was also com-piling the *Casebook on the Beat*. When I was being considered for a promotion my then chairman asked for a description of recent publica-tions and current research, and after I handed him a bibliography, I re-

marked that I was compiling an anthology on the Beat writers. He replied that it would be wiser not to mention it because there might be
somebody on the Budget Committee who lacked a sense of humor. I
have always treasured that moment. That was the first critical approach to the Beat writers—ignore them, don't take them seriously,
they are a bunch of clowns. But the fact is that they could not be ignored, that they went on to become the common reading of millions of
young people, and my chief pride in the *Casebook* is that not one of the
writers included in it has failed to be continuously productive, that
Gary Snyder won the Pulitzer Prize and Ginsberg the National Book
Award and that, alas, those writers have become part of academic
study.

I say alas, because there is something mildly depressing in considering the distance from 1959 to 1977, from the chairman who thought
the Beat writers were funny to the full majesty of the Modern Language Association turned toward the study of William S. Burroughs.
Naked Lunch is now, in Chaucer's terms, to be considered by the members of "A solempne and a great fraternitee," rather than in unpublish-
able form by a few young people reading a typescript.

The danger in making the contemporary respectable is that we
might at the same time make it dull. Serious study tends toward sol-
emnity, and I have the uneasy feeling in reading Eric Mottram's *William Burroughs* that a handful of very uneven books and a rather goofy
theory of composition are being treated as if they were the major works
and theories of a Conrad, Hardy or James. I am mildly relieved when
I note that Mottram has absolutely no clue about how to handle routine
matters like bibliographies and notes and is no scholar, but when the
question of Burroughs' world view is given so Germanic a presentation, I become irreverent, as I do at times with Professor Tytell's excellent long essay on Burroughs in his *Naked Angels*.

The primary critical problem is what is the ground of the appeal of
this work? Does *Ulysses*, for instance, get its overwhelming charm from
the series of literary and philosophical and historical correspondences
that can be found through patient labor and a little bending of the
truth? Does Yeats' later poetry appeal to us because of the endless delight of comparing perfectly clear poems with irrelevant and obscure
prose selected from *A Vision*? Do *The Tropic of Cancer* and *The Tropic of
Capricorn* command attention because of their Emersonean vision of individual value? Do we read *Naked Lunch* because it is one phase in the
development of a vision of defiance against cosmic authoritarianism?
Do we read the notes to *The Waste Land* rather than the poem because
we don't want to face the funny frightening poem that Eliot actually

wrote? I suspect that we read Yeats because he is bold, sexy, and wise, and that we read *Naked Lunch* because it is outrageously funny.

This brings us back to Ginsberg's perception of the funny side of Whitman. What he had in mind can be epitomized in a single line: "I dote on myself. There is that lot of me and all so luscious." This is on the surface as hilarious as Mark Twain's essay on the literary offenses of James Fenimore Cooper or Faulkner's "Spotted Horses" episode from *The Hamlet*. The English are capable of humor, the French of wit, but only Americans are capable of hilarity: boisterous merriment. I am speaking of literature not life; the English are capable of boisterous merriment, but except for the Anglo-Irish, notably Joyce, it is beyond them in literature. "No, Sir; wine gives not light, gay, ideal humour; but tumultuous, noisy, clamorous merriment" (O.E.D.). Outrageous fun.

Humor for Dr. Johnson was ideal; he loved Shakespeare's comedies and had little use for the tragedies. Burroughs is frequently compared to Swift, especially the Swift of *A Modest Proposal*, but there is a more appropriate sense in which he should be compared to Twain and Faulkner, and perhaps most of all to Henry Miller, all part of that special tradition of hilarity that distinguishes American literature and would seem hopelessly out of place in English or French, not to mention our earnest German and Russian friends. When Russian writers are hilarious, the tone is entirely different, and there are many times when to think of their work as hilarious is to insult them. Woody Allen's *Love and Death* is a marvelous parody of an American trying to keep a straight face when he treats characteristic situations and plots in Russian fiction. Even so solemn a fellow as Woody Allen cannot quite bring it off.

What is the special hilarious quality of American humor? It has not been defined, though my suspicion is that many members of this audience have an immediate reaction to the effect that, yes, the same tradition that produced Hemingway's "Today is Friday" could as properly produce the famous hanging cum buggery/fornication scenes of *Naked Lunch*. It is hard to believe, however, that Hemingway would excuse his travesty of the crucifixion as an argument against captial punishment. Burroughs says of the disgusting and fascinating hanging cum buggery/fornication passages that they were written ". . . as a tract against Capital Punishment in the manner of Jonathan Swift's Modest Proposal. These sections are intended to reveal capital punishment as the obscene barbaric and disgusting anachronism that it is. . . ." Now this is hogwash. Swift's *Modest Proposal* is written in a somberly rational tone, and it is a kind of hoax writing—like Defoe's *The Shortest Way with Dissenters* (suppress them totally, even if the cost is mass slaughter)—that was taken literally by part of its audience, even though it was written by the Dean of Dublin's St. Patrick's Cathedral, just as Defoe's ironic tract was written by a notorious dissenter. Now nobody in his right mind would take Burroughs' "tract" as in any way a literal or probable recommendation. It boggles my mind to imagine any reader of the text, without Burroughs' intervention, stumbling unaided on the notion that those obscene, barbaric and disgusting passages are anything more than an exhibit of the kind of depravity that the human mind can sink to, and of which to the guilt and sorrow of humanity, we are all capable. But the text itself gives no clue to Burroughs' intended effect. If Burroughs really intended to write an attack on Capital Punishment, what he managed was a much more fundamental indictment of humanity. That he did so through savage hilarity superficially comparable to that of Apollinaire's *The Debauched Hospodar* and his *Memoirs of a Young Rakehell* (which have absolutely no redeeming social importance, except that they were written by a great poet) places him firmly in the tradition of Miller and the late Twain. Burroughs is not a social critic but a nihilist intent on wiping out all conventional and civilized human values.

The appeal of *Naked Lunch* resides in the fact that it expresses the plight of a decadent capitalist culture in which the audience does not believe. The conventional and civilized values that it flouts are accepted superficially by the audience, and they delight in seeing them reduced to sexual and violent horror. The same principle makes the figure of Doctor Benway so numbingly funny:

> Dr. Benway is operating in an auditorium filled with students: "Now, boys, you don't see this operation performed very often and there's a reason for that. . . . You see it has absolutely no medical value. No one knows what the purpose of it originally was or if it had a purpose at all. Personally I think it was a pure artistic creation from the beginning.
> "Just as a bull fighter with his skill and knowledge extricates himself from danger he has himself invoked, so in this operation the surgeon deliberately endangers his patient, and then, with incredible speed and celerity, rescues him from death at the last possible split second. . . . Did any of you ever see Dr. Tetrazzini perform? I say perform advisedly because his operations were performances. He would start by throwing a scalpel across the room into the patient and then make his entry like a ballet dancer. His speed was incredible: 'I don't give them time to die,' he would say. Tumors put him in a frenzy of rage. 'Fucking undisciplined cells!' he would snarl, advancing on the tumor like a knife-fighter."
> A young man leaps down into the operating theatre and, whipping out a scalpel, advances on the patient.
> Dr. Benway: "An espontaneo! Stop him before he guts the patient!"
> (Espontaneo is a bull-fighting term for a member of the audience who leaps down into the ring, pulls out a concealed cape and attempts a few passes with the bull before he is dragged out of the ring.)

The orderlies scuffle with the espontaneo, who is finally ejected from the hall. The anesthetist takes advantage of the confusion to pry a large gold filling from the patient's mouth. . . .

Now, does anybody in the audience think that this is an argument for socialized medicine? It is an hilarious presentation of all our unconscious fears of doctors, their absolute authority over life and death, their indifference to their patients, their pride in their skill, even their vainglory, and finally the opportunistic greed of the anesthetist. Since modern medicine has saved my life on three separate occasions because of its recent technological developments, I respect it immensely, and number among my friends several devoted radiotherapists· and surgeons. But this episode makes me laugh heartily and with a sense of relief. Burroughs writes many such brilliant scenes in *Naked Lunch*, including the unprintable (!) section on the day that Roosevelt appointed nine baboons to the Supreme Court. Is this a satire on the judicial system? Or is it a terribly funny presentation of the fears that Roosevelt haters had of him and his intentions? Anybody who understands or remembers the New Deal will also understand why otherwise rational men in their seventies will drool with rage at the mention of NRA, WPA, and FDR. And much of *Naked Lunch* is full of such topical fun. I find it hard to think of it, however, as satirical. Burroughs and his readers are just having a good time. But since this means that we share low motives and are capable of being moved by gleefully unrestricted obscenity, we try to convince ourselves that we are reading a noble tract against Capital Punishment or the AMA or the judicial system. I think that one deficiency in criticism of *Naked Lunch* is that critics are wary of being caught appreciating the book for laughs. Hence the "solempne" tone. And until some serious critic of Burroughs writes a frank and uninhibited appreciation of the book, really serious criticism of Burroughs cannot begin.

When it does, I think that certain results will follow, and one of them will be a depreciation of the succeeding books. I am a tireless reader of science fiction, and Burroughs apparently has also read E. E. (Doc) Smith's *Lensman* series. Those books with their Intergalactic Patrol, their Arisians contemplating the Cosmic All, the monstrous Eichs who cut their victims to pieces molecule by molecule and then assimilate them by a gruesome method that a Burroughs character would characterize as "disgustin"—they are the exact and adequate parallel to the "serious" novels that follow *Naked Lunch* and strike me as pretentious bores.

As for critical approaches to Burroughs, my own feeling is that the central need for determining the ground of the work's appeal has not been satisfied. First, I should suggest that evaluations of the individual books have not seriously been entertained. The negative critics merely call names; the friendly critics take refuge in allegories that, to my mind, inhabit the banks of the Nile. The special humor of Burroughs has not been defined, and his place in the history of the peculiar American tradition of hilarity not approached. In contemplating the subject for the purposes of this brief chapter, I have concluded that wit divides man from man; humor brings them together in a community of biological good sense; hilarity destroys the individual person as the author transcends and violates reality by a sense of outrageously uninhibited fun. Burroughs is no Swift or Defoe. Works like the *Bickerstaff Papers, A Modest Proposal,* or *The Shortest Way with Dissenters* are rational wit with a certain extravagance. Burroughs belongs with the authors of *The Mysterious Stranger, Pudd'nhead Wilson, Fenimore Cooper's Literary Offenses, The Tropic of Cancer* and *The Tropic of Capricorn,* and Faulkner's classic *The Hamlet.*

Beyond that, there simply has to be some more rational examination of science fiction that would clarify what Burroughs is up to in his cosmic works. There is a special genre of science fiction that can only be called fascist—some of the works of Robert Heinlein (especially *Farnham's Freehold*), most of the grand panoramic works, but especially Doc Smith's *Lensman* series. Burroughs uses many of Smith's devices for anarchist purposes, and this seems to have evaded sensible notice.

Finally, there is the entire question of Burroughs' theories of composition. They are goofy, and the cut-up method and all the nonsense about electronic fooling around neglect the fact that Burroughs' sensibility is what makes the work interesting, not all the gimmicks. The trouble is that there is no young Kenneth Burke around to make a responsible analysis of the folly of the entire theory. My own experience with Ginsberg, Kerouac, and Burroughs is that they rationalize their practice when they theorize, and with the exception of Ginsberg—who has real knowledge of the poetic tradition—they lack the training and good sense to shape any kind of rational and usable theory. There is something dreary in watching that chameleon Norman Mailer try to use Burroughs' style in *Why We Are in Viet Nam.* All that Mailer proves in that book is that Burroughs' manner is peculiarly suited to his sensibility, not to Mailer's.

In my view the best description of Burroughs' idea of the novel is Wyatt Blassingame's conclusion that Mark Twain "was not so interested in the novel as a compact whole as in the individual scenes on which he could release his full flamboyant genius."

Hence there is a great deal to re-think about Burroughs, evaluatively, with some sense of literary continuities and parallels, socially with some sense of the post-fascist nature of the later works. A good Marxist critique of Burroughs might also clarify matters. But above all, I should like to see the serious students of Burroughs confess that they like *Naked Lunch* because it is outrageously funny, hilarious in the manner of Faulkner, Miller, and Twain. Seriousness about hilarity becomes unconsciously hilarious. Years ago I consented to do an individual study project on Miller with a rather solempne student. Finally, at one of our weekly conferences, I asked him with a feeling of despair, why he liked Miller. He looked shifty and said, "Well, remember the passage at the Paris Opera where the soprano has an immense menstrual flow that inundates the orchestra and boxes and leaves the audience floundering for their lives? Well, I used to have visions like that all the time, and until I read Miller, I thought I was abnormal." All right, I could understand that, but he was deeply offended when I said that I liked Miller because he was hilariously funny. I hope that nobody in the audience is offended when I affirm that in approaching *Naked Lunch*, we should keep our real motives in mind.

Reprinted from *Occident*, Spring 1980.

Index